THE JOHN HARVARD LIBRARY

THE LIFE OF WASHINGTON

By

MASON L. WEEMS

Edited by Marcus Cunliffe

THE BELKNAP PRESS OF
HARVARD UNIVERSITY PRESS

Cambridge, Massachusetts
London, England

Twelfth printing, 2001

Library of Congress Catalog Card Number 62–20253
ISBN 0–674–53251–1

Printed in the United States of America

CONTENTS

THE LIFE OF

WASHINGTON

CONTENTS

ILLUSTRATIONS

following page 164

INTRODUCTION

I
THE MAN

Mason Locke Weems is known today mainly for one book, his *Life of Washington,* and indeed for one anecdote in the book—that of young George and the cherry-tree. Largely on the strength of his single, immortal, and dubious anecdote, Weems has become a test-case in American historiography. His name and reputation have evoked reactions ranging from exasperation and indulgence to delight. But Weems made other contributions to American mythology. His life was busy, varied, and prolific; before it was over he, too, in his humbler way had passed into American folklore. His story presents problems that, in a minor key, are no less interesting than the problems of the greater men whom he celebrated.

Weems was born at Marshes Seat, Herring Bay, Anne Arundel County, Maryland, on October 11, 1759. He was the youngest of the nineteen children of David Weems, who was of Scottish descent; twelve of the children were by David Weems's second wife, Esther Hill Weems. Not much is known about the early life of Mason Weems. He had some schooling in Maryland and may have made some voyages in the trading vessels owned by his two older brothers. It seems likely that in 1777–1779 he was in Edinburgh or London, studying medicine. There is a story that at the outset of the Revolutionary War he was serving as a surgeon in the Royal Navy. Weems does seem fond of nautical descriptions and maritime metaphors. But this is conjecture. There is surer evidence that he returned to Maryland in 1779, when his father died. For part of the next three or four years the supposition is that he was back in England, studying for another profession—the ministry. With the end of the Revolutionary War he ran into difficulties. He wished to be ordained in the Anglican church. But when independence was secured, the status of the Church of England needed to be redefined in relation to the former American colonies. An American citizen could not be expected to take an oath of allegiance to the British crown, and yet such an oath was required of an ordinand. In his plight Weems appealed for help to the American Minister at The Hague, John Adams. This was late in 1783, or possibly early in 1784. On July 9, 1784, he wrote a letter in the same vein to Benjamin Franklin in Paris and got a courteous answer. A way out of Weems's dilemma was found, and he was fully ordained as a priest, by the Archbishop of Canterbury, on September 12, 1784.

By the end of 1784 he was installed as Rector of All Hallows, at South River, Herring Creek, in the county of his birthplace. He remained there until 1789. About two years later he was Rector of St. Margaret's, Westminster, Maryland. During the same year (1791) Weems appears to have launched himself upon his long career as a promoter and seller of books and pamphlets, and after about 1793, though he remained an Episcopalian minister, he had no further permanent clerical connections.[1]

His first publishing activities involved merely the reissue of other men's works, usually at the hands of printers in Baltimore or elsewhere in Maryland. The title pages stated that these productions were "printed for the Rev. M. L. Weems." Among the earliest examples, in 1791–1793, were collections of sermons by Robert Russel and Hugh Blair, and

[1] The main sources of information about Weems are Lawrence C. Wroth, *Parson Weems: A Biographical and Critical Study* (Baltimore, 1911), a rather slight work; Harold Kellock, *Parson Weems of the Cherry-Tree* (New York, 1928), which adds a little new material but relies principally on Wroth; and Mrs. Emily E. Ford Skeel, ed., *Mason Locke Weems: His Works and Ways,* 3 vols. (Norwood, Mass., 1929), an important collection originally assembled by Paul Leicester Ford. Vol. I is biographical and bibliographical; Vols. II and III are devoted to Weems's letters, mostly to the publisher Mathew Carey.

Hannah More's *Religion of the Fashionable World.* These were blameless enough productions. He seems, though, to have provoked both amusement and embarrassment by sponsoring the publication (in 1791 or 1792) of a pamphlet entitled *Onania,* which warned the reader against the dangers of masturbation.[2] At any rate we catch a glimpse of him in the manuscript diary of a fellow churchman, the Rev. William Duke, who notes at Annapolis on June 1, 1792, that he "walked into the country and lodged with M[r] Weems and M[r] Coleman. Subscribed Weems's proposals for 2 books and paid 1/10." On September 12, 1792, Duke records:

> Went to Church and preached. the Rev[d] M[r] Weems came in the meantime. . . . Was sorry to see Weems's pedling way of life but God knows best by what methods we can most directly answer to designations of his Providence.[3]

Perhaps in the course of a bookselling tour, Weems became acquainted with Colonel Jesse Ewell of Bel Air, near Dumfries, in Prince William County, Virginia. In July 1795 Weems married Colonel Ewell's daughter Frances; he was thirty-five, his bride a good deal younger. He moved to Dumfries, a small tobacco port on Quantico creek, which flowed into the Potomac some eighteen miles down river from George Washington's Mount Vernon home. He bought a house in Dumfries and some years later, possibly on the death of Colonel Ewell in 1806, established himself at Bel Air, which was to be his home or at least his base of operations for the rest of his life.[4]

His operations ramified. In 1794 he began to act as agent for the young publisher Mathew Carey, an Irishman who had emigrated to America in 1784 and settled in Philadelphia. The two men were to be associated for another thirty years, and much of what we know of Weems derives from their

2 Wroth, p. 3; Kellock, pp. 57–58; Skeel, I, 259.

3 Skeel, I, 257–258.

4 Van Wyck Brooks, *The World of Washington Irving* (New York, 1944), p. 278, confuses this with Bellair or Bel Air in Harford County, Maryland.

vigorous correspondence. Carey was an able and enterprising man. In addition to the items which he himself had had printed, Weems was soon offering works published by Carey, such as William Guthrie's *New System of Modern Geography* and Oliver Goldsmith's *Animated Nature.* He sold them on commission; and little by little his journeys grew longer and more ambitious. Though at first he traveled mainly in Maryland, Pennsylvania and Virginia, with occasional forays into New Jersey and New York, by degrees his journeys extended and took him further south, into the Carolinas and to Georgia. Sometimes in concert with Carey and sometimes on his own account, he added to the list of publications which bore his own name somewhere on the title page. In the next decade, for instance, he promoted *The Lover's Almanac, The Bachelor's Almanac,* and *The Grand Republican Almanac.* In 1799 he brought out a pamphlet, dedicated to George Washington, called *The Philanthropist; Or, A Good Twelve Cents Worth of Political Love Powder, for the Fair Daughters and Patriotic Sons of Virginia.*[5]

In the following year appeared the first edition of his life of Washington, the history of which will be discussed in a moment. For some years thereafter he acted as agent for another Philadelphia publisher, Caleb P. Wayne, though he did not sever his connection with Carey. More and more publications came from Weems's pen: further editions of *Washington;* biographies of Francis "Swamp Fox" Marion (*c.* 1810), Benjamin Franklin (1815) and William Penn (1822); and pamphlets recommending matrimony (*Hymen's Recruiting Sergeant, c.* 1805), and condemning sundry vices: *God's Revenge Against Murder* (1807), *God's Revenge Against Gambling* (*c.* 1810), *The Drunkard's Looking Glass* (*c.* 1812), *God's Revenge Against Adultery* (1815), *God's Revenge Against Duelling* (1820), and the *Bad Wife's Look-*

[5] Skeel I, 150–152. Though Weems added comments of his own, the pamphlet was culled from William Laurence Brown's *Essay on the Natural Equality of Man,* first printed in America in 1793.

ing Glass (1823).[6] For much of the time Weems was on the road, selling his own and other works wherever there promised to be a likely audience. He died far from home, at Beaufort, South Carolina, on May 23, 1825.[7]

II
THE LIFE OF WASHINGTON

Weems's biography of George Washington was thus only one of many enterprises during his career. But it was his most successful venture, and its evolution tells us a good deal about the temperament of Weems and the climate of his day.

The first editions of the work appeared in 1800, only a few months after Washington's death at Mount Vernon on December 14, 1799. The event produced a huge crop of memorial sermons and tributes. Weems's earlier biographers, Lawrence C. Wroth and Harold Kellock, have supposed that his little book grew out of a sermon he had himself preached. Perhaps he did preach such a sermon—few clergymen in America seem to have missed the opportunity—but William A. Bryan argues convincingly that Weems was already writing a biography of sorts when Washington died.[8] As early as January 22, 1797, he told Mathew Carey:

[6] The full history of all these publications is set out in Skeel, vol. I, though the record is intricate and in some cases incomplete. Next to *Washington*, Weems's *Marion* was by far the most successful of his creations. It had reached the twelfth edition by 1825 and went on being reprinted up to 1891. *Franklin*, which enjoyed a fair success, seems to have had its last reprinting in 1876. *Penn*, though it too sold fairly well, was the least popular of the biographies. First published by Carey in 1822, it reappeared in editions of 1829, 1836, 1845, 1850, 1854, and possibly 1859.

[7] The last known letter from Weems, postmarked February 11, 1825, and sent to Henry Carey, is reprinted in William A. Bryan, "Three Unpublished Letters of Parson Weems," *William & Mary Quarterly*, 2nd series, 23: 272–277 (July 1943). Weems writes that he is "very ill of the *strangury*." According to Bryan, this may have been urethritis or one of several other diseases.

[8] William A. Bryan, "The Genesis of Weems's 'Life of Washington,'" *Americana*, 36: 147–165 (April 1942)—a valuable article. There is also much of interest in the same author's *George Washington in American Literature, 1775–1865* (New York, 1952).

Experience has taught me that small, i.e. quarter of dollar books, on subjects calculated to *strike* the Popular Curiosity, printed in very large numbers and properly *distributed,* w^{d} prove an immense revenue to the prudent and industrious Undertakers. If you cou^{d} get the life of Genl. Wayne, Putnam, Green[e] &c., Men whose courage and Abilities, whose patriotism and Exploits have won the love and admiration of the American people, printed in small volumes and with very interesting frontspieces [*sic*], you w^{d}, without doubt, sell an immense number of them. People here think nothing of giving 1/6 (their quarter of a dollar) for anything that pleases their fancy. Let us give them something worth their money.[9]

This was at a period when Weems was trying to dispose of certain expensive publications such as Guthrie's *Geography,* which apparently sold at over ten dollars a set.[10] Carey did not respond to the suggestion; so in 1799 one guesses that Weems set out to meet the demand by composing a short, popular account of the prime Revolutionary hero, George Washington. On June 24 of that year he was far enough along to write to Carey:

I have nearly ready for the press a piece christen^{d}, or to be christen^{d}, "The Beauties of Washington." Tis artfully drawn up, enliven^{d} with anecdotes, and in my humble opinion, marvellously fitted, *"ad captandum—gustum populi Americani*! ! ! ! ["] What say you to printing it for me and ordering a copper plate Frontispiece of that Heroe, something in this way. George Washington Esqr. The Guardian Angel of his Country "Go thy way old George. Die when thou wilt we shall never look upon thy like again" M. Carey inver. &^{c}

NB. The whole will make but four sheets and will sell like flax seed at quarter of a dollar. I cou'd make you a world of pence and popularity by it.[11]

9 Skeel, II, 72.

10 Weems to Carey, June 6, 1796, from Dumfries: "Draw me up 300 elegant subscription papers. . . . I sh^{d} like to see an eloquent little preamble on the pleasures and advantages which a Gentleman may promise himself from so complete a system of Geography. . . . You talk of 13 Dol. exclusive of binding. I *must* you know have them bound." Skeel, II, 16.

11 Skeel, II, 120.

A month after Washington's sudden, fatal illness, Weems was urgently pressing Carey, in another exuberant letter that deserves to be quoted at length:

I've something to whisper in your lug. Washington, you know is gone! Millions are gaping to read something about him. I am very nearly prim^{d} and cock^{d} for 'em. 6 months ago I set myself to collect anecdotes of him. My plan! I give his history, sufficiently minute—I accompany him from his start, thro the French & Indian & British or Revolutionary wars, to the Presidents chair, to the throne in the hearts of 5,000,000 of People. I then go on to show that his unparrelled [*sic*] rise & elevation were due to his Great Virtues.

Washington's virtues, as Weems enumerated them, were:

1 his Veneration for the Diety [*sic*] or Religious Principles. 2 His Patriotism. 3^{d} his Magninmity [*sic*]. 4 his Industry. 5 his Temperance & Sobriety. 6 his Justice, &^{c}. &^{c}. Thus I hold up his great Virtues . . . to the imitation of Our Youth.

"All this," Weems went on,

I have lin^{d} & enliven^{d} with *Anecdotes apropos interesting* and *Entertaining*. I have read it to several Gentlemen whom I thought good judges, such as Presbyterian Clergymen, Classical Scholars, &^{c}. &^{c}. and they all commend it much. . . . We may sell it with great rapidity for 25 or 37 Cents and it w^{d} not cost 10 . . . it will be the first. I can send it on, half of it, immediately.[12]

Again Carey seems to have been unresponsive, for Weems wrote on February 2, 1800:

I sent you on a sample of [the] History of Washington. In consequence of not hearing from you I resolv^{d} to strike off a few on my own acc^{t}. . . .[13]

As a result, Weems's first edition (1800) was probably printed for him by another Dublin-born figure, George Keatinge of Baltimore. It was entitled *The Life and Memorable Actions of George Washington* and ran to 80 pages, more or less along the lines indicated in Weems's correspondence with

12 "Jan. 12 or 13," 1800; Skeel, I, 8–9.
13 Skeel, I, 9.

Carey. The pamphlet was anonymous. However, another edition, probably also of 1800, was printed in Georgetown, "for the Rev. M. L. Weems of Lodge No. 50, Dumfries." This Masonic designation was followed on many of Weems's title pages. A third edition of 1800, described on the title page as "A Second Edition Improved," was printed for the author by John Bioren of Philadelphia. The second and third of these were dedicated to George Washington's widow, Martha. There may have been a fourth edition in the same year.

The pamphlet continued to sell extremely well, with minor changes of text, and eventually began to appear under Carey's imprint. But in the meantime Weems went to work as an agent for C. P. Wayne. In this capacity he found himself soliciting subscriptions for a much more ambitious undertaking. This was the official biography of George Washington entrusted to Chief Justice John Marshall. There was widespread interest in the project, though some apprehension that it would be unduly Federalist in tone. Weems drummed up plenty of advance trade. But, to Weems not least of all, Marshall's book proved to be a considerable disappointment. The first two volumes did not reach the impatient subscribers until 1804, in some cases two years after their money had been committed. Of these volumes, the first was a general history of the American colonies up to 1760, with only incidental references to Washington. The second volume dismissed Washington's boyhood and early manhood in a single page. The third and fourth volumes, published a year later, provided a survey of the Revolution but again failed to focus on George Washington. The fifth and final volume (1807) dealt with the years 1783–1799 in seven hundred cramped pages. They were an improvement on the previous contents, but were stiff and impersonal. Weems, struggling to appease his public, became increasingly disgusted, as his letters to Wayne testify. The subscribers were complaining, he said. The work was too voluminous, too formal. Worse than that, the publisher was trying to cut his costs by bringing out later volumes in cheap bindings with inferior paper. Weems insisted, no doubt correctly, that the customers would still buy the set as an act of piety, if it were handsomely produced. As it was, they felt cheated.[14]

This is the background to Weems's renewed attention to his own piece of Washingtoniana. In 1806 Carey brought out the so-called fifth edition of Weems's *Washington.* The author still identified himself as of Lodge No. 50; the text was still only 80 pages. Yet it had been rewritten completely and divided for the first time into chapters. Moreover, two new anecdotes were included, both destined for a long life and both referring to Washington's childhood. One of them, in fact, was the tale of the cherry-tree (see pp. 11–12 of the present edition) which young George admitted to cutting "with my little hatchet"—the word "little" disappeared in later editions. The other story (see pp. 13–16 of the present edition) was of the cabbage-seed which George's father secretly planted so that on sprouting it would spell out the letters of "GEORGE WASHINGTON."

The next development, a more decisive one, was revealed in 1808, with the sixth edition. By then Weems had ceased to peddle John Marshall's mammoth potboiler and could devote some leisure to his own creation. The outcome was no longer a pamphlet, but a book of over 200 pages (216 in one version, 228 in another). *The Life of George Washington; With Curious Anecdotes, Equally Honourable To Himself and Exemplary To His Young Countrymen* was now almost in its final form. On the title page, now and in all subsequent editions of *Washington,* Weems styled himself "Formerly Rector of Mount-Vernon Parish." The text was much amplified. Among the fresh material was the story of the Quaker named

[14] There is a long and entertaining description of this venture in Albert J. Beveridge, *The Life of John Marshall,* 4 vols. (Boston, 1916–1919), III, 223–274. William Foran, "John Marshall as a Historian," *American Historical Review,* 43: 51–64 (October 1937), reveals that Marshall "borrowed" extensively from the *Annual Register.*

Potts (see pp. 181–182) who saw General Washington on his knees in prayer at Valley Forge. The vivid dream of Washington's mother, Mary Ball Washington (see pp. 55–57), was also newly introduced. Indeed, these had already in a sense been tested on the public. Weems had described himself as Rector of Mount Vernon as far back as 1804, in some Georgia newspaper announcements of Sunday services at which he was to officiate. He had likewise used the Potts anecdote in 1804, as a newspaper advertisement for Marshall's *Washington*. The dream too had been recounted as part of an advertisement, in the *Columbia Museum and Savannah Advertiser* of June 12, 1807, with the additional comment:

> This little dream tho' presenting Washington as *in crayons,* and dimly seen like Ossian's "Half viewless Heroes," bending forward from their clouds, yet does it surprisingly mark the characteristic features of that unequall'd man. . . . A complete and elegant history of this great man, compiled from his own papers, by Chief Justice John Marshall, five volumes in calf and gilt, with an atlas of military charts, are now for sale at DR. GEORGE HARRAL'S at 20 dollars to subscribers, and 21 to non-subscribers. M. L. Weems tenders his best thanks to those of his numerous *subscribers* whom he has had the honour to see, for the truly filial cheerfulness with which they have generally receiv'd the History of their POLITICAL FATHER.[15]

Thereafter, only minor changes were made in the text. The seventh edition (1808) contained 228 pages, as did the eighth and ninth. It still had a rather improvised air: it was an inflated pamphlet, with an introduction, eleven chapters of biography, and four more expatiating on Washington's character, benevolence, industry and patriotism. Some time in 1808 Weems apparently sold the copyright of the work to Carey, for about $1,000. He soon began to regret the arrangement, not only because he seemed to have got the worst of the bargain, but also because he felt the book could be much improved. "You have a great deal of money lying in the

[15] Skeel, I, 32–33.

bones of old George," he told Carey in January 1809, "if you will but exert yourself to extract it."[16] A few days later Weems returned to the theme:

> Believe me I sometimes mourn that I ever let it go out of my hand,—but *chiefly* because it is not *half finished,* not *half* finish[d]. Several most valuable chapters . . . ought still to be added. And in the work, as it now stands, there are many passages that are capable of being wrought up to a far *more interesting height,* but which can hardly be done except by a mind peculiarly prone to the thing like mine, and enthusiastically heated.[17]

Weems offered to do the necessary adding and polishing for "some trifling douceur." Carey was unreceptive.

For several more years, at intervals, Weems renewed the suggestion. "Washington outsells anything I have, no comparison," he told Carey in 1810. With embellishments it could be a gold-mine. So he urged the publisher, seemingly without response, to issue an "elegant edition" at three or four dollars.

In 1814 he said wistfully, "I have some noble anecdotes to add to it." In January 1816 he tried another tack:

> I wish you w[d] instantly give me orders to finish Washington. It cries aloud for 60 or 70 pages more, for it is much clamour[d] against as far too small for a dollar book. Ramsay's is nearly *twice the size,* & better plates, & yet Cushing says he prints it for 40 cents.[18]

All this to no avail: Weems's *Washington* remained the same, in edition after edition. Other writing engrossed his attention, and his fertile mind sought other expedients.

[16] January 13, 1809; Skeel, I, 47.

[17] January 19, 1809; Skeel, I, 47.

[18] February 4, 1810; postmarked March 19, 1814; January 4, 1816. Skeel I, 50, 62, 64. The *Life of George Washington* by David Ramsay (New York, 1807), though largely military and political in treatment, was smoothly written and quite popular: further editions appeared in 1811, 1814, 1815, 1818, 1825, 1832 and 1840. Unlike Weems, Ramsay had the honor of being reprinted abroad, in English and French editions (1807, 1809) and in various Spanish translations. See W. S. Baker, *Biblioteca Washingtoniana* (Philadelphia, 1889), *passim.*

He seems, for example, to have envisaged his Washington, Franklin, and Marion biographies as a trio, to be sold accordingly, if possible. Such would appear to be the implication of an advertisement, probably inserted by Weems, in a North Carolina newspaper in 1821:

> . . . Where also may be had, the Biographies of the three NOBLEST FOUNDERS of our LIBERTIES;—WASHINGTON,— . . . of whom not even admiring strangers speak without exclaiming—"FAVOR'D, HAPPY AMERICA! The Lightnings of Heaven bowed to thy Franklin! The Temptations of Earth could not seduce thy Washington! The Demons of Hell were vanquish'd by thy Marion!" N.B.—A liberal part of the profit will be given to the Sunday Schools of Newbern.[19]

No matter what its imperfections, the *Washington* kept on selling. By 1825, the year of Weems's death, it had reached its twenty-ninth "edition"—or more accurately, printing (a century afterward the number had risen to eighty). It had come out in German translations.[20] Its anecdotes were being borrowed by other biographers, with or without attribution. The story of the cherry-tree was the favorite and gained still wider notoriety when it was included in one of McGuffey's *Readers*. Close behind in popular esteem came the story of the cabbage-seed, and of the little boy in the apple-orchard. Other much-cited bits of Weemsiana were Potts and the Valley Forge prayer; Mary Washington's dream;

[19] Skeel, I, 73.

[20] This twenty-ninth "edition" was the last to be numbered separately. It was the first to be published not by Carey but by Joseph Allen, also of Philadelphia. The text had long since become final, though the illustrations had undergone some modification in style and number. Apart from the frontispiece portrait, the illustrations were wretchedly bad—battle-scenes vaguely fashioned after the paintings of John Trumbull. During the 1850's the book came under the imprint of J. B. Lippincott, who reprinted at regular intervals until 1892, when there was a pause until 1918. The most recent edition (New York, Macy-Masius, 1927) carries the title borne by some of the 1800 pamphlet-versions of the book: *A History of the Life and Death, Virtues & Exploits of General George Washington*. German translations appeared in 1810 ("Libanon," Penn.) and 1817 (Baltimore). Both were taken from the ninth edition of Weems; and both described the author as "ehemaligen Prediger der Mount-Vernon Kirche."

and the story of the "famous Indian warrior" (see p. 42) who fired seventeen times at Washington, at the Monongahela in 1755, but was mysteriously unable to hit him. Various details of Washington's childhood were also frequently adapted from Weems—the information that his first schooling was at the hands of old Hobby the sexton (see p. 8); that George's schoolmates submitted their disputes to his adjudication (see p. 19); that he prevented them from fighting, but that he nevertheless organized mock-battles; and that he was an admirable athlete, who was often seen to "throw a stone across Rappahannock, at the lower ferry of Fredericksburg" (pp. 20–21).

Material of this nature was reproduced—to give a few instances—in Anna C. Reed, *The Life of George Washington* (New York, 1829), which was written for the American Sunday School Union; in "Peter Parley" (Samuel G. Goodrich), *The Life of George Washington, Illustrated by Tales, Sketches and Anecdotes* (New York, 1832), a little book designed for use in schools; in the Reverend E. C. M'Guire, *The Religious Opinions and Character of Washington* (New York, 1836); in S. G. Arnold, *The Life of George Washington, First President of the United States* (New York, 1840), written for the Sunday School Union of the Methodist Episcopal Church; in Horatio Hastings Weld, *Pictorial Life of George Washington* (Philadelphia, 1845); in another book of the same title by John Frost (Philadelphia, 1854); in Caroline Matilda Kirkland, *Memoirs of Washington* (New York, 1857); and so on.[21] Americans all over the Union have

[21] Anna Reed's biography, published anonymously, came out in revised form in 1832 and 1842. The 1832 edition includes Potts and the prayer; the cherry-tree does not turn up until 1842. M'Guire's *Religious Opinions* cites the apple-orchard and cherry-tree episodes in Weems's own words and paraphrases the cabbage-seed story (pp. 33–37). S. G. Arnold's *Life* introduces the cherry-tree and cabbage-seed (pp. 14–16). Horatio H. Weld's anonymous *Pictorial Life* makes no use of the cherry-tree but does adopt other Weemsian anecdotes—for example, the Valley Forge prayer (p. 88): "The inhabitants of the surrounding country, knowing the condition of the army, were alarmed; one of them left his home one day, and, as he was passing thoughtfully the edge of a

testified to the influence that Weems and the Weemsian anecdotes exercised over them. William Russell Smith of Alabama (1815–1890) was one; and his more famous contemporary Abraham Lincoln confessed that "away back in my childhood, the earliest days of my being able to read, I got hold of a small book, . . . Weem's [*sic*] Life of Washington."[22] Some of Weems's successors improved on the Weemsian canon. Thus in 1864 Morrison Heady produced a juvenile work on Washington, *The Farmer Boy, and How He Became Commander-in-Chief.* In this the cherry-tree tale was set at Christmas time, and the hatchet was described as a little Indian tomahawk brought by Santa Claus. George first used it, virtuously, to chop some firewood for the family, then mischievously upon the cherry-tree. His father, finding the damaged tree, suspected a little slave-boy, Jerry, and was about to whip him when George arrived upon the scene:

"O papa, papa!" cried he, "don't whip poor Jerry: if somebody must be whipped, let it be me; for it was I and not Jerry, that cut the cherry-tree."

Ever after, Heady assures us, Jerry "loved his noble little

---

wood near the camp, heard low sounds. . . . He paused to listen, and . . . saw Washington engaged in prayer. He passed quietly on . . . ; and, on returning home, told his family he knew the Americans would succeed, for their leader did not trust in his own strength, but sought aid from the Hearer of prayer. . . . Many, who, in prosperity, have forgotten to worship their Creator, call upon him earnestly in the day of trouble, when they feel that His power only can deliver them; but with Washington it was a custom. . . ." Frost's *Pictorial Life* quotes the anecdotes of the apple-orchard and the cherry-tree *verbatim* (pp. 17–18), together with Weemsian information on Washington's schooling. Caroline M. Kirkland relegates to an appendix the story of Mary Washington's dream, as "too vivid and picturesque to be omitted, yet too evidently fabulous to deserve admission into the text" (p. 30); but she praises Weems's style and reproduces several other anecdotes in full. See also Bryan, *Washington in American Literature,* pp. 97–107.

[22] Smith, who led a full and varied career, read Weems at the age of ten: "It was true to its great office . . . , and that was, to make the American youth feel and believe that Washington was the greatest man that ever lived . . . , and that the country he delivered was the greatest country on the globe." See Jay B. Hubbell, *The South in American Literature* (Durham, N.C., 1954), pp. 233–234, 628–629; and see Roy P. Basler, ed., *The Collected Works of Abraham Lincoln,* 9 vols. (New Brunswick, 1953), address to the New Jersey Senate at Trenton, February 21, 1861, IV, 235.

master to distraction." A few pages earlier, Heady says that it would be pleasant to record some stories of George Washington's childhood,

> but we must keep within the bounds of true history, and content ourselves with . . . that which really did happen. With this safe rule for our guidance, we will therefore proceed at once to take up the thread . . . at that period of George's boyhood, concerning which some certain record has come down to our time.[23]

A generation later, though popular biographers were less sure of the strict accuracy of the canon, they showed themselves reluctant to abandon it. For example, Virginia F. Townsend writes of her efforts in 1887:

> The material for a biography is, at this early period, rather scanty. The story of the hatchet and the cherry sapling, whether true or not, is singularly characteristic. It shows the strong impression which the sensitive conscience of the child must have made on those around him. Nobody would ever have thought of relating such a story in connection with the boyhood of Napoleon Bonaparte.[24]

With similar equivocations, this approach is evident in a children's book published as recently as 1954:

> Stories about George Washington as a boy have been retold so often through the years that even though we're not sure they really did happen, they have become a part of the story of America. And they do tell us something of the kind of boy he was.[25]

[23] [Morrison Heady], *The Farmer Boy, and How He Became Commander-in-Chief,* by Uncle Juvinell (Boston, 1864), pp. 41–45, 36–37; Bryan, *Washington in American Literature,* p. 110.

[24] Virginia F. Townsend, *Life of Washington* (New York, 1887), pp. 18–19.

[25] Bella Koral, *George Washington: The Father of Our Country* (New York, 1954), no pagination.

III
CRITICISM OF WEEMS

There can be no doubt that either directly or through borrowings Weems has, to quote Albert J. Beveridge, "profoundly influenced the American conception of Washington." Beveridge goes on, though, to assert that the "grotesque and wholly imaginary stories" that Weems propagated have depicted Washington, "that intensely human founder of the American Nation," as "an impossible and intolerable prig." Another scholarly commentator, John S. Bassett, while admitting that Weems's *Washington* was "the most successful historical book of the day," dismisses it as "a romance, interlarded with pious stories. It was slightly esteemed by educated men of the day but was acceptable to the unsophisticated. Except as a curiosity, it is beneath contempt or criticism." William Roscoe Thayer, who published a biography of Washington in 1922, spoke even more sharply of the biographer's disadvantage in "having to counteract the errors and absurdities which the Reverend Mason L. Weems made current. . . ." Thayer declared:

> Owing to the pernicious drivel of . . . Weems no other great man in history has had to live down such a mass of absurdities and deliberate false inventions. At last after a century and a quarter the rubbish has been mostly cleared away, and only those who wilfully prefer to deceive themselves need waste time over an imaginary Father of His Country amusing himself with a fictitious cherry-tree and hatchet.

Rupert Hughes, another Washington biographer of the 1920's, remarked that there was a gap in our knowledge of Washington's early life: "It was this gap that Parson Weems filled up with such slush of plagiarism and piety."[26]

[26] Beveridge, *Marshall,* III, 231–232n.; John S. Bassett, *Cambridge History of American Literature,* 4 vols. (New York, 1917–1921), II, 105–106; William R. Thayer, *George Washington* (Boston, 1922), pp. 2, vii; Rupert Hughes, *George*

Indeed, the validity of his material was questioned during his lifetime. The *Washington* pamphlet of 1800 was described by a reviewer as "eighty pages of as entertaining and edifying matter as can be found in the annals of fanaticism and absurdity."[27] The enlarged version of a decade later was wittily analyzed by Dr. Bigelow of Boston:

With a style of rotundity and bombast which may distance Macpherson himself, he has intermingled the ludicrous quaintness of Joe Miller; and he often transports us from a strain of religious moralizing . . . to the low cant and balderdash of the drinking table . . . We have questioned whether the book before us may not be termed a novel founded on fact. Second thoughts would induce us to style it rather an epick poem; for, besides its figures, characters, battles, and episodes, it is duly provided with a suitable quantity of preternatural machinery. The exploits and future greatness of Washington are . . . foretold by a wonderful dream . . . which happened to his mother while he was a boy . . .[28]

This slightly condescending skepticism seems to have been common among educated Americans. John Neal, who contributed some impressionistic sketches of American writers to *Blackwood's Edinburgh Magazine* in 1824–25, had only a brief verdict on Weems:

Washington: The Human Being and The Hero, 1732–1762 (New York, 1926), pp. 23–24. This was the first of a three-volume set (1926–1930), which took Washington's career up to 1781.

27 *Monthly Magazine and American Review,* 3: 210 (September 1800), quoted in Skeel, I, 14.

28 Quoted in Skeel, I, 55–56. Dr. Bigelow's report was read to the Anthology Society of Boston on December 11, 1810. The *Macpherson* he mentions is James Macpherson (1736–1796), a Scottish poet who aroused enormous interest by publishing "translations" from Ossian and other bards from the shadowy Gaelic past. Weems was indeed acquainted with Macpherson's Ossian (see note 15). As for Joe Miller, a collection of what might be called gags was published in 1739, under the title of *Joe Miller's Jests.*

Another review, in the Boston *Panoplist,* 5: 525 (April 1810), quoted in Frank Luther Mott, *A History of American Magazines,* 4 vols. (Cambridge, Mass., 1930–1957), I, 263, commended Weems for having "collected a number of facts particularly relating to the childhood and youth of the American sage, and presented them . . . in such an interesting, and frequently comic dress, that it will require the most immoveable gravity of disposition to preserve a composure of muscles in reading this book."

WEAMS, Dr:—a D.D. perhaps: Rector of MOUNT VERNON—the seat of George Washington, whom he knew from his boyhood: author of A WASHINGTON'S LIFE—not one word of which we believe. It is full of ridiculous exaggeration.[29]

Neal's note does not suggest a close acquaintance with Weems or his work. But an 1817 review of Weems's *Franklin* would indicate that the Parson was becoming a semi-legendary figure, endowed with "the power of doing considerable good, and considerable mischief, among the lower orders of readers in this country":

Our readers should know, that he is an author, a pedlar, and a preacher. He writes a book, and carries it about the country; holding forth a godly sermon in every village, and taking occasion to exhort all manner of persons to read fructifying books. The cart stands ready at the door; and, after a congregation have heard a sermon for nothing, they will seldom be so hard-hearted as not to pay for a book.[30]

Though the reviewer admitted that he could not vouch for the accuracy of this account, it was corroborated and amplified by Bishop William Meade, who was fairly well acquainted with Weems. Meade, half-amused, half-scandalized, pictured the Parson as a man "of a very enlarged charity in all respects." Weems, he said,

was in the habit of having the servant[s], assembled in private houses, where he would spend the night, and would recite a portion of Scripture, for he never read it out of the book. . . . I do not think he could have long even pretended to be the rector of any parish. From my earliest knowledge of him he was a travelling bookseller for Mr. Matthew [*sic*] Carey, of Philadelphia, visiting all the States south of Pennsylvania, and perhaps north of it, in a little wagon, with his fiddle as a constant companion to amuse himself and others. . . . One instance of his good-nature is well attested. At the old tavern in Caroline county, Virginia, . . .

[29] *Blackwood's Edinburgh Magazine*, 27: 203 (February 1825). Neal (1793–1876), an American author of great facility, was in England at the time and so wrote from memory.

[30] *Analectic Magazine*, 9: 389–391 (May 1817), quoted in Skeel, I, 132–133.

Mr. Weems and some strolling players or puppet-showmen met together one night. A notice of some exhibition had been given, and the neighbours had assembled to watch it. A fiddle was necessary to the full performance, and that was wanting. Mr. Weems supplied the deficiency. . . . Though calling himself an Episcopal minister, he knew no distinction of Churches. He preached in every pulpit to which he could gain access, and where he could recommend his books. His books were of all kinds. . . . On an election or court-day at Fairfax Court-House, I once . . . found Mr. Weems, with a bookcaseful for sale, in the portico of the tavern. On looking at them I saw Paine's "Age of Reason," and, taking it into my hand, turned to him, and asked if it was possible that he could sell such a book. He immediately took out the Bishop of Llandaff's answer, and said, "Behold the antidote. The bane and antidote are both before you." He carried this spurious charity into his sermons. In my own pulpit . . . in my absence, it being my Sunday in Winchester, he extolled Tom Paine and one or more noted infidels . . . , and said if their ghosts could return to the earth they would be shocked to hear the falsehoods which were told of them. I was present the following day, when my mother charged him with what she had heard of his sermon, and well remember that he was confused and speechless.

Bishop Meade conceded that some of Weems's pamphlets on drunkenness and gambling would be valuable, "but for the fact that you know not what to believe of the narrative." The same must be said of Weems's "very popular" biographies of Washington and Marion: "You know not how much of fiction there is in them."[31]

At least one outraged contemporary was in no doubt on that score. This was a Carolinian named Peter Horry, who had fought under General Marion and tried to set down his reminiscences. Finding that he lacked the necessary flair, Horry turned his notes over to Weems. On December 13,

31 William Meade, *Old Churches, Ministers, and Families of Virginia,* 2 vols. (Philadelphia, 1857), II, 234–236. The Bishop of Llandaff in this passage was Richard Watson (1737–1816). His "antidote" was *An Apology for the Bible* (1796), a copy of which is said to have been presented to every Harvard undergraduate of the period. See Vernon L. Parrington, *Main Currents in American Thought,* 3 vols. (New York, 1927–1930), I, 324.

1809, Weems informed Horry that the book was finished. He added: *"I told you I must write it in my own way, and knowing the passion of the times for novels, I have endeavoured to throw your ideas and facts about Gen. Marion into the garb . . . of a military romance."* A year later Weems wrote that he was astonished to hear that Horry was displeased: how *could* he be? Horry answered, on February 4, 1811, with some dignity:

> *A history of realities turned into a romance!* The idea alone, militates against the work. The one as a history of real performance, would always be read with pleasure. The other as a fictitious invention of the brain, once read would suffice. Therefore, I think you injured yourself, notwithstanding the quick sales of the book. *Nor have the public received the real history of General Marion. You have carved and mutilated it with so many erroneous statements,* [that] your embellishments, observations and remarks must necessarily be erroneous as proceeding from false grounds. *Most certainly 'tis not* MY history, but YOUR romance.[32]

Horry and others may have wondered, too, about the nature of Weems's devotion to George Washington, in view of the couplet he inserted on the title page of *Marion:*

> On VERNON's Chief, why lavish all our lays?
> Come, honest Muse, and sing great Marion's praise.

Weems's eccentricity and unreliability were, then, known to at least some persons during his lifetime. All the more sober and ambitious biographers of Washington avoided his prize anecdotes. There is no hint of the cherry-tree in the biographies of Washington produced in 1807 by Aaron Bancroft and David Ramsay. Jared Sparks, who published the first large collection of Washington's writings and com-

[32] These exchanges, quoted in Skeel, I, 100–102, are taken from William Gilmore Simms, "Weems, the Biographer and Historian," *Views and Reviews, Second Series* (New York, 1845), pp. 123–141. The Simms article first appeared in the *Southern and Western Monthly Magazine and Review* (Charleston), I: 35–47 (January 1845). The *Second Series,* though dated 1845, was not published until 1847.

pleted the set with a biographical volume (1837), may have had Weems in mind when he said of his own book:

Anecdotes are interwoven, and such incidents of a private and personal nature as are known; but it must be confessed, that these are more rare than could be desired. I have seen many particulars of this description which I knew not to be true, and others which I did not believe. These have been avoided; nor have I stated any fact for which I was not convinced there was credible authority. If this forbearance has been practised at the expense of the reader's entertainment, he must submit to the sacrifice as due to truth and the dignity of the subject.[33]

In Sparks there is no mention of the cherry-tree, Mary's dream, Potts and the prayer, and so on; nor in *A Life of George Washington in Latin Prose* (New York, 1835), written by an Ohio teacher named Francis Glass; nor in James Kirke Paulding's more sprightly *Life of Washington* of the same year. Paulding also may have been thinking of Weems when he maintained, rather too confidently:

It has hitherto been found impossible to mar the severe simplicity of Washington's greatness by coupling it with puerilities that have neither the merit of illustrating his character or increasing our stores of useful knowledge.[34]

Although Washington Irving probably consulted Weems in the course of preparing his own extensive biography of Washington (1855–1859), he, like Sparks, eschewed the more fanciful anecdotes. So did the dignified Edward Everett (1860) and Woodrow Wilson (1897).[35] It was the producers

[33] Jared Sparks, *The Writings of George Washington; . . . with A Life of the Author,* 12 vols. (Boston, 1834–1837), I, xiii.

[34] James Kirke Paulding, *A Life of Washington,* 2 vols. (New York, 1835), I, 43–44.

[35] Washington Irving, *Life of George Washington,* 5 vols. (New York, 1855–1959); Edward Everett, *The Life of George Washington* (New York, 1860; originally compiled as an article for the *Encyclopaedia Britannica*); Woodrow Wilson, *George Washington* (New York, 1897). Irving, who began to collect material for his biography as early as 1841, asked his bookseller to send him Weems's biography in addition to Paulding and others: Bryan, *Washington in American Literature,* pp. 103–104.

of juvenile, Sunday School, and semi-fictional biographies who perpetuated the cherry-tree.

Anyone who examined the Weemsian *oeuvre* at all methodically could not help being suspicious of his claims as a biographer. He wrote, as Dr. Bigelow observed, in a grotesque medley of styles. He had no hesitation in rendering conversations as if he had been present with a shorthand notebook. He was a free, undiscriminating, and often ludicrous adapter of well-known material. For example, he modified for his own purpose the famous epitaph on the Countess of Pembroke, attributed to Ben Jonson:

Underneath this sable hearse
Lies the subject of all verse,—
Sidney's sister, Pembroke's mother.
Death, ere thou hast slain another,
Learn'd and fair and good as she,
Time shall throw a dart at thee.

"A little altered," these lines became in Weems's *Washington* an epitaph (see p. 54) on Martha Custis:

Underneath this marble hearse,
Lies the subject of all verse.
Custis' widow—great George's wife—
Death! ere thou robb'st another life,
Virtuous, fair and good as SHE,
Christ shall launch a dart at thee.

Weems's pamphlet *Hymen's Recruiting Sergeant* contained a very free version of Proverbs, chapter 31, "with a touch or two of an American brush:"

Verse 10. Behold a virtuous woman, for her price is above rubies. . . .
15. She regardeth not the snow; for her household are clothed in *fearnought.*
16. By her much industry her cheeks are made ruddy like the rose of Sharon; yea, her nerves are strengthened, so that when she heareth talk of the hysterics, she marvelleth thereat. . . .
21. Her poultry multiply exceedingly in the land, even as the

black-birds in the corn field for multitude; so that she feedeth her household daintily on chicken pies. . . .[36]

Nevertheless, there was reason for contemporaries to accept at least some of Weems's statements. After all, he *had* lived near to George Washington. If his data seemed to be casually assembled, the historical standards of the day were not very exact. The full attack on Weems was delayed until the latter part of the nineteenth century. By then, American historians were far more professional in technique; they had accumulated a great deal of information about Washington and his era; Washington was no longer quite so sacred a figure; and so his biographers felt that it was feasible and desirable to present him in more human guise. Much of the previous Washington historiography was criticized. Jared Sparks was blamed for editing the humanity out of Washington's correspondence. Weems was thoroughly discredited. He had turned Washington into a prig and influenced generations of young Americans into accepting his version; he was exposed as shamelessly inaccurate and irresponsible. Scholars pointed out that only in his *Washington* did Weems claim to be "formerly Rector of Mount-Vernon Parish"; on other title pages he was Weems "of Lodge No. 50, Dumfries." The reason was obvious: Weems meant to lay claim to special knowledge of Washington. But there was no such parish as "Mount Vernon." Washington had once attended Pohick church, in Truro Parish, where Weems was an occasional preacher. But there was no proof that Weems ever preached before George Washington. In this respect, to start with, Weems was a fraud.

On investigation, other features of his *Washington* appeared equally dubious. "You know not how much of fiction there is . . ."; the cabbage-seed anecdote was detected as a

36 Mason L. Weems, *Three Discourses* [*Hymen's Recruiting Sergeant, The Drunkard's Looking Glass, God's Revenge Against Adultery*], ed. by Emily E. Ford Skeel (New York, 1929), pp. 31–32. Fearnought was a rough woollen cloth, often worn by sailors.

plagiarism from the Scottish poet-philosopher James Beattie. In 1799 Beattie published a commemorative account of his dead son, as part of an edition of his works. In this Beattie describes how he imparted instruction to the little boy:

The first rules of morality I taught him were, to speak truth, and keep a secret; and I never found that in a single instance he transgressed either. . . . I was desirous to make a trial how far his own reason could go in tracing out . . . the . . . first principle of all religion, the being of God. . . .

He had reached his fifth (or sixth) year, knew the alphabet, and could read a little. . . . In a corner of a little garden, . . . I wrote in the mould, with my finger, the three initial letters of his name; and sowing garden-cresses in the furrows, covered up the seed, and smoothed the ground. Ten days after, he came running to me, and with astonishment . . . told me, that his name was growing in the garden. I smiled at the report . . . ; but he insisted on my going to see what had happened. "Yes," said I carelessly, on coming to the place, "I see it is so; but there is nothing in this worth notice; it is mere chance:" and I went away. He followed me, and . . . said, with some earnestness, "It could not be mere chance. . . ."[37]

Nor could Weems's use of the story, to make the same homiletic point about George's "*true* Father."

What Weems did not borrow, he seemed gaily to invent. Later investigators could find little or no substance in several of his anecdotes, and good cause to suspect that they came out of Weems's imagination. For the seminar-trained historians of a later generation, proud of their diligence and objectivity, Weems furnished an object-lesson in how *not* to write history. Their position is eloquently summarized in the biography of Washington (1889) by Henry Cabot Lodge, who had worked at Harvard under Henry Adams and earned a Ph.D.:

In regard to the public life of Washington, Weems took the facts known to every one, and drawn for the most part from the

[37] Sir William Forbes, *An Account of the Life and Writings of James Beattie, LI.D.*, 2 vols. (London, 1824), II, 286–287; Rupert Hughes, *Washington,* I, 24, 501.

gazettes. He then dressed them up in his own peculiar fashion and gave them to the world. All this, forming of course nine tenths of his book, has passed, despite its success, into oblivion. The remaining tenth described Washington's boyhood . . . and this, which is the work of the author's imagination, has lived. Weems, having set himself up as absolutely the only authority as to this period, has been implicitly followed, and has thus come to demand serious consideration. Until Weems is weighed and disposed of, we can not even begin an attempt to get at the real Washington.

Lodge goes on to say that Weems was " a man destitute of historical sense, training, or morals, ready to take the slenderest fact and work it up for . . . the market until it became almost as impossible to reduce it to its original dimensions as it was for the fisherman to get the Afrit back into his jar":

Weems says that his stories were told him by a lady, and "a good old gentleman," who remembered the incidents. . . . To a writer who invented the rector of Mount Vernon, the further invention of a couple of Boswells would be a trifle. I say Boswells advisedly, for these stories are told with the utmost minuteness.

The real point, for Lodge, is that the Weemsian tales are *unhistorical:*

No English-speaking people, certainly no Virginians, ever thought or behaved or talked in 1740 like the personages in Weems's stories. . . . These precious anecdotes belong to the age of Miss Edgeworth and Hannah More and Jane Taylor. They are engaging specimens of the "Harry and Lucy" and "Purple Jar" morality, and accurately reflect the pale didacticism which became fashionable in England at the close of the last century.

Lodge concludes:

To enter into any serious historical criticism of these stories would be to break a butterfly. So much as this has been said only because these wretched fables have gone throughout the world, and it is time that they were swept away into the dust-heaps of history. They represent Mr. and Mrs. Washington as affected and priggish people, given to cheap moralizing, and, what is far worse, they have served to place Washington himself in a ridiculous light to an age which has outgrown the educational foibles of seventy-five years ago.[38]

In a word, the objection to Weems is that he was slapdash and even fraudulent; and that he forced upon the world a false and repellent picture of George Washington.

IV
EXTENUATIONS

It is useless to try to pass Weems off as a scrupulous historian. His main claim to our attention must rest on other grounds. But he has been perhaps too roughly handled, and too much singled out as a scapegoat. Emily E. Ford Skeel, who took over the large collection of Weemsiana assembled by her brother Paul Leicester Ford, an experienced historian and author of *The True George Washington* (1896), notes that in early drafts Ford dismissed Weems as a "fabricator and sensation-monger"; whereas later estimates "showed a larger toleration and understanding born of sympathy and wider knowledge."[39] A previous champion of Weems, the South Carolina novelist William Gilmore Simms, spoke of him as a "person to whom . . . full justice has never been done, as a man of talent." After weighing all the evidence in the case of the Horry-Weems biography of Marion, Simms concluded that there had been little real distortion of the truth about Marion. This, of course, is the viewpoint of a writer of fiction, who would be disposed to look favorably on history dressed as romance.[40]

38 Henry Cabot Lodge, *George Washington,* 2 vols. (Boston, 1889), I, 39–45. If Lodge had been in need of any more ammunition, he might have noted how remarkably lachrymose Weems's short book is. There are more than thirty references to weeping and in several cases Washington himself is the weeper.

39 Skeel, I, ix.

40 Simms to Benjamin Franklin Perry, October 30, 1842, in *The Letters of William Gilmore Simms,* ed. by Mary C. Simms Oliphant *et al.,* 5 vols. Columbia, S.C., 1952–1956), I, 328; Skeel, I, 100–102. For Simms's discussion of history for purposes of art, see his essay in *Views and Reviews, First Series,* republished (1962) in the John Harvard Library.

Yet by more rigorous standards Weems's *Washington* is not altogether unreliable. Sometimes, no doubt, this was because Weems got his facts "from the gazettes." For example, the story of how Washington at fourteen or fifteen almost became a midshipman in the British navy, and was dissuaded by his mother (see p. 27), seems to have been widely current—and true in essentials.[41] Other stories which look like pure Weemsian inventions turn out to be true or at least plausible. There is, for example, the tale of the Indian chief who failed to shoot Washington (see p. 42). According to Jared Sparks, the tradition rests upon the authority of Dr. Craik, an intimate friend of Washington who was with him in the battle and who journeyed with him to the Western country fifteen years after. An Indian chief came to see them and told them through an interpreter that

> during the battle of the Monogahela, he had singled [Washington] out as a conspicuous object, fired his rifle at him many times, and directed his young warriors to do the same, but to his utter astonishment none of their balls took effect. He was then persuaded, that the youthful hero was under the special guardianship of the Great Spirit, and ceased to fire at him any longer. He was now come to pay homage to the man, who was the particular favorite of Heaven, and who could never die in battle.[42]

A detailed investigation might show that in this instance as in others, a Weemsian invention had passed into folklore, and perhaps secured lodgment in the recesses of Dr. Craik's mind, so that what he thought he remembered he had in fact merely read. If so, this would illustrate the process by which, in the opinion of Henry Cabot Lodge and others, Weems

41 See, for example, Aaron Bancroft, *An Essay on the Life of George Washington* (Worcester, Mass., 1807), p. 2: "At his own importunity, the birth [*sic*] of a midshipman . . . was obtained in the British navy. His views in this instance were defeated by the anxiety of an affectionate mother." The episode is thoroughly investigated in Douglas Southall Freeman, *George Washington: A Biography*, 6 vols. (New York, 1948–1954), I, 190–199.

42 Sparks, *Writings of George Washington*, I, 68–69; II, 475.

established himself as the Father of the Father of His People.[43] But it is at least conceivable that Weems heard the story from Dr. Çraik in the first place; for Craik was married to the sister of Colonel Ewell, Weems's father-in-law, and may well have talked to Weems at Bel Air or in Dumfries. By the same token, it is arguable that Weems's sin in styling himself rector of Mount Vernon was no more than venial. Though the label was an advertising dodge, letters to Carey show that he preached quite often at Pohick during 1802, and we cannot prove that he did not sometimes take services there while Washington was still alive. He was in touch with Washington's literary executor, Bushrod Washington, probably in connection with his "subscriptioneering" for the Marshall biography, and with the rest of "the Mount Vernon Family." Moreover, as Emily Skeel notes, he convinced *himself* in this matter: see for instance his letter to Carey of July 10, 1816, from New Holland, Pennsylvania:

'Tis 11 o'clock P.M. and I have just finish[d] a Sermon to a host of good Dutch People, who are mightily taken with me for having been Chaplain to the Great Gen[l] Washington, and the writer of his wonderful Life.[44]

In another instance two reputable biographers of Washington are inclined to give the benefit of the doubt to Weems. Nathaniel W. Stephenson and Waldo H. Dunn discuss the uncertainty surrounding Washington's appointment to Gen-

43 A complicated instance is the story of Potts and the Valley Forge prayer, which is discussed at some length in Hughes, *Washington,* III, 270–287. In seeking to demonstrate the intensity of Washington's religious beliefs, Weems, like a great many other patriotic chroniclers, confused what he wished to discover with what the real facts showed. Yet there is some kind of factual basis in Weems, no matter how shadowy. There are several different versions of the Potts story. It is possible that they all derive in part from Weems. But there *was* an inhabitant of the Valley Forge area named Potts; and a reference in E. C. M'Guire, *The Religious Opinions and Character of Washington,* p. 159, to a second source suggests that the anecdote may have been in existence, perhaps already in variant forms, when Weems first brought it into print. Thus in Weems, Potts seems an enthusiastic patriot: in M'Guire he is a Tory.

44 Skeel, I, 19, 34–36. And, according to a laconic entry in Washington's diary for March 3, 1787, Weems and Craik had stayed at Mount Vernon for

eral Braddock's staff in 1755. They point out that the circumstances are obscure, but that Weems's explanation—that Braddock talked with Governor Dinwiddie about Washington (see pp. 37–38)—fits the facts.[45]

On a further and more circumstantial matter Weems emerges with credit. He recounts at some length an alleged dispute between Washington and a man named Payne, who knocked him down. According to Weems (see pp. 188–189), Washington felt that he was in the wrong and so apologized to Payne. Lodge dismisses the episode as one of the Weemsian stories "so silly and so foolishly impossible that they do not deserve an instant's consideration." Yet Washington's foremost biographer, Douglas Southall Freeman, confirms that apart from minor inaccuracies the Weemsian version is correct.[46]

This is not to pretend that all the Weemsian anecdotes (except for the cabbage-seed) are authentic. From what we know of Weems and of Washington's mother, her dream is almost certainly a fabrication. So are the details of his early schooling. The story of young George refusing to fight and refusing to let other children fight is distinctly fishy. Washington's death-scene (see pp. 165–168) is fictitious and absurdly overblown. Nevertheless the real complaint is not that Weems recorded impossible tales, but rather that he drew such unctuous lessons from them. The cherry-tree incident could have happened to any small boy let loose with a hatchet; the unforgivable offense, in critics' eyes, was to moralize about it.

That Weems was an inveterate sermonizer is undeniable.

---

the night. William S. Baker, *Washington After the Revolution* (Philadelphia, 1898), p. 70.

45 Nathaniel W. Stephenson & Waldo H. Dunn, *George Washington*, 2 vols. (New York, 1940), I, 122–123, 424–427.

46 Lodge, I, 44. Lodge's view is shared by Paul Van Dyke, who in *George Washington: The Son of His Country, 1732–1775* (New York, 1931), pp. 147–148, asserts that the Payne story is "much more inherently improbable than the cherry-tree." Freeman, II, 146, offers a decisive answer; he arrives at much the same conclusion as John Corbin, *The Unknown Washington* (New York, 1930), pp. 43–46.

One of his reasons for disliking Marshall's *Washington* was that it "is not half so moralizing & Republican as my own."[47] But by "Republican" in this context, Weems meant "human." His own intention, while drawing moral lessons for young Americans, was also to reveal Washington's private life and private virtues. His motives and his styles were certainly mixed. But we miss much of the nature of Weems and of his appeal to bygone generations, if we fail to note how much the early chapters, at any rate, seek to avoid the marmoreal, "Federalist" tone of John Marshall. Weems did *try*—unlike Marshall—to show that Washington was once a child. Though his moralizing tendency ran away with him, Weems did also try to make young George plausible. If what George said sounded sanctimonious, the way in which he said it was remarkably colloquial:

—"Well, Pa, only forgive me this time; see if I ever be so stingy any more. . . ."

—"High, Pa, an't *you* my *true* father, that has loved me, and been so good to me always?"

The father's answers are less colloquial and more uplifting. But there is a certain gusto in these early chapters, turgid in places though they are. It is instructive to compare the Weemsian prose with that of writers who paraphrased him. His successors, though more even in tone, are more dull and formal. One of them, for instance, modifies Weems's *"I can't tell a lie, Pa"* to "Father, I can not tell a lie."[48]

[47] Weems to Carey, Savannah, May 24, 1807; Skeel, II, 362.

[48] John S. C. Abbott, "George Washington," *Harper's New Monthly Magazine,* 12: 291 (February 1856). John Abbott (1805–1877) was the brother of Jacob Abbott, author of the "Rollo" series of juvenile works. The article is derivative and sententious—a standard specimen of patriotic journalism. One can see that according to the taste of such authors, Weems came very near to offending against a sacred image of Washington. Thus, though M'Guire quotes freely from Weems, he does so with a prefatory apology: "What these little domestic occurrences shall be found to want in historical dignity, we think they will make up in real worth and useful intimations" (*Religious Opinions and Character,* pp. 32–33). Similar caution is apparent in John Frost, *Pictorial Life,* p. 17: "The moral tendencies . . . of childhood, are

Again, Lodge is only partly justified in saying that Weems portrayed Washington's parents as "affected and priggish people." The truth is that Weems is one of the few biographers of the nineteenth century who allowed any prominence at all to Washington's father. Most of them hustled him off the stage with hardly a mention. They did so to make way for Washington's mother; indeed, for Washington's Mother. As Moncure D. Conway observed:

> The Washington family has passed into a conventionalization curiously resembling that of the Holy Family: the saviour of his country has for his mother a saintly Mary; his father is kept in the background like Joseph; he is born in a mean abode.[49]

The comparison with Jesus and the Virgin Mary is made explicit in a gushing passage by Rufus Griswold. There is a glowing picture of Mary Washington in Jared Sparks:

> Her good sense, assiduity, tenderness, and vigilance overcame every obstacle; and, as the richest reward of a mother's solicitude . . . , she had the happiness to see all her children . . . filling the sphere allotted to them in a manner equally honorable to themselves, and to the parent who had been the *only* guide of their principles, conduct, and habits. . . . It has been said, that there never was a great man, the elements of whose greatness might not be traced to the original characteristics or early influence of his mother. If this be true, how much do mankind owe to the mother of Washington.

Edward Everett echoes the sentiment. "Washington," he says, "is unquestionably to be added to the list of eminent men

---

seldom eradicated in after life. It is with this conviction, and at the risk perhaps of being considered as detracting from the dignity of our subject, that we give some incidents of Washington's life, which illustrate his father's system of early training."

49 Quoted in Francis Rufus Bellamy, *The Private Life of George Washington* (New York, 1951), pp. 7–8. Bellamy remarks that though Washington's father did not die until George was eleven, he has been oddly neglected. Conway, a Virginian by origin and an unconventional scholar, "regretted this neglect . . . because Captain Washington . . . was a vigorous man in his own right and moreover exceeded his wife in both family and education."

whose characters have been moulded by a mother's influence."[50]

Weems is certainly not hostile to Mary Washington: she is not the pipe-smoking crone that we encounter in the pages of Rupert Hughes, nor even the limited, self-centered old woman that Douglas Southall Freeman depicts.[51] Yet on inspection Weems's Mary Washington seems closer to these than to the Ideal Mother of nineteenth-century biography. The first mention of her character is a remark that George could not have inherited his martial spirit from her: "For as some of the Virginia officers, just after the splendid actions of Trenton and Princeton, was [*sic*] complimenting her on the generalship and *rising glory* of her son, instead of showing the exultation of a Spartan dame, she replied . . . , *"Ah, dear me! This fighting and killing is a sad thing! I wish George would come home and look after his plantation!!"* (see p. 27). And the story of her reluctance to let George go away to sea, as Weems tells it, illustrates his obedience more than her generosity.

This leads to another consideration. Weems was far from being the only purveyor of Washington anecdotes. We have seen that he was not responsible for the glorification of Mary Washington. Nor did he contribute the tale of George Washington, Betsy Ross, and the American flag to national

50 Rufus Wilmot Griswold, *The Republican Court; or, American Society in the Days of Washington* (New York, 1855): "There is no fame in the world more pure than that of the mother of Washington, and no woman since the Mother of Christ has left a better claim to the affectionate reverence of mankind" (p. 125, 1867 edition); Sparks, *Writings of George Washington,* I, 5; Everett, *Washington,* p. 35; and Margaret C. Conkling, *Memoirs of the Mother and Wife of Washington* (Auburn, N.Y., 2nd ed., 1850). After quoting the famous passage from Sparks (p. 67), Miss Conkling goes on to say of Mary Washington (p. 72): "Enshrined in the *Sanctuary of Home,* her sublime example is the peerless boast of her country. . . ." The writer was the sister of Senator Roscoe Conkling, who did not always maintain so fine a sense of the sanctity of the home; see Thomas Graham Belden and Marva Robins Belden, *So Fell the Angels* (Boston, 1956), pp. 287–319.

51 Hughes, II, 44–46; Freeman, I, 193; II, 17–18; III, 597; V, 281–282, 491–492; VI; 228–231; and see Paul Leicester Ford, *The True George Washington* (Philadelphia, 1896), pp. 17–21.

mythology. He did introduce the legend that young Washington threw a stone across the Rappahannock; it was left to others to add the news that George also threw stones over the Natural Bridge in Virginia and into the Hudson from the New Jersey Palisades.[52] Weems did not plant the notion that the youthful Washington composed out of his own head the "Rules of Behaviour in Company and in Conversation" which were found among the Washington papers—though Weems would no doubt have fastened upon them avidly if he had had the chance. Nor, despite assertions to the contrary, did he have anything to do with a legend that has attained almost as much prominence as the cherry-tree. This is the story of the sorrel colt, a fiery animal which was a great favorite of his mother's. Egged on by some companions when he was in his early 'teens, Washington is said to have managed to mount and "break" the colt, a fine piece of horsemanship—only to have it drop dead from bursting its "noble heart." He confessed what had happened to his mother:

> The hectic of a moment was observed to flush on the matron's cheek, but like a summer cloud, it soon passed away, and all was serene and tranquil, when she remarked: "It is well; but while I regret the loss of my favorite, *I rejoice in my son, who always speaks the truth.*"

The anecdote first appeared in the *United States Gazette,* in an article by George Washington Parke Custis, the grandson of Martha Washington, on May 13, 1826. It was later incorporated in an influential book, *Recollections and Private Memoirs of Washington.*[53] The story of the sorrel colt was

52 For instance, [Horatio Hastings Weld], *Pictorial Life of George Washington* (Philadelphia, 1845), pp. 184–185.

53 George Washington Parke Custis, *Recollections and Private Memoirs of Washington . . . with . . . Illustrative and Explanatory Notes by Benson J. Lossing* (New York, 1860), pp. 132–134. The book was posthumous: Custis died in 1857. An example of incorrect attribution can be found in Edward H. O'Neill, *A History of American Biography, 1800–1935* (Philadelphia, 1935), p. 156: "It was in the fifth edition that Weems introduced the cherry tree incidents, the cabbage and the colt incidents. The cherry tree and colt stories were pure fiction. . . ."

widely repeated, sometimes by biographers such as James K. Paulding, who did not include the cherry tree.[54] Custis did more than anyone to propagate the cult of the Mother of Washington. He wrote historical plays as a pastime; and as the extract from his *Recollections* may indicate, he does not carry conviction as a historian. The colt, as Henry Cabot Lodge discerned, is probably as apocryphal as the cherry-tree and suffers from the same didactic tendency.

In commenting upon it though, Lodge unwittingly reveals one reason why it enjoyed such popularity. Arguing that Custis' narrative was hopelessly anachronistic, like Weems's, Lodge nevertheless says:

> It may be accepted as certain that [Washington] rode and mastered many unbroken thoroughbred colts, and it is possible that one of them burst a blood-vessel in the process and died, and that the boy promptly told his mother of the accident.[55]

The language is oddly positive for a cautious historian. One senses that Lodge would *like* to have accepted this particular anecdote, as others had unquestioningly done before him. Indeed, several gentlemanly biographers who balked at certain Weems stories had unhesitatingly borrowed the Weemsian details of Washington's military and athletic prowess. As Stephenson and Dunn remark of Washington biographers, "they have an amusing way of discovering that whenever [Weems's] subject matter appeals to them he must for once have been correct."[56] Here is Edward Everett on young Washington:

[54] Paulding, I, 41–42; and also, to take some random instances, M'Guire, pp. 37–39; S. G. Arnold, pp. 14–16; Weld, pp. 12–13; Frost, pp. 20–22; Hughes, I, 31–32. Caroline M. Kirkland, *Memoirs of Washington* (New York, 1857), p. 59, is more circumspect: "The story of his having ridden to death a fiery colt of his mother's . . . sounds a little too much like a modernized version of Alexander's taming Bucephalus; so we shall not repeat it here." Paulding, incidentally, dedicated his biography to "the pious, retired, domestic MOTHERS OF THE UNITED STATES, . . . for the use of their children. . . ."

[55] Lodge, I, 44.

[56] Stephenson & Dunn, I, 123. Hughes (I, 31) cheerfully accepts the

According to still existing traditions, he evinced in his boyhood the military taste, which seems to have been hereditary in his family. The self-elected but willingly obeyed leader of his comrades, he formed them into companies for their juvenile battles. His early repute for veracity and justice, with his athletic prowess beyond his years, made him the chosen umpire of their disputes. He wrestled, leaped, ran, threw the bar, and rode with the foremost. A spot is still pointed out, where, in his boyhood, he threw a stone across the Rappahannoc [*sic*]; he was proverbially strong of arm; . . . and he was through life a bold and graceful horseman.[57]

This improves on Weems, who suggested that the source of Washington's military talent was a mystery.

The point is that Weems supplied distinct needs for the American imagination in the nineteenth century; that he was not a figure apart, uniquely unprincipled or uniquely priggish; that the reasons for his remarkable success lie largely, though not entirely, in the quality of his writing; and that where he failed, his failure has been shared by almost everyone who has sought to capture the essence of George Washington. He should be seen in context, as a stage in the history of American nationalism; of popular and juvenile literature; and of Washington biography, which also has certain timeless aspects.

American nationalism was a self-conscious creation, and George Washington was its chief symbol. Traveling widely and continuously, Weems discovered by experiment what Americans wanted to read. They were religiously minded, so they would buy Bibles, sermons, tracts. They were eager for color and excitement, so they would buy novels by the cartload. They were, when stimulated, ferociously patriotic, so they would buy works that ministered to their national pride. What better literary fare than the Weemsian biog-

---

Rappahannock stone-throwing, and the story of young Washington playing soldier and fighting mock battles. He finds them useful touches in his own picture of Washington as a powerful adolescent with "extraordinarily big feet" and "freakishly huge hands."

[57] Everett, pp. 31–32.

raphies, which satisfied all their wants—religion (or religiosity), romanticism, patriotism—simultaneously? They were stirred by his would-be epic strain, edified by his preachments, tickled by his knockabout farce. If he was the most garish of the purveyors of popular nationalist literature, he was one of a numerous company. Gilbert J. Hunt, who produced a *Historical Reader* of the War of 1812, wrote and arranged it in a biblical style which nowadays reads like a burlesque, though it was meant seriously. A textbook of *Arithmetical Questions,* by William Butler, coupled mathematics and nationalism in this way:

> No. 201. FEMALE PATRIOTISM. The generous exertions of the American daughters of liberty in Philadelphia, and the neighbourhood, to assist the continental soldiers, in the war with England, are mentioned . . . by Dr. Gordon. Desirous of sharing with the gentlemen of America in the splendors of patriotism, . . . they formed a female association. . . . Their donations, says the historian, purchased a sufficient quantity of cloth, and their hands made the same into two thousand one hundred and seven shirts, which were delivered to . . . General WASHINGTON. . . . Supposing each shirt contained 3 yards and ¼, how many pieces, each consisting of 25 yards and ½, must the American ladies have purchased, to accomplish their patriotic purpose?
> *Ans.* 268 pieces, 13 yards ¾.[58]

Washington, up to about the Civil War, was so venerated that no biographer would dream of criticizing him. On the contrary, biographers vied in finding new ways of praising him. "He was as fortunate as great and good," said Aaron Bancroft. For Peleg Sprague, Washington was "The Patriot Hero of our Revolution, the Christian Statesman of our Republic, great in goodness, and good in greatness." Edward Everett did not hesitate "to pronounce Washington, of all men that have ever lived, THE GREATEST OF GOOD

[58] Gilbert J. Hunt, *The Historical Reader . . . Written in the Ancient Historical Style* (New York, 3rd edition, 1819). The problem in arithmetic is quoted in Albert Bushnell Hart, "Imagination in History," *American Historical Review,* 15: 250 (January 1910).

MEN AND THE BEST OF GREAT MEN." Even a humorist—Artemus Ward in this case—picked his words carefully:

G. Washington was abowt the best man this world ever sot eyes on. . . . He luved his country dearly. . . . He was a human angil in a 3 kornered hat and knee britches. . . .

So it is wrong to suppose that Weems on his own determined the nation's view of George Washington. The American public demanded to be told of a Washington who was a "human angil"—spotless, pious, dauntless. Along with many others, Weems helped to supply the demand.[59]

He was of course unusually enterprising. He was one of the first to realize the size of the market for popular and juvenile literature and to exploit it. His methods of salesmanship were probably somewhat in advance of his time. He tried to bring inexpensive editions direct to the public. He proposed ingenious methods of disposing of books in quantity, as in 1796–97, when he petitioned the Virginia legislature to establish a charity school, by means of a state lottery—the prizes payable in Mathew Carey's books.[60] He used the pulpit

59 Aaron Bancroft, *An Essay on the Life of George Washington*, p. 531; Peleg Sprague, "Remarks at the Centennial Celebration of Washington's Birthday, February 22, 1832," reprinted in *Speeches and Addresses* (Boston, 1858), p. 427; Everett, pp. 262–263; Ward, "4th of July Oration at Weathersfield, Conn., 1859," in Charles Farrar Browne, *The Complete Works of Artemus Ward* (London, 1899), p. 125.

It is not quite accurate to say, as Kellock does (p. 97), that Weems's enlarged *Washington* "had the field to itself, with no competition in sight." During the early years of Weems's efforts at Washingtoniana he faced competition from David Ramsay, Aaron Bancroft, and from two other enterprising compilers: Thomas Condie and John Corry. Condie was a Philadelphia book-binder who first issued his *Memoirs of George Washington* in 1798, and brought out a revised edition in 1800. Later editions of varying length appeared up to about 1814. Corry, a more vigorous challenger, was an Irish journalist who worked in London. His *Life of George Washington* first appeared there in 1800. It was reprinted in Philadelphia in 1801 and in the next quarter of a century ran through a quantity of American editions. See Baker, *Biblioteca Washingtoniana*, pp. 6–61.

60 Weems to Carey, October 15, 1796 (Skeel, II, 48): "The lottery shall contain 20,000 tickets at one dollar per ticket. The number and size of the prizes as also the sum to be rais[d], is all left to your arrangement. To all good

as an advertising agency. He timed his journeys to coincide with court-days, revival meetings, legislative assemblies and the like, where crowds might be expected. He offered discounts. He composed eye-catching slogans and newspaper advertisements:

M. L. WEEMS begs leave very respectfully to inform the Honourable the Gentlemen of the Legislature, that his FLYING LIBRARY will leave town on Friday morning. Those who mean to procure some good books will please honour him with their attention. . . . Liberal allowance made to those benevolent characters who take several copies of Washington and Marion for Christmas Boxes to their young relations.[61]

He always envisaged his biographies as works for the unlettered and the young. Sending a copy of his *Washington* to Thomas Jefferson in 1809, he solicited "a line or two in favor of it—as a school book."[62] He suggested to Carey in 1821–22 that it would be sensible to have the *Washington* translated into French: "Many w^{d} sell in that dress for scholastic purposes."[63]

Christians the education of the poor and fatherless is a *primary wish.* And when there is a prospect of doing this at the very cheap rate of 7/6, and a chance that even this trifle may burn into our bosoms with a ten-fold usury of favorite books, who will not heartily approve . . . ? I am well acquainted with . . . the Governor of this State, and also with numbers of those who are . . . most eminent for Wealth & influence . . . , with the co-operation of these and the divine benediction I have no doubt but I shall be enabled to sell you 16,000 dollars worth of books more briefly than you apprehend." Carey heartily approved of the scheme, but the Virginia legislature was less impressed. The petition was not accepted.

[61] *Georgia Journal,* November 28, 1810, quoted in Skeel, I, 97.

[62] Weems to Jefferson, February 1, 1809, in Skeel, I, 39–40. As early as July 12, 1800, Weems suggested to Carey that his *Washington* might be bound in duodecimo "& Sold as a School Book." Skeel, I, 12; and see Bryan, "Genesis," *Americana,* 36: 148–150. The possibility occurred to others. John Marshall's *Washington* eventually came out in a condensed edition (Philadelphia, 1838) "for the use of Schools." Marshall himself may have prepared this version, shortly before his death in 1835. Irving's *Washington* was likewise abridged for use in schools (Boston, 1887), by John Fiske. Beveridge, *Marshall,* III, 273; Baker, *Biblioteca Washingtoniana,* pp. 83, 161–162.

[63] Skeel, I, 74. No such edition appeared. But the idea was obviously sound. Arsène N. Girault brought out a *Vie de George Washington* (Philadelphia,

But again he was not alone in the field. He was an agent—true, with a stronger commercial tinge than most—in the great didactic and humanitarian mood that was overtaking Britain and America. The techniques of Methodism, the tracts and campaigns of the English Evangelicals were familiar and pervasive influences upon Weems. Henry Cabot Lodge is correct in noting the affinity of Weems's writings with those of high-minded ladies like Hannah More, Maria Edgeworth, and Sarah Trimmer. Among other things they evolved a new "improving" literature for children, long before Queen Victoria. The "moral tale" was prominent in such literature—for example, the tale to which Lodge alludes, of Little Rosamund, who "spent her money on a purple jar from the chemist's window instead of on a pair of shoes, only to find that the colour was in the liquid, not in the glass, while the lack of the shoes led to all kinds of disappointments and disasters."[64] Weems read and peddled such stories; they helped to form his world. Before he died, the American Bible Society and the American Tract Society were busy in somewhat similar ways to his. The pamphlet-vending missionaries of the Tract Society moved among much the same audiences as his. Weems anticipated these "colporteurs," but not by much.[65]

1835), based on the biography written by Anna C. Reed for the American Sunday School Union. Girault's text ran through four editions in the first year and sold briskly for another quarter of a century. It was used at the U.S. Naval Academy at Annapolis, where Girault became an instructor in 1845. The version of Anna Reed's biography translated by Girault included the colt but not the cherry-tree. Baker, *Biblioteca Washingtoniana,* p. 72.

64 Muriel Jaeger, *Before Victoria: Changing Standards of Behaviour, 1787–1837* (London, 1956), p. 107.

65 "Thanks to the promoting genius of Mathew Carey, . . . book agents such as Parson Weems traveled up and down the land peddling . . . biographies, histories, and manuals designed for the use and moral uplift of people in the ordinary walks of life. Moralistic and anecdotal chapbooks found a place in the wagons of the two hundred peddlers that by 1823 were canvassing the country." Merle Curti, *The Growth of American Thought* (New York, 1943), p. 229; and see Clifford S. Griffin, *Their Brothers' Keepers: Moral Stewardship in the United States, 1800–1865* (New Brunswick, N.J., 1960), esp. pp. 23–43.

As the classroom and Sunday-school audience enlarged, so did the demand for appropriate texts and tracts. Weems's arguments against drunkenness, gambling, and adultery were hardly suitable; but his biographies were ideal. They remained popular in their own right or were pillaged by later rivals, because in one vital respect they catered to juvenile readers. Not only was his *Washington* simply written; unlike the abbreviated school-editions of Irving's and Marshall's biographies, his account told American children about the hero's childhood. Without his anecdotes, what was there to visualize about young Washington? The anecdotes were indispensable. The same was true to a lesser extent of Washington's later life, though here Weems was not so accommodating. Ordinary people had always needed and cherished brief, vivid characterizations of their heroes. Now that the market was widened to include children the need was all the greater. It was greater because the United States lacked a folklore of its own. The Scots could take pride in their tale of Bruce and his spider, the English in the story of Drake playing bowls while he awaited the Armada, the Swiss in the vignette of William Tell shooting the apple from his little son's head. What would America have, without a cherry-tree?[66]

Moreover, such anecdotes, while almost always apocryphal, do not endure unless they express some sort of general truth about the persons they describe. Does not the cherry-tree tale, after all, tell us something about Washington which fits surprisingly well into the known facts of his life[67]—apart from

66 The Rev. Henry F. Harrington, "Anecdotes of George Washington . . . ," *Godey's Lady's Book,* 38: 427–429 (June 1849), discussing the scarcity and utility of Washington stories, notes "how eagerly every little anecdote of his hours of boyhood or manly relaxation . . . has been seized upon. . . . How many children have been stimulated to inflexible truth . . . , by the story that is told of him . . . when he injured with his hatchet one of his father's favorite trees. . . . What a bearing this little anecdote alone has exerted over many minds . . . !"

67 Robert Birley, "The Undergrowth of History: Some Traditional Stories of English History Reconsidered" (London: Historical Association, 1955),

the American idolization of him, which is a historical fact of another kind?

All Washington biographers, from Marshall and Weems onward, have faced well-nigh insoluble problems. Despite the more intimate knowledge of him accumulated through research, his childhood and youth remain somewhat shadowy; while his mature years were *public* years: the man became merged with his country, with his own legend. Washington is a great national hero. Biographers have naturally wished to convey his transcendent merit, as it struck his contemporaries and as a more objective phenomenon. But they have also, naturally, wished to treat him as a man, not a demigod. More particularly they have sought to render the Americanness of him, to be on visiting terms with him, as they are with Abraham Lincoln. They have wanted to emphasize what was "normal" about him, what practical lessons his actions held for other Americans, what his countrymen could do to be like him. Yet how to accomplish this without suggesting that Washington had blemishes? And even if biographers should wish to point to his faults, how to do so when he appears to have *had* none, except of the most minor order? How to make such a being credible, when he has proved invulnerable even

---

comments sensibly on the origin and function of such stories. Birley points out that while some are plainly fictions, others rest on better evidence, and all survived (p. 28) "because they brought out most emphatically the particular traits in the characters of the heroes which the popular imagination considered to be most significant." Eric Robinson, "James Watt and the Tea Kettle: A Myth Justified," *History Today*, 6: 261–265 (April 1956), supplies striking evidence in support of the historical antecedents of one of these legends. The cherry-tree, too, has some faint corroboration in the shape of an earthenware mug, "apparently made in Germany between 1770 and 1790, decorated with a quaint illustration of the cherry tree story, a large hatchet, the letters G. W., and the numerals 1776." See Hughes, I, 501; Skeel, I, 26–27. The mug was first described in R. T. Haines Halsey, *Pictures of Early New York on Dark Blue Staffordshire Pottery* (New York, 1899), pp. 302–306. It is reproduced in Skeel. If, however, the story of the cherry-tree had really been current in 1776, there would surely have been other illustrations and references. The power of the story, though, as in the case of King Alfred and the cakes, or Francis Drake playing bowls at Plymouth, rests on considerations that have very little to do with precise evidence.

to the debunkers, so that they have found themselves deriding not Washington but rather Washington's previous biographers—poor Weems foremost among the targets?

Grappling with these difficulties, biographers often begin by declaring their humanizing intent. *Other* biographers, they say, have missed the living man. So John Neal, in a historical novel, makes one of the characters say:

George Washington had his infirmities, in the same measure as his virtues. And thanks be to God that he *had!* Now we have an example to encourage us. . . . [H]is character is not understood by his own countrymen. . . . They have so long listened to hyperbolical eulogy, intemperate, and unmeaning praise, that he has lost to their eyes, the chief attributes of humanity—and become a God.

Washington Irving tells a correspondent that

I have availed myself of the licence of biography to step down occasionally from the elevated walk of history, and . . . depict the heroes of Seventy-Six as they really were—men in cocked hats, regimental coats, and breeches, and not classical warriors, in shining armour and flowing mantles, with brows bound with laurel. . . .

John B. McMaster says:

General Washington is known to us, and President Washington. But George Washington is an unknown man. When at last he is set before us as he lived, we shall read less of the cherry-tree and more of the man. Naught surely that is heroic will be omitted, but side by side . . . will appear much that is commonplace.

Worthington Chauncey Ford declares in the preface of his own scholarly biography: "In one respect Washington has lost in definition. His name and renown are taken for granted, and his individuality has thus lost." And Douglas Southall Freeman introduces the first volume of his huge study by remarking on "the extent to which the personality of young Washington has been ignored":

Apparently there have been two orthodox approaches . . .—one forward through Weems and the other backward from Gilbert Stuart and John Marshall. If Weems were followed, Washington was a cross between a prig and a paragon. When seen through the eyes of the Chief Justice or those of the Rhode Island painter, he was so awesome . . . that he never could be credited with a youth.[68]

Yet Weems makes very much the same observation, in his introduction:

IT is not then in the glare of *public,* but in the shade of *private life,* that we are to look for the man. . . . Of these private deeds of Washington very little has been said. . . . No! this is not the Washington you see; 'tis only Washington the HERO, and the Demigod. . . .

But in spite of their humanizing efforts, the biographers end in panegyric. Washington recedes into public life and into near-apotheosis. He certainly does in Weems. But the transformation is evident in all the others: in Sparks, and Irving, and so on. The same person in John Neal's novel who asserted that Washington was fallible scolds James Fenimore Cooper for bringing him into a novel "profanely . . . , in situations totally unworthy of him. . . ." Another character in Neal's novel, moreover, says: "I cannot write or speak the name of GEORGE WASHINGTON, without a contraction, and dilation of the heart, if I do it irreverently." W. R. Thayer, after pouring scorn initially upon Weems and Sparks as sentimental falsifiers, concludes his book by hinting at almost supernatural attributes in Washington. Dumas Malone comments on the "devastating candor" with which Freeman, in his first two volumes, analyzed Washington as "a bold and dashing but ambitious and calculating young man"; but he notes the gradual emergence, in subsequent volumes, of the lineaments that Washington's countrymen "have so long recognized and so long honored." Or in Freeman's words, "The more I study

68 John Neal, *Randolph,* 2 vols. (Philadelphia, 1823), II, 62–66, quoted in Bryan, *Washington in American Literature,* p. 201; Irving to H. Tuckerman, January 8, 1856 (on the reception of the second volume of his *Washington*), in Pierre E. Irving, *The Life and Letters of Washington Irving,* 2 vols. (London, 1877), II, 903; John B. McMaster, *A History of the People of the United States* . . . , 8 vols. (New York, 1883–1913), II, 452–453; Worthington C. Ford, *George Washington,* 2 vols. (New York, 1900), I, viii; Freeman, I, xiii.

George Washington, the more am I convinced that the great reputation he enjoyed with his contemporaries and with men of the next generation was entirely justified. He was greater than any of us believed he was."[69]

Washington biographers have sought another compromise between the real and ideal. They have argued that, though great, Washington was not a genius; he was the ordinary man raised to the highest power. He was not, they indicate, an intellectual, or a fine orator, or of unusually magnetic personal appeal. He was great in his *character*. He had not very much formal education, and no gift for abstract theorizing. Biographers dwell therefore on his simplicity, his rural upbringing, his physical strength, his athletic feats: for these features make him more acceptably "American," and bring him closer to the average American, who can hope to imitate and emulate him in at least some respects.[70] Once again, Weems anticipates an aspect of Washington biography. His Washington was not born "with a silver spoon in his mouth," but "in humble circumstances," and spent his early manhood

69 Neal, *Randolph*, II, 213; I, 65; quoted in Bryan, *Washington in American Literature*, pp. 200–202; Thayer, *Washington*, p. 260; Dumas Malone, introduction to Freeman, *Washington* (New York, 1954), VI, xxx and xliv.

70 See, for example, David Ramsay, *The Life of George Washington*, pp. 429–430: "Youths of the United States! Learn from WASHINGTON what may be done by an industrious improvement of your talents, and the cultivation of your moral powers. . . . You cannot all be commanders of armies or chief magistrates, but you may all resemble him in the virtues of private and domestic life, in which he excelled, and in which he most delighted." Or see Caroline M. Kirkland, *Memoirs of Washington*, pp. 41–42: "The plain, humble home on Pope's Creek; the stout, kind, planter papa, and serious, housewifely mother; that primitive and retired mode of life, . . . influenced . . . the whole future of the General, President, Benefactor of nations. . . . Through the whole of his grand career, whenever the pressure of duty relented, he sprang back to rural life . . . as the half-weaned child to its mother's bosom. . . ." Ruth Miller Elson, "American Schoolbooks and 'Culture' in the Nineteenth Century," *Mississippi Valley Historical Review*, 46: 417–420 (December 1959), notes how in these Washington is shown as "brave, charitable, industrious, religious, courteous, and a paragon of the domestic virtues. The best qualities of the self-made man are his. . . . But in no instance are intelligence, learning, or disinterested inquiry associated with Washington. Indeed, in some of the later books he is specifically shown as a practical man who rejected the intellectual life." Compare this with Weems's (probably correct) insistence that Washington knew no Latin.

in "the laborious life of a woodsman" (see pp. 24, 211). Weems, of course, overdoes this line in order to present Washington as a "poor young man" who "from a sheep-cot ascended the throne of his country's affections" (p. 216), and who may therefore provide a genuine example for aspiring young Americans. Where Weems expresses a general truth, or a notion that is echoed by later biographers, he sometimes does so for his own peculiar reasons. He hits the truth by accident, we might say. Nevertheless, he *is* the prototype of all Washington biographers. His respectable successors have adopted without question the anecdotes dealing with Washington's physical strength, because these fit their own picture of Washington. They have avoided the more celebrated anecdotes because of Weems's way of telling them. But in either case, he has somehow managed to embody almost all the possible approaches to Washington. Those who came after have written more comprehensively and with more sophistication; none has altogether escaped the traps into which he tumbles so awkwardly and so engagingly.

V
WEEMS: HIS WORKS AND WAYS

The exasperation of historians like Lodge and Thayer was usually qualified by the admission that they found something endearing in Weems. Albert J. Beveridge thought him a curious mixture of Whitefield and Villon—Methodist pioneer and vagabond poet. He has been described as a "Livy of the common people."[71] Some scholars imply that Weems took Washington away from the Federalists and portrayed him as a self-made man on the Republican, Jeffersonian

[71] Beveridge, *Marshall,* III, 231. The Livy reference comes from the *Cyclopaedia of American Literature,* 2 vols. (New York, 1855), compiled by Evart A. and George L. Duyckinck: "He went to work in stout heart and faith, a Livy of the common people. He first gave the fact and then the moral, and neither of them was dull." It is quoted in C. A. Ingraham, "Mason Locke Weems: A Great American Author and Distributor of Books," *Americana,* 25: 484 (October 1931).

model. Even in brief accounts of Weems's career, the story is often cited of Weems selling Paine's deistic *Age of Reason*—a radical document.[72] Weems's biographer Harold Kellock reminds us that Weems was absorbed into the folklore of Jacksonian America, when he appeared in the third part of the *Autobiography of David Crockett*—ten years after his death—as an amiable old pilgrim who plays the fiddle for a traveling showman in Little Rock, Arkansas. Though the cleric's name is not given, he is obviously modeled on Weems; and indeed he reads aloud from *God's Revenge Against Drunkenness*.[73]

This indulgent view of Weems obviously expresses a large part of the truth about him. But not, one feels, the whole truth. He is something more and something less than a Johnny Appleseed of letters, a quaint old humanitarian. Why did he change his career from medicine to the ministry? Why did he become an Episcopalian clergyman and not, say, a Presbyterian or a Methodist? Why did he cease to hold a permanent parish? Why did he became an itinerant book-salesman? He was apparently an affectionate husband and parent. Why choose a life that entailed long and frequent absences from home?

[72] Van Wyck Brooks, *The World of Washington Irving*, pp. 1–4, portrays Weems as a jovial, Paine-selling Jeffersonian, whose "views were liberal, to say the least." Bryan, *Washington in American Literature*, pp. 94–95, though more cautiously and with reservations, presents a man "politically in tune with his time," i.e., Jeffersonian. So does Michael Kraus, *The Writing of American History* (Norman, Okla., 1953), p. 87.

[73] Kellock, pp. 206–212. Crockett (or whoever wrote the posthumous part of his autobiography for him) says that the old gentleman "looked . . . more like a lunatic than a moral lecturer." The account goes on: "I learnt that he was educated for the church, but not being able to obtain a living, he looked upon the whole earth as his altar, and all mankind as his flock. . . . Being unable to earn his bread as an itinerant lecturer,—for in those cases it is mostly poor preach and worse pay—he turned author and wrote histories which contained but little information, and sermons which, like many others, had nothing to boast of. . . . He succeeded in obtaining a sulky, and a horse to drag it, by a plea of mercy, which deprived the hounds of their food, and with these he traveled over the western states, to dispose of the product of his brain. . . ." *Davy Crockett's Own Story* (New York, 1955), pp. 249–250.

The answers may be straightforward. Any man is entitled to change his mind and his career. When Weems decided to become a minister, it was appropriate enough for him to enter the Episcopal church—the established church of Maryland and Virginia. It was unfortunate for him that the Episcopalians were so closely tied with the mother country; for this made his ordination difficult, and the situation in Maryland chaotic. More credit to him, we might say, for persevering in the matter of ordination and for doing his best to preach the faith in the post-Revolutionary years, when his denomination was disorganized and somewhat unpopular (over two-thirds of the Anglican clergy in Maryland had been loyalists).[74] With the loss of their former privileges, no wonder the Episcopalians fell upon hard times: no wonder Weems, with a family to support, should turn to the writing and selling of improving literature. Since there is no sign that he ever lost his faith, there was no need for him to renounce his Episcopal connection. Since he had apparently no desire to resume full-time, formal religious activities, there was no reason for him to switch allegiance to another denomination, even if his wife and some of his children became Methodists. As for his wandering, we may suppose that like many men he retained a fondness for travel and adventure even after he became a family man. It seems clear that he was something of a misfit as a clergyman: that he was high-spirited, perhaps rather loose in doctrine, and rather undignified. Bishop Meade says that no one could hear him preach without wanting to laugh.[75] Perhaps then there is no mystery. Weems may have turned naturally and sensibly to the kind of activity that best suited his temperament.

Perhaps Weems is also to be seen as a novelist or poet

74 Kellock, pp. 25–30, 39–40; Claude H. Van Tyne, *The Loyalists in the American Revolution* (New York, 1929), p. 112.

75 "Whether in private or public, in prayers or preaching, it was impossible that either the young or old, the grave or the gay, could keep their risible faculties from violent agitation." Meade, *Old Churches . . . of Virginia,* II, 234.

manqué, a man who in another time or society—in Britain for example—might have had a more conventionally successful career in letters. As it is, he stands before us as one of the great bad authors, the enthusiastic amateurs, the primitives whose virtues are also their defects. Perhaps we see the buried novelist/poet struggling for expression in all his writing—the tracts as well as the biographies. His writing takes on vitality whenever it breaks into dialogue or into imaginative passages. There is a humorous novelist's insight, as well as a moralist's, in Weems's *Washington* when (see pp. 3–4) he says of "private virtues" that

These old fashioned commodities are generally thrown into the back ground of the picture, and treated, as the grandees at the London and Paris routs, treat their good old *aunts* and *grandmothers,* huddling them together into the *back rooms,* there to wheeze and cough by themselves, and not depress the fine laudanum-raised spirits of the *young sparklers.*

There is a delightful comic evocation of war-fever in Britain during the 1750's (see pp. 34–35); and a nice humor in the observation (see p. 88) that

The British officers gave Washington full credit for such fine strokes of generalship, and *began to look thoughtful whenever his name was mentioned.*

Some of his extravagant images are both bad and brilliant, as when he says that "the Augusta, a heavy 64 gun ship, took fire, and blew up, *the horrible balloon of many of the crew*" (see p. 90), or emphasizes the casualties at Cowpens (see p. 111): "The tops of the aged pines shook with the ascending ghosts. . . ." We can see why a perceptive contemporary reviewer felt that the liveliest part of Weems's *William Penn* was the account of Penn's admiral-father, whom Weems rendered in a manner reminiscent of Uncle Toby in *Tristram Shandy.*[76]

[76] The Rev. Dr. Abercrombie of Philadelphia, in the *Charleston Courier,* April 11, 1822, quoted in Skeel, I, 143–144: "there is a peculiar vein of wit

Yet Weems appears to have had little of the dedication and none of the typical stigmata of authorship: the touchiness, the inwardness, the yearning for recognition. The first edition of his highly popular *Marion,* for example, was anonymous; and in all subsequent editions P. Horry, not Weems, was cited as the author. Weems's main concern seems to have been with *sales.* And though there may have been faults on both sides, the picture we get of him through the uninhibited correspondence with Carey is of a rather greedy and even unprincipled promoter. "Mr. Carey," he cries out in one letter,

> I have ever glow[d] with a book vending enthusiasm. I believe in the Immortality of the Soul, and the future reign of Light, Liberty & Love. I believe too that in those Gorgeous Worlds, those who have here aided the diffusion of Light & Love shall outshine the stars. Hence my enthusiasm to vend good books.

Here we encounter Weems the lovable, the wandering cleric whose favorite text for a sermon is said to have been "God is Love." The letter continues, however:

> But the Sun soaring eaglet must not get limed. You wou[d] lime me, you w[d] so clip the wings of my wages, as to bring me down flopping in the mire of meanness, baseness & dishonesty, w[h] w[d] soon drive me like an Owl to the shade of insignificance & uselessness. Oh that you did but consider the consequence of giving me the character of a Consciencious Book Seller, and the cheapest bookseller in Virginia! I tell you it w[d] be worth thousands to us both.[77]

This is hardly the expression of disinterested piety; and it could be matched in a score of other letters from Weems to Carey.

Nor will it do to visualize Weems as a man of strongly

---

and raciness, and an originality of thought, in his writings, which are seldom to be met with, and which never fail to seize the hearts of his readers, especially the young, with sentiments the most friendly to Virtue and Happiness."

[77] Weems to Carey, February 16, 1801, from Dumfries, Va.; Skeel, II, 172–173.

egalitarian sentiments. It is true that the Federalists tried to appropriate George Washington as their own patron saint, and that Weems recommended his biography to Thomas Jefferson as a portrait not of "an Aristocrat" but "a pure Republican."[78] He knew very well that Marshall's *Washington,* especially the final volume, smacked of Federalist propaganda. But it is unlikely that Weems had any fixed political opinions. In 1801 he referred to his pamphlet *The Philanthropist* as "my political Placebo, my aristocratico-Democratico political Anodyne." As later editions show, he regarded it in exactly that light.[79] When Weems was selling Marshall's *Washington* on subscription, there is no implication in his letters that he disagreed with Marshall's views, but simply that he regarded Marshall's Federalism as a tactical mistake. Weems speaks solely as a salesman in this letter of 1803, from Carlisle, Pennsylvania:

> The place had been represented to me, as a Nest of Anti Washingtonian Hornets who w[d] draw their Stings at mention of his name. . . . However, I dash[d] in among them and *thank God* have obtain[d] already 17 good names.[80]

Possibly there are Federalist tinges in Weems's *Philanthro-*

[78] Weems to Jefferson, February 1, 1809, in Skeel, II, 389; Bryan, *Washington in American Literature,* pp. 13–15. And see Samuel Eliot Morison, *The Life and Letters of Harrison Gray Otis, Federalist, 1765–1848,* 2 vols. (Boston, 1913), I, 300–303, for a discussion of the political role of the Washington Benevolent Societies. Weems's humanitarian instincts are said to have led him to free his slaves. Quite possibly he does deserve credit for this act. But the evidence is unclear. He owned some slaves as late as *c.* 1823, and did not emancipate them in his will (he died intestate). Kellock, pp. 8, 23.

[79] Weems to Carey, September 28, 1801; Skeel, I, 156. One edition, *The Philanthropist; Or, A Good Twelve Cents Worth of Political Love Powder, for the Fair Daughters and Patriotic Sons of Virginia* (1799), was dedicated to George Washington. Having solicited and got a polite acknowledgment from Washington, Weems immediately added the Washington letter to an otherwise identical new edition (1799), which he marketed at a higher price and with a less parochial title, as *The Philanthropist; Or, A Good Twenty-Five Cents Worth of Political Love Powder, for Honest Adamites and Jeffersonians.* In 1809 it was still appearing in the same format, except for an altered title: *The Philanthropist; Or Political Peace-maker Between All Honest Men of Both Parties.* Skeel, I, 153–156.

[80] Weems to Caleb Wayne, April 18, 1803, in Beveridge, *Marshall,* III, 234.

pist, and here and there in his *Washington,* as when (see p. 179) he refers to "certain blind patriots" involved in the Pennsylvania Whiskey Rebellion. But on the whole he is careful to avoid controversy. There is no mention of the "Conway Cabal" or of disagreements over the ratification of the Constitution. Jay's Treaty is sympathetically described (see p. 137): but Weems adds that it was no doubt "entirely execrated by great numbers of sensible and honest men." He deals somewhat critically with Alexander Hamilton (e.g., p. 174), but mainly because of Hamilton's recourse to duelling. He makes no allusion, in the very sketchy account of Washington's presidency, to any conflict between Hamilton and Jefferson; the only reference to the emergence of political parties is (see p. 170) a remark that Federalists and Republicans were united by the death of Washington. The defense of the Union and the Embargo (see pp. 218–219) is, if "Republican" in tone, no evidence of partisanship when set against previous statements.

As for Tom Paine, Bishop Meade recalls that Weems sold both Paine *and* the "antidote" in the shape of Watson's *Apology for the Bible.* Moreover, if Weems once had a soft spot for Paine, he turned decisively against him in *God's Revenge Against Adultery* (1815), which includes the cautionary tale of Dr. Theodore Wilson of Delaware:

According to his friend and kinsman governor Hall, this elegant young man owed his early downfal [*sic*] to reading 'PAINE'S AGE OF REASON.' He was in the full vigour of twenty-five when he heard of this libertine publication. The noise which it made in the world ensured to it an eager reader in doctor Wilson; and by his boundless ardour for animal pleasures he was already prepared to give Mr. Paine rather more than fair play, and even to swallow with delight his bold slanders of the bible, and his still bolder conclusions that all revelation is but a trick of self-seeking priests. . . . He might then riot and revel in the sties of brutal pleasure and never more dread the gospel trumpet sounding the dismal doom of adulterers.[81]

81 Weems, *Discourses,* ed. Skeel, pp. 146–147.

A change of heart or a change of pitch? Similar uncertainties surround Weems's attitude to lotteries. In 1796–97 he eagerly recommended such schemes. Perhaps later he began to have moral qualms, like other Americans who had once unhesitatingly supported lotteries for worthy purposes. Perhaps he was simply going with the current when, in *The Drunkard's Looking Glass* (*c.* 1812), he listed "joy-fevered drawers of prizes in lotteries" as among the unstable individuals who are apt to turn to the bottle.[82] At any rate he shows no embarrassment at his own *volte-face.*

When we pull together all the testimony, what estimate do we form of Parson Weems? It is of a man of varied and unfocussed talents, of exuberant and unwinking assurance—and yet in political and other matters a trimmer, a Vicar of Bray more than a Vicar of Wakefield. He expresses himself dashingly, racily—and yet *safely.* Maybe he is something of an artificial patriot. Consider again his early career. His father was born in Scotland; Weems himself was in Britain for part of the War of Independence and did not enlist on the American side; his Anglican connections may have been slightly ambiguous; Dumfries, before the war, was very much a Scottish tobacco-factors' settlement, and therefore presumably housed a number of loyalists; and as late as 1814 Weems's brother-in-law James Ewell was accused of being too friendly with the British during their raid on Washington, D.C., where he was living.[83] This is of course not to contend that Weems was a concealed Tory, but merely to suggest that his temperament and his early experiences led him to trim

[82] Weems, *Discourses,* ed. Skeel, p. 126. Apart from the charity-school scheme already mentioned (Skeel, II, 48), Weems in 1797 unsuccessfully petitioned the Virginia House of Delegates to allow him to sell his books by lottery, a part of the proceeds to be devoted to the construction of bridges on the post road from Fredericksburg to Dumfries. John S. Ezell, *Fortune's Merry Wheel: The Lottery in America* (Cambridge, Mass., 1960), p. 131, citing "Petition of Mason L. Weems," *Tyler's Quarterly Historical and Genealogical Magazine,* 5: 237–238 (1923).

[83] Sketch of James Ewell (1773–1832) in *Dictionary of American Biography,* 22 vols. (New York, 1928–1944), VI, 229.

and compromise, and that his acute sense of popular appetites may have derived from these uncertain circumstances. He had the desire to please more strongly than the desire to preach. He expounded an enthusiastic but innocuous gospel. He assumed an identity and identified himself with America, once it was a country—with its heroes, its dialect, its landscape.

The portrait is not altogether likeable. It shows too much concern for cash, too much of the cynic and the barker to permit us altogether to accept the indulgent version of Weems. His lip-smacking relish for misconduct may strike some readers as further evidence of a disingenuous character. There is a touch of the confidence-man in him. Rather than combining Whitefield and Villon in his make-up, he is a mixture of, say, P. T. Barnum and Horatio Alger. There is a good deal of hokum and crude moralizing in his *Washington,* as in Weems's other work. He exhibits George Washington in the guise of an American marvel, much as Barnum was to exhibit an ancient Negro woman as George Washington's nurse. They genuinely love Washington and genuinely love the profit in him. Weems rubs in the practical value of being virtuous, much as Horatio Alger did in novelette after novelette. He is, like them, a demonstrator of Americanism. We never quite know when he is sincere; we feel he does not himself know.

We warm to him, though, because he is buoyant, bizarre, and—at least according to the popular accounts of him—a little pathetic. He is Alfred Jingle, the strolling player in *Pickwick Papers,* who has his own strikingly flamboyant style of utterance; and Colonel Sellers in Twain's *The Gilded Age.* Neither Jingle nor Sellers would be tolerable if his semi-corrupt dreams came true. Weems as a millionaire-entrepreneur would be detestable. In fact, take away his fiddle and we would at once begin to suspect him. Instead, there is a healing innocence in his long saga. He achieves a kind of integrity through the very single-mindedness and duration of his travels. It is as if he were after all a second Johnny Appleseed: a wayfarer who set out with the idea of lining his pockets and then gradually forgot his intention in the pleasure of the journey. There is even a hint of this in early letters from Carey which reproach him for absent-minded inefficiency.[84] Little by little Weems, like Washington, merges with the terrain. He acquires and is acquired by a country. The taint runs clear, as so often in the American legend of the harmless trickster. W. C. Fields is cast as Mr. Micawber: fraudulence becomes indistinguishable from benevolence.

Weems's writings have another sort of timelessness. What intrigues us in them is the possibility that despite himself he may have conveyed valuable truths about George Washington and about the United States. Far from being ruined by his tales, we decide that American history would be thinner without them.

Marcus Cunliffe

December 1961

NOTE ON THE TEXT

Since the history of Weems's *Life of Washington* is fully discussed in the Introduction, it is necessary to add only that the text of the present edition follows that of the ninth, issued in 1809, "greatly improved." The only changes made are slight modifications in the use of quotation marks and of a few other typographical details.

[84] See, e.g., Carey to Weems, October 17, 1796; Skeel, II, 46.

THE LIFE

OF

GEORGE WASHINGTON;

WITH

CURIOUS ANECDOTES,

EQUALLY HONOURABLE TO HIMSELF

AND

EXEMPLARY TO HIS YOUNG COUNTRYMEN

A life how useful to his country led!
How loved! while living!.....how revered! now dead!
Lisp! lisp! his name, ye children yet unborn!
And with like deeds your own great names adorn.

NINTH EDITION....GREATLY IMPROVED.

EMBELLISHED WITH SEVEN ENGRAVINGS.

BY M. L. WEEMS,

FORMERLY RECTOR OF MOUNT-VERNON PARISH.

" The author has treated this great subject with admirable suc-
" cess in a new way. He turns all the actions of Washington to the
" encouragement of virtue, by a careful application of numerous
" exemplifications drawn from the conduct of the founder of our
" republic from his earliest life. No Biographer deserves more
" applause than he whose chief purpose is to entice the young
" mind to the affectionate love of virtue, by personifying it in the
" character most dear to these states."

H. Lee, Major General Army U. S.

PHILADELPHIA:
PRINTED FOR MATHEW CAREY
1809.

Original Title Page

BOOKS

PUBLISHED BY MATHEW CAREY,

No. 122, Market-street, Philadelphia.

(*PRICE ONE DOLLAR.*)

The Life of Gen. Washington,

WITH CURIOUS ANECDOTES,

EQUALLY HONOURABLE TO HIMSELF, AND EXEMPLARY TO HIS YOUNG COUNTRYMEN.

By the Rev. MASON L. WEEMS.

Embellished with a Portrait, and
Six Historical Engravings.

Criticisms on Weems's Life of Washington.

"Although the people of the United States have conferred eulogiums on Washington, so general and great, both during his life and after his decease, it is a fact that his character has not been duly appreciated by many. The reasons are evidently these;—The multitude know him, principally, as the ILLUSTRIOUS CHIEF in the war for Independence. The comparatively few that have perused the histories of our country, or the accounts of his public life, find indeed a copious display of his military and political talents, but little information concerning his *private virtues*. Yet, without these, he could not have been that great commander and statesman! Without them, our Independence might, probably, not have been acquired! or, might not have proved a blessing.

"Many patriotic and intelligent persons have therefore wished for a true and popular account of these; not only as a debt of gratitude to this great man, but as an important mean of promoting imitation of them in this nation, and even in others.

Advertisement from the Ninth Edition

CHAPTER I

OH! as along the stream of time thy name
Expanded flies, and gathers all its fame;
May then these lines to future days descend,
And prove thy COUNTRY's good thine *only end!*

"AH, *gentlemen!*"—exclaimed Bonaparte—'twas just as he was about to embark for Egypt . . . some young Americans happening at Toulon, and anxious to see the mighty Corsican, had obtained the honour of an introduction to him. Scarcely were past the customary salutations, when he eagerly asked, "*how fares your countryman, the great* WASHINGTON?" "He was very well," replied the youths, brightening at the thought that they were the countrymen of Washington; "he was very well, general, when we left America."—"*Ah, gentlemen!*" rejoined he, "*Washington can never be otherwise than well:—The measure of his fame is full—Posterity shall talk of him with reverence as the founder of a great empire, when my name shall be lost in the vortex of Revolutions!*"

Who then that has a spark of virtuous curiosity, but must wish to know the history of him whose name could thus awaken the sigh even of Bonaparte? But is not his history *already* known? Have not a thousand orators spread his fame abroad, bright as his own Potomac, when he reflects the morning sun, and flames like a sea of liquid gold, the wonder and delight of all the neighbouring shores? Yes, they have indeed spread his fame abroad . . . his fame as Generalissimo of the armies, and first President of the councils of his nation. But this is not *half* his fame. . . . True, he is there seen in *greatness,* but it is only the greatness of public character, which is no evidence of *true greatness;* for a public character is often an artificial one. At the head of an army or nation, where gold and glory are at stake, and where a man feels himself the *burning focus* of unnumbered eyes; he must be a paltry fellow indeed, who does not play his part pretty handsomely . . . even the common passions of pride, avarice, or ambition, will put him up to his metal, and call forth his best and bravest doings. But let all this heat and blaze of public situation and incitement be withdrawn; let him be thrust back into the shade of private life, and you shall see how soon, like a forced plant robbed of its hot-bed, he will drop his false foliage and fruit, and stand forth confessed in native stickweed sterility and worthlessness. . . . There was Benedict Arnold—while strutting a BRIGADIER GENERAL on the public stage, he could play you the *great man,* on a handsome scale . . . he out-marched Hannibal, and out-fought Burgoyne . . . he chaced the British like curlews, or cooped them up like chickens! and yet in the *private walks of life,* in Philadelphia, he could swindle rum from the commissary's stores, and, with the aid of loose women, retail it by the gill!! . . . And there was the great duke of Marlborough too—his public character, a thunderbolt in war! Britain's boast, and terror of the French! But his private character, what? Why a *swindler* to whom not *Arnold's self* could hold a candle; a perfect nondescript of baseness; a shaver of farthings from the poor sixpenny pay of his own brave soldiers!!!

It is not then in the glare of *public,* but in the shade of *private life,* that we are to look for the man. Private life is always *real* life. Behind the curtain, where the eyes of the million are not upon him, and where a man can have no motive but *inclination,* no excitement but *honest nature,* there he will always be sure to act *himself;* consequently, if he act greatly, he must be great indeed. Hence it has been justly said, that, "our *private deeds,* if *noble,* are noblest of our lives."

Of these private deeds of Washington very little has been said. In most of the elegant orations pronounced to his praise, you see nothing of Washington below *the clouds*—nothing of Washington the *dutiful son*—the affectionate brother—the cheerful school-boy—the diligent surveyor—the neat draftsman—the laborious farmer—and widow's husband—the orphan's father—the poor man's friend. No! this is not the Washington you see; 'tis only Washington the HERO, and the Demigod. . . . Washington the *sun beam* in council, or the *storm* in war.

And in all the ensigns of character, amidst which he is generally drawn, you see none that represent him what he really was, *"the Jupiter Conservator," the friend and benefactor of men.* Where's his bright ploughshare that he loved—or his wheat-crowned fields, waving in yellow ridges before the wanton breeze—or his hills whitened over with flocks—or his clover-covered pastures spread with innumerous herds—or his neat-clad servants, with songs rolling the heavy harvest before them? Such were the scenes of *peace, plenty,* and *happiness,* in which Washington delighted. But his eulogists have denied him *these,* the only scenes which belong to man the GREAT, and have trick'd him up in the vile drapery of man the *little.* See! there he stands! with the port of Mars *"the destroyer,"* dark frowning over the fields of war . . . the lightning of Potter's blade is by his side—the deep-mouthed cannon is before him, disgorging its flesh-mangling balls—his war-horse paws with impatience to bear him, a speedy thunderbolt, against the pale and bleeding ranks of Britain!—These are the drawings usually given of Washington; drawings masterly no doubt, and perhaps justly descriptive of him in some scenes of his life; but scenes they were, which I am sure his soul *abhorred,* and in which at any rate, you see nothing of his *private virtues.* These old fashioned commodities are generally thrown into the back ground of the picture, and treated, as the grandees at the London and Paris routs, treat their good old *aunts* and *grandmothers,* huddling them together into the *back rooms,* there to wheeze and cough by themselves, and not depress the fine laudanum-raised spirits of the *young sparklers.* And yet it was to those *old-fashioned virtues* that our hero owed every thing. For they in fact were the food of the great actions of him, whom men call Washington. It was they that enabled him, first to triumph over *himself,* then over the *British,* and uniformly to set such bright examples of *human perfectibility* and *true greatness,* that compared therewith, the history of his capturing Cornwallis and Tarleton, with their buccaneering legions, sounds almost as *small* as the story of old General Putnam's catching his wolf and her lamb-killing whelps.

Since then it is the private virtues that lay the foundation of all human excellence—since it was these that exalted Washington to be *"Columbia's first* and *greatest Son,"* be it our first care to present these, in all their lustre, before the admiring eyes of our *children.* To *them* his private character is *every thing;* his public, hardly *any thing.* For how glorious soever it may have been in Washington to have undertaken the emancipation of his country; to have stemmed the long tide of adversity; to have baffled every effort of a wealthy and warlike nation; to have obtained for his countrymen the completest victory, and for himself the most unbounded power; and then to have returned that power, accompanied with all the weight of his own great character and advice to establish a government that should immortalize the blessings of liberty . . . however glorious, I say, all this may have been to himself, or instructive to future generals and presidents, yet does it but *little* concern our *children.* For who among us can hope that his son shall ever be called, like Washington, to direct the storm of war, or to ravish the ears of deeply listening Senates? To be constantly placing him then, before our children, in this high character, what is it but like springing in the clouds a golden Phœnix, which no mortal calibre can ever hope to reach? Or like setting pictures of the Mammoth before the *mice* whom "not all the manna of

Heaven" can ever raise to equality? Oh no! give us his *private virtues!* In *these,* every youth is interested, because in these every youth may become a Washington—a Washington in piety and patriotism,—in industry and honour—and consequently a Washington, in what alone deserves the name, SELF ESTEEM and UNIVERSAL RESPECT.

CHAPTER II

BIRTH AND EDUCATION

Children like tender osiers take the bow;
And as they first are form'd for ever grow.

To this day numbers of good Christians can hardly find faith to believe that Washington was, bona fide, *a Virginian!* "*What! a buckskin!*" say they with a smile, "*George Washington a buckskin! pshaw! impossible! he was certainly an European: So great a man could never have been born in America.*"

So *great a man could never have been born in America!*— Why that's the very *prince of reasons* why he should have been born here! Nature, we know, is fond of *harmonies;* and *paria paribus,* that is, *great things to great,* is the rule she delights to work by. Where, for example, do we look for the *whale* "the biggest born of nature?" not, I trow, in a *millpond,* but in the main ocean; "*there go the great ships,*" and there are the spoutings of whales amidst their boiling foam.

By the same rule, where shall we look for Washington, the greatest among men, but in *America?* That greatest Continent, which, rising from beneath the frozen pole, stretches far and wide to the south, running almost "*whole the length of this vast terrene,*" and sustaining on her ample sides the roaring shock of half the watery globe. And equal to its size, is the furniture of this vast continent, where the Almighty has reared his cloud-capt mountains, and spread his sea-like lakes, and poured his mighty rivers, and hurled down his thundering cataracts in a style of the *sublime,* so far superior to any thing of the kind in the other continents, that we may fairly conclude that great men and great deeds are designed for America.

This seems to be the verdict of honest analogy; and accordingly we find America the honoured cradle of Washington, who was born on Pope's creek, in Westmoreland county, Virginia, the 22d of February, 1732. His father, whose name was Augustin Washington, was also a Virginian, but his grandfather (John) was an Englishman, who came over and settled in Virginia in 1657.

His father fully persuaded that a marriage of virtuous love comes nearest to angelic life, early stepped up to the *altar* with glowing cheeks and joy sparkling eyes, while by his side, with soft warm hand, sweetly trembling in his, stood the angel form of the lovely Miss Dandridge.

After several years of great domestic happiness, Mr. Washington was separated, by death, from this excellent woman, who left him and two children to lament her early fate.

Fully persuaded still, that *"it is not good for man to be alone,"* he renewed, for the second time, the chaste delights of matrimonial love. His consort was Miss Mary Ball, a young lady of fortune, and descended from one of the best families in Virginia.

From his intermarriage with this charming girl, it would appear that our Hero's father must have possessed either a very pleasing person, or highly polished manners, or perhaps *both; for,* from what I can learn, he was at that time at least 40 years old! while she, on the other hand, was universally toasted as the belle of the Northern Neck, and in the full bloom and freshness of love-inspiring sixteen. This I have from one who tells me that he has carried down many a sett dance with her; I mean that amiable and pleasant old gentleman, John Fitzhugh, Esq. of Stafford, *who* was, all his life, a neighbour and intimate of the Washington family. By his first wife, Mr. Washington had two children, both sons—Lawrence and Augustin. By his second wife, he had five children, four sons and a daughter—George, Samuel, John, Charles, and Elizabeth. Those *over delicate* ones, who are ready to faint at thought of a second marriage, might do well to remember, that the greatest man that ever lived was the son of this second marriage!

Little George had scarcely attained his fifth year, when his father left Pope's creek, and came up to a plantation which he had in Stafford, opposite to Fredericksburg. The house in which he lived is still to be seen. It lifts its low and modest front of faded red, over the turbid waters of Rappahannock; whither, to this day, numbers of people repair, and, with emotions unutterable, looking at the weatherbeaten mansion, exclaim, *"Here's the house where the Great Washington was born!"*

But it is all a mistake; for he was born, as I said, at Pope's creek, in Westmoreland county, near the margin of his own roaring Potomac.

The first place of education to which George was ever sent, was a little *"old field school,"* kept by one of his father's tenants, named Hobby; an honest, poor old man, who acted in the double character of sexton and schoolmaster. On his skill as a gravedigger, tradition is silent; but for a teacher of youth, his qualifications were certainly of the humbler sort; making what is generally called an A. B. C. schoolmaster. Such was the preceptor who first taught Washington the knowledge of letters! Hobby lived to see his young pupil in all his glory, and rejoiced exceedingly. In his cups—for, though a *sexton,* he would sometimes drink, particularly on the General's birth-days—he used to boast, that *"'twas he, who, between his knees, had laid the foundation of George Washington's greatness."*

But though George was early sent to a schoolmaster, yet he was not on that account neglected by his father. Deeply sensible of the *loveliness* and *worth* of which human nature is capable, through the *virtues* and *graces* early implanted in the heart, he never for a moment, lost sight of George in those all-important respects.

To assist his son to overcome that selfish spirit which too often leads children to fret and fight about trifles, was a notable care of Mr. Washington. For this purpose, of all the presents, such as cakes, fruit, &c. he received, he was always desired to give a liberal part to his play-mates. To enable him to do this with more alacrity, his father would remind him of the love which he would hereby gain, and the frequent presents which would in return be made *to him;* and also would tell of that great and good God, who delights above all things to see children love one another, and will assuredly reward them for acting so amiable a part.

Some idea of Mr. Washington's plan of education in this respect, may be collected from the following anecdote, related to me twenty years ago by an aged lady, who was a distant relative, and when a girl spent much of her time in the family.

"On a fine morning," said she, *"in the fall of* 1737, *Mr. Washington, having little George by the hand, came to the door and asked my cousin Washington and myself to walk with him to the orchard, promising he would show us a fine sight. On arriving at the orchard, we were presented with a fine sight indeed. The whole earth, as far as we could see, was strewed with fruit: and yet the trees were bending under the weight of apples, which hung in clusters like grapes, and vainly strove to hide their blushing cheeks behind the green leaves. Now, George, said his father, look here, my son! don't you remember when this good cousin of yours brought you that fine large apple last spring, how hardly I could prevail on you to divide with your brothers and sisters; though I promised you that if you would but do it, God Almighty would give you plenty of apples this fall. Poor George could not say a word; but hanging down his head, looked quite confused, while with his little naked toes he scratched in the soft ground. Now look up, my son, continued his father, look up, George! and see there how richly the blessed God has*

made good my promise to you. Wherever you turn your eyes, you see the trees loaded with fine fruit; many of them indeed breaking down, while the ground is covered with mellow apples more than you could ever eat, my son, in all your life time."

George looked in silence on the wide wilderness of fruit; he marked the busy humming bees, and heard the gay notes of birds, then lifting his eyes filled with shining moisture, to his father, he softly said, *"Well, Pa, only forgive me this time; see if I ever be so stingy any more."*

Some, when they look up to the oak whose giant arms throw a darkening shade over distant acres, or whose single trunk lays the keel of a man of war, cannot bear to hear of the time when this mighty plant was but an acorn, which a pig could have demolished: but others, who know their value, like to learn the soil and situation which best produces such noble trees. Thus, parents that are *wise* will listen well pleased, while I relate how moved the steps of the youthful Washington, whose single worth far outweighs all the oaks of Bashan and the red spicy cedars of Lebanon. Yes, they will listen delighted while I tell of their Washington in the days of his youth, when his little feet were swift towards the nests of birds; or when, wearied in the chace of the butterfly, he laid him down on his grassy couch and slept, while ministering spirits, with their roseate wings, fanned his glowing cheeks, and kissed his lips of innocence with that fervent love which makes *the Heaven!*

Never did the wise Ulysses take more pains with his beloved Telemachus, than did Mr. Washington with George, to inspire him with an *early love of truth.* "Truth, George," (said he) "is the loveliest quality of youth. I would ride fifty miles, my son, to see the little boy whose heart is so *honest,* and his lips so *pure,* that we may depend on every word he says. O how lovely does such a child appear in the eyes of every body! His parents doat on him; his relations glory in him; they are constantly praising him to their children, whom they beg to imitate him. They are often sending for him, to visit them; and receive him, when he comes, with as much joy as if he were a little angel, come to set pretty examples to their children.

"But, Oh! how different, George, is the case with the boy who is so given to lying, that nobody can believe a word he says! He is looked at with aversion wherever he goes, and parents dread to see him come among their children. Oh, George! my son! rather than see you come to this pass, dear as you are to my heart, gladly would I assist to nail you up in your little coffin, and follow you to your grave. Hard, indeed, would it be to me to give up my son, whose little feet are always so ready to run about with me, and whose fondly looking eyes and sweet prattle make so large a part of my happiness: but still I would give him up, rather than see him a common liar.

"Pa, (said George very seriously) do I ever tell lies?"

"No, George, I *thank God* you do not, my son; and I rejoice in the hope you never will. At least, you shall never, from me, have cause to be guilty of so shameful a thing. Many parents, indeed, even compel their children to this vile practice, by barbarously beating them for every little fault; hence, on the next offence, the little terrified creature slips out a *lie!* just to escape the rod. But as to yourself, George, you know I have *always* told you, and now tell you again, that, whenever by accident you do any thing wrong, which must often be the case, as you are but a poor little boy yet, without *experience* or *knowledge,* never tell a falsehood to conceal it; but come *bravely* up, my son, like a *little man,* and tell me of it: and instead of beating you, George, I will but the more honour and love you for it, my dear."

This, you'll say, was sowing good seed!—Yes, it was: and the crop, thank God, was, as I believe it ever will be, where a man acts the true parent, that is, the *Guardian Angel,* by his child.

The following anecdote is a *case in point.* It is too valuable to be lost, and too true to be doubted; for it was communicated to me by the same excellent lady to whom I am indebted for the last.

"When George," said she, "was about six years old, he was made the wealthy master of a *hatchet!* of which, like most little boys, he was immoderately fond, and was constantly going about chopping every thing that came in his way. One day, in the garden, where he often amused himself hacking his mother's pea-sticks, he unluckily tried the edge of his hatchet on the body of a beautiful young English cherry-tree, which he barked so terribly, that I don't believe the tree ever got the better of it. The next morning the old gentleman finding out what had befallen his tree, which, by the by, was a great favourite, came into the house, and with much warmth asked for the mischievous author, declaring at the same time, that he would not have taken five guineas for his tree. Nobody could tell him any thing about it. Presently George and his hatchet made their appearance. *George,* said his father, *do you know who killed that beautiful little cherry-tree yonder in the garden?* This was a *tough question;* and George staggered under it for a moment; but quickly recovered himself: and looking at his father, with the sweet face of youth brightened with the inexpressible charm of all-conquering truth, he bravely cried out, *"I can't tell a lie, Pa; you know I can't tell a lie. I did cut it with my hatchet."—Run to my arms, you dearest boy,* cried his father in transports, *run to my arms; glad am I, George, that you killed my tree; for you have paid me for it a thousand fold. Such an act of heroism in my son, is more worth than a thousand trees, though blossomed with silver, and their fruits of purest gold.*

It was in this way, by interesting at once both his *heart* and *head,* that Mr. Washington conducted George with great ease and pleasure along the happy paths of virtue. But well knowing that his beloved charge, soon to be a man, would be left exposed to numberless temptations, both from himself and from others, his heart throbbed with the tenderest anxiety to make him acquainted with that GREAT BEING, whom to know and love, is to possess the surest defence against vice, and the best of all motives to virtue and happiness. To startle George into a lively sense of his Maker, he fell upon the following very curious but impressive expedient:

One day he went into the garden, and prepared a little bed of finely pulverized earth, on which he wrote George's name at full, in large letters—then strewing in plenty of cabbage seed, he covered them up and smoothed all over nicely with the roller. This bed he purposely prepared close along side of a gooseberry walk, which happening at this time to be well hung with ripe fruit, he knew would be honoured with George's visits pretty regularly every day. Not many mornings had passed away before in came George, with eyes wild rolling, and his little cheeks ready to burst with *great news.*

"O Pa! come here! come here!"

"What's the matter, my son, what's the matter?"

"O come here, I tell you, Pa, come here! and I'll show you such a sight as you never saw in all your life time."

The old gentleman suspecting what George would be at, gave him his hand, which he seized with great eagerness, and tugging him along through the garden, led him up point blank to the bed whereon was inscribed, in large letters, and in all the freshness of newly sprung plants, the full name of

GEORGE WASHINGTON

"There, Pa!" said George, quite in an ecstasy of astonishment, "did you ever see such a sight in all your life time?"

"Why it seems like a curious affair, sure enough, George!"

"But, Pa, who did make it there, who did make it there?"

"It grew there by *chance,* I suppose my son."

"By *chance,* Pa! O no! no! it never did grow there by *chance,* Pa; indeed that it never did!"

"High! why not, my son?"

"Why, Pa, did you ever see any body's name in a plant bed before?"

"Well, but George, such a thing might happen, though you never saw it before!"

"Yes, Pa, but I did never see the little plants grow up so as to make *one single* letter of my name before. Now, how could they grow up so as to make *all* the letters of my name! and then standing one after another, to spell *my name* so *exactly!*—and all so neat and even too, at top and bottom!! O Pa, you must not say *chance* did all this. Indeed *somebody* did it; and I dare say now, Pa, *you* did do it just to scare *me,* because I am your little boy."

His father smiled, and said, "Well George, you have guessed right—I indeed *did* it; but not to *scare* you, my son; but to learn you a great thing which I wish you to understand. I want, my son, to introduce you to your *true* Father."

"High, Pa, an't *you* my *true* father, that has loved me, and been so good to me always?"

"Yes, George, I am your father as the world calls it: and I love you very dearly too. But yet with all my love for you, George, I am but a poor good-for-nothing sort of a father in comparison of one you have."

"Aye! I know, well enough whom you mean, Pa. You mean God Almighty, don't you?"

"Yes, my son, I mean him indeed. *He is* your *true* Father, George."

"But, Pa, where is God Almighty? I did never *see* him yet."

"True, my son; but though you never *saw* him, yet he is always with you. You did not see me when ten days ago I made this little plant bed, where you see your name in such beautiful green letters; but though you did not *see* me here, yet you know I was here!!"

"Yes, Pa, that I do—I know you was here."

"Well then, and as my son could not believe that *chance*

had made and put together so exactly the *letters* of his name, (though only sixteen) then how can he believe that *chance* could have made and put together all those millions and millions of things that are now so exactly fitted to his good? That my son may look at every thing around him, see! what fine eyes he has got! and a little pug nose to smell the sweet flowers! and pretty ears to hear sweet sound! and a lovely mouth for his bread and butter! and O, the little ivory teeth to cut it for him! and the dear little tongue to prattle with his father! and precious little hands and fingers to hold his play-things! and beautiful little feet for him to run about upon! and when my little rogue of a son is tired with running about, then the still night comes for him to lie down, and his mother sings, and the little crickets chirp him to sleep! and as soon as he has slept enough, and jumps up fresh and strong as a little buck, there the sweet golden light is ready for him! When he looks down into the water, there he sees the beautiful silver fishes for him! and up in the *trees* there are the apples, and peaches, and *thousands* of sweet fruits for him! and *all, all around* him, wherever my dear boy looks, he sees every thing just to his *wants and wishes;*—the bubbling springs with cool sweet water for him to drink! and the wood to make him sparkling fires when he is cold! and beautiful horses for him to ride! and strong oxen to work for him! and the *good* cows to give him milk! and bees to make sweet honey for his sweeter mouth! and the little lambs, with snowy wool, for beautiful clothes for him! Now, these and all the *ten thousand thousand other good things* more than my son can ever think of, and all so exactly fitted to his *use* and *delight*. . . . Now how could chance ever have done all this for my little son? Oh George! . . ."

He would have gone on, but George, who had hung upon his father's words with looks and eyes of all-devouring attention, here broke out—

"Oh Pa, that's enough! that's enough! It can't be chance,

indeed, it can't be chance, that made and gave me all these things."

"What was it then, do you think, my son?"

"Indeed, Pa, I don't know, unless it was *God Almighty!*"

"Yes, George, he it was, my son, and nobody else."

"Well, but Pa, (continued George) does God Almighty give me *every thing?* Don't you give me *some things,* Pa?"

"I give *you* something, indeed! Oh! how can I give you any thing, George! I, who have nothing on earth that I can call my own, no, not even the breath I draw!"

"High, Pa! isn't that great big house your house, and this garden, and the horses yonder, and oxen, and sheep, and trees, and every thing, isn't all yours, Pa?"

"Oh no! my son! no! Why you make me shrink into nothing, George, when you talk of all these belonging to *me,* who can't even make *a grain of sand!* Oh, how could I, my son, have given life to those great oxen and horses, when I can't give life even to a fly?—no! for if the poorest fly were killed, it is not your father, George, nor all the men in the world, that could ever make him alive again!"

At this, George fell into a profound silence, while his pensive looks showed that his youthful soul was labouring with some idea never felt before. Perhaps it was at that moment, that the good Spirit of God ingrafted on his heart that germ of *piety,* which filled his after life with so many of the precious fruits of *morality.*

CHAPTER III

George's father dies—his education continued by his mother—his behaviour under school-master Williams

THUS pleasantly, on wings of down, passed away the few short years of little George's and his father's *earthly* acquaintance. Sweetly ruled by the sceptre of REASON, George almost adored his father; and thus sweetly *obeyed* with all the cheerfulness of LOVE, his father doated on George. . . . And though very different in their years, yet parental and filial love rendered them so mutually dear, that the old gentleman was often heard to regret, that *the school took his little companion so much from him*—while George, on the other hand, would often quit his playmates to run home and converse with his more beloved father.

But George was not long to enjoy the pleasure or the profit of such a companion; for scarcely had he attained his tenth year, before his father was seized with the gout in the stomach, which carried him off in a few days. George was not at home when his father was taken ill. He was on a visit to some of his cousins in Chotank, about twenty miles off; and his father, unwilling to interrupt his pleasures, for it was but seldom that he visited, would not at first allow him to be sent for. But finding that he was going very fast, he begged that they would send for him in all haste . . . he often asked if he was come, and said how happy he should be, once more to see his little son, and give him his blessing before he died. But alas! he never enjoyed that last mournful pleasure; for George did not reach home until a few hours before his father's death, and then he was speechless! The moment he alighted, he ran into the chamber where he lay. But oh! what were his feelings when he saw the sad change that had passed upon him! when he beheld those eyes, late so *bright* and *fond,* now reft of all their lustre, faintly looking on him from their hollow sockets, and through swelling tears, in mute but melting language, bidding him a LAST, LAST FAREWELL! . . . Rushing with sobs and cries, he fell upon his father's neck . . . he kissed him a thousand and a thousand times, and bathed his clay-cold face with scalding tears.

O happiest youth! Happiest in that love, which thus, to its enamoured soul strained an aged an[d] expiring sire. O! worthiest to be the founder of a JUST and EQUAL GOVERNMENT, lasting as thy own deathless name! And O! happiest old man! thus luxuriously expiring in the arms of such a child! O! well requited for teaching him that LOVE OF HIS GOD (*the only fountain of every virtuous love*) in return for which he gave thee ('twas all he had) *himself*—his *fondest company*—his *sweetest looks and prattle.* He now gives thee his little strong embraces, with artless sighs and tears; faithful to thee still, his feet will follow thee to thy grave: and when thy beloved corse is let down to the stones of the pit, with streaming eyes he will rush to the brink, to take *one more* look, while his bursting heart will give thee its last trembling cry. . . . *O my father! my father!*

But, though he had lost his best of friends, yet he never lost those divine sentiments which that friend had so carefully inculcated. On the contrary, interwoven with the fibres of his heart, they seemed to "grow with his growth, and to strengthen with his strength." The *memory* of his father, often bathed with *a tear*—the memory of his father now sleeping in his grave, was felt to impose a more sacred obligation to do what, 'twas known, would rejoice his departed shade. This was very happily displayed, in every part of his deportment, from the moment of his earliest intercourse with mankind.

Soon after the death of his father, his mother sent him

down to Westmoreland, the place of his nativity, where he lived with his half-brother Augustin, and went to school to a Mr. Williams, an excellent teacher in that neighbourhood. He carried with him his virtues, *his zeal for unblemished character, his love of truth, and detestation of whatever was false and base.* A gilt chariot with richest robes and liveried servants, could not half so substantially have befriended him; for in a very short time, so completely had his virtues secured the love and confidence of the boys, his *word* was just as current among them as a *law.* A very aged gentleman, formerly a school-mate of his, has often assured me, (while pleasing recollection brightened his furrowed cheeks,) that nothing was more common, when the boys were in high dispute about a question of fact, than for some little shaver among the mimic heroes, to call out *"well boys! George Washington was there; George Washington was there; he knows all about it; and if he don't say it was so, then we will give it up,"*—*"done,"* said the adverse party. Then away they would trot to hunt for George. Soon as his verdict was heard, the party favoured would begin to crow, and then all hands would return to play again.

About five years after the death of his father, he quitted school for ever, leaving the boys in tears for his departure: for he had ever lived among them, in the spirit of a brother. He was never guilty of so brutish a practice as that of fighting them himself, nor would he, when able to prevent it, allow them to fight one another. If he could not disarm their savage passions by his arguments, he would instantly go to the master, and inform him of their barbarous intentions.

"The boys," said the same good old gentleman, "were often angry with George for this"—But he used to say, "angry or not angry, you shall never, boys, have my consent to a practice so shocking! shocking even in *slaves* and *dogs;* then how utterly scandalous in little boys at school, who ought to look on one another as brothers. And what must be the feelings of our tender parents, when, instead of seeing us come home smiling and lovely, as the JOYS OF THEIR HEARTS! they see us creeping in like young *blackguards,* with our heads *bound up, black eyes,* and *bloody clothes!* And what is all this for? Why, that we *may get praise!!* But the truth is, a quarrelsome boy was never sincerely praised! Big boys, of the *vulgar sort,* indeed may praise him; but it is only as they would a silly game cock, that fights for their *pastime*—and the little boys are sure to praise him, but it is only as they would a bull dog—to keep him from tearing them!!"

Some of his historians have said, and many believe, that Washington was a *Latin scholar!* But 'tis an error. He never learned a syllable of Latin. His second and last teacher, Mr. Williams, was indeed a capital hand—but not at Latin; for of that he understood perhaps as little as Balaam's ass—but at *reading, spelling, English grammar, arithmetic, surveying, book-keeping and geography,* he was indeed famous. And in these useful arts, 'tis said, he often boasted that he had made *young George Washington as great a scholar as himself.*

Born to be a soldier, Washington early discovered symptoms of nature's intentions towards him. In his 11th year, while at school under old Mr. Hobby, he used to divide his play-mates into two parties, *or armies.* One of these, for distinction sake, was called *French,* the other *American.* A big boy at the school, named William Bustle, commanded the former, George commanded the latter. And every day, at play-time, with corn-stalks for muskets, and calabashes for drums, the two armies would turn out, and march, and counter-march, and file off or fight their mimic battles, with great fury. This was fine sport for George, whose passion for active exercise was so strong, that at play-time no weather could keep him within doors. His *fair cousins,* who visited at his mother's, used to complain, that *"George was not fond of their company, like other boys; but soon as he had got his task, would run out to play."* But such trifling play as marbles and tops he could never abide. They did not afford him exercise enough. His delight was in that of the manliest sort, which, by stringing the limbs and swelling the muscles, promotes the kindliest flow of blood and spirits. At jumping with a long pole, or heaving heavy weights, for his years he hardly had an equal. And as to running, the swift-footed Achilles could scarcely have matched his speed.

"Egad! he ran wonderfully," said my amiable and aged friend, John Fitzhugh, esq. who knew him well. *"We had nobody here-abouts, that could come near him. There was young Langhorn Dade, of Westmoreland, a confounded clean made, tight young fellow, and a mighty swift runner too . . . but then he was no match for George: Langy, indeed, did not like to give it up; and would brag that he had sometimes brought George to a tie. But I believe he was mistaken: for I have seen them run together many a time; and George always beat him easy enough."*

Col. Lewis Willis, his play-mate and kinsman, has been heard to say, that he has often seen him throw a stone across Rappahannock, at the lower ferry of Fredericksburg. It would be no easy matter to find a man, now-a-days, who could do it.

Indeed, his father before him was a man of extraordinary strength. His gun, which to this day is called *Washington's fowling-piece,* and now the property of Mr. Harry Fitzhugh, of Chotank, is of such enormous weight, that not one man in a hundred can fire it without a rest. And yet throughout that country it is said, that he made nothing of holding it off at arms-length, and blazing away at the swans on Potomac; of which he has been known to kill *rank* and *file,* seven or eight at a shot.

But to return to George. . . . It appears that from the start he was a boy of an uncommonly warm and noble heart; insomuch that Lawrence, though but his *half-brother,* took such a liking to him, even above his *own* brother Augustin, that he would always have George with him when he could get him;

and often pressed him to come and live with him. But, as if led by some secret impulse, George declined the offer, and went up, as we have seen, to work, in the back-woods, as Lord Fairfax's surveyor! However, when Lawrence was taken with the consumption, and advised by his physicians to make a trip to Bermuda, George could not resist any longer, but hastened down to his brother at Mount Vernon, and went with him to Bermuda. It was at Bermuda that George took the small-pox, which marked him rather agreeably than otherwise. Lawrence never recovered, but returned to Virginia, where he died just after his brother George had fought his hard battle against the French and Indians, at Fort Necessity, as the reader will presently learn.

Lawrence did not live to see George after that; but he lived to hear of his fame; for as the French and Indians were at that time a great public terror, the people could not help being very loud in their praise of a youth, who with so slender a force had dared to meet them in their own country, and had given them such a check.

And when Lawrence heard of his favourite young brother, that he had fought so gallantly for his country, and that the whole land was filled with his praise, he *wept* for joy. And such is the victory of love over nature, that though fast sinking under the fever and cough of a consumption in its extreme stage, he did not seem to mind it, but spent his last moments in fondly talking of his brother George, who, he said, *"he had always believed, would one day or other be a great man!"*[1]

On opening his will, it was found that George had lost

[1] It is pointless to explore every error of fact in Weems's biography. But this page illustrates how he gets his facts wrong but not entirely wrong, and how he re-arranges time sequences for greater dramatic effect. Thus, George and his half-brother Lawrence actually went to Barbados, not Bermuda. Yet Lawrence did return to Virginia *via* Bermuda; and at one stage it had been planned that George should bring Lawrence's wife there. As for Lawrence's death, this took place in July 1752, a whole year before the fight at Fort Necessity.

nothing by his dutiful and affectionate behaviour to his brother Lawrence. For having now no issue, (his only child, a little daughter, lately dying) he left to George all his rich lands in Berkley, together with his great estate on Potomac, called MOUNT VERNON, in honour of old Admiral Vernon, by whom he had been treated with great politeness, while a volunteer with him at the unfortunate siege of Carthagena, in 1741.

CHAPTER IV

George leaves school—is appointed a private surveyor to Lord Fairfax, of the Northern Neck—wishes to enter on board of a British man of war—providentially prevented by his mother—the first lightnings of his soul to war

HAPPILY for America, George Washington was not born with *"a silver spoon in his mouth."* The Rappahan[n]ock plantation left him by his father, was only in *reversion*—and his mother was still in her prime. Seeing then no chance of ever rising in the world but by his own merit, on leaving school he went up to Fairfax to see his brother Lawrence; with whom he found Mr. William Fairfax, one of the governor's council, who was come up on a visit to his sister, whom Lawrence had married. The counsellor presently took a great liking to George, and hearing him express a wish to get employment as a surveyor, introduced him to his relative, Lord Fairfax, the wealthy proprietor of all those lands generally called the *Northern Neck,* lying between the Potomac and Rappahan[n]-ock, and extending from Smith's Point, on the Chesapeake, to the foot of the Great Allegheny. At the instance of the counsellor, Lord Fairfax readily engaged George as a surveyor, and sent him up into the back-woods to work. He continued in his lordship's service till his 20th year, closely pursuing the laborious life of a woodsman.

From the manner in which Washington used to amuse his leisure hours during this period, one is almost inclined to think, that he had a presentiment of the great labours that lay before him. While in Frederick, which at that time was very large, containing the counties now called Berkley, Jefferson, and Shenandoah, he boarded in the house of the widow

Stevenson, generally pronounced *Stinson.* This lady had seven sons—William and Valentine Crawford, by her first husband; and John, and Hugh, and Dick, and Jim, and Mark Stinson, by her last husband. These seven young men, in Herculean size and strength, were equal, perhaps, to any seven sons of any one mother in Christendom. This was a family exactly to George's mind, because promising him an abundance of that manly exercise in which he delighted. In front of the house lay a fine extended green, with a square of several hundred yards. Here it was every evening, when his daily toils of surveying were ended, that George, like a young Greek training for the Olympic games, used to turn out with his sturdy young companions, *"to see,"* as they termed it, *"which was the best man,"* at running, jumping, and wrestling. And so keen was their passion for these sports, and so great their ambition to out-do one another, that they would often keep them up, especially on moon-shining nights, till *bed-time.* The Crawfords and Stinsons, though not taller than George, were much heavier men; so that at *wrestling,* and particularly at the *close* or *Indian hug,* he seldom gained much matter of triumph. But in all trials of *agility,* they stood no chance with him!

From these Frederick county gymnastics or *exercises,* there followed an effect which shows the very wide difference between participating in *innocent* and *guilty* pleasures. While companions in raking and gambling, heartily despise and hate one another, and, when they meet in the streets pass each other, with looks cold and shy as sheep-thieving curs—these virtuous young men, by spending their evenings together in innocent and manly exercises, contracted a friendship which lasted for life. When George, twenty-five years after this, was called to lead the American armies, he did not forget his old friends, the Stinsons and Crawfords, but gave commissions to all of them who chose to join his army; which several of them did. William Crawford, the eldest of them, and as brave a man as ever shouldered a musket, was advanced as high as the rank of colonel, when he was burnt to death by the Indians at Sandusky. And equally cordial was the love of these young men towards George, of whom they always spoke as of *a brother*. Indeed, Hugh Stinson, the second brother, who had a way of snapping his eyes when he talked of any thing that greatly pleased him, used to brighten up at the name of Washington, and would tell his friends, that *"he and his brother John had often laid the conqueror of England on his back."* But, at the same time, would agree, that *"in running and jumping they were no match for him."*

Such was the way in which George spent his *leisure hours* in the service of Lord Fairfax. Little did the old nobleman expect that he was educating a youth, who should one day dismember the British empire, and break his own heart—which truly came to pass. For on hearing that Washington had captured Cornwallis and all his army, he called out to his black waiter, *"Come, Joe! carry me to my bed! for I'm sure 'tis high time for me to die!"*

Then up rose Joe, all at the word,
And took his master's arm,
And to his bed he softly led,
The lord of Green-way farm.

There oft he call'd on Britain's name,
"And oft he wept full sore."—
Then sigh'd—thy will, O Lord, be done—
"And word spake never more."

It was in his 15th year, according to the best of my information, that Washington first felt the kindlings of his soul for war. The cause was this—In those days, the people of Virginia looked on Great Britain as the *mother country,* and to go thither was in common phrase, *"to go home."* The name of OLD ENGLAND was music in their ears: and the bare mention of a blow meditated against her, never failed to rouse a something at the heart, which instantly flamed on the cheek and flashed in the eye. Washington had his full share of these virtuous feelings: on hearing, therefore, that France and Spain were mustering a black cloud over his MOTHER COUNTRY, his youthful blood took fire, and he instantly tendered what aid *his little arm* could afford. The rank of midshipman was procured for him on board a British ship of war, then lying in our waters, and his trunk and clothes were actually sent on board. But when he came to take leave of his mother, she wept bitterly, and told him *she felt that her heart would break if he left her*. George immediately got his trunk ashore! as he could not, for a moment, bear the idea of inflicting a wound on that dear life which had so long and so fondly sustained his own.

Where George got his great military talents, is a question which none but the happy believers in a *particular Providence* can solve: certain it is, his earthly parents had no hand in it. For of his father, tradition says nothing, save that he was a most amiable old gentleman; one who made good crops, and scorned to give his name to the quill-drivers of a counting room. And as to his mother, it is well known that she was none of Bellona's fiery race. For as some of the Virginia officers, just after the splendid actions of Trenton and Princeton, was complimenting her on the generalship and *rising glory* of her son, instead of showing the exultation of a Spartan dame, she replied, with all the sang froid of a good old Friend, *"Ah, dear me! This fighting and killing is a sad thing! I wish George would come home and look after his plantation!!"*

Nor does it appear that nature had mixed much of gunpowder in the composition of any of his brothers: for when one of them, in the time of Braddock's war, wrote him a letter, signifying something like a wish to *enter into the service;* George, it is said, gave him this short reply, *"Brother, stay at home, and comfort your wife."*

But though not destined to figure on the quarterdeck of a

man of war, yet he ceased not to cultivate that talent which had been given for higher uses. From adjutant Muse, a Westmoreland volunteer, who had gained much credit in the war of Cuba, whence he had lately returned with Lawrence Washington, he learnt to go through the manual exercise with great dexterity; and by the help of good treatises on the art of war, which were put into his hands, by the same gentleman, he soon acquired very clear ideas of the evolutions and movements of troops. And from Mons. Vanbraam, who afterwards accompanied him as interpreter to Venango, he acquired the *art of fencing,* at which, 'tis said, he was extremely expert. A passion, so uncommon for war, joined to a very manly appearance, and great dignity of character, could scarcely fail to attract on him the attention of the public. In fact the public sentiment was so strong in his favour, that at the green age of nineteen, he was appointed major and adjutant general of the Virginia forces, in the Northern Neck, when training, as was expected, for immediate service.

For his services as an adjutant general, he was allowed by the crown 100*l.* sterling per annum.

CHAPTER V

French encroachments on the Ohio—Washington volunteers his services to governor Dinwiddie—his hazardous embassy to the French and Indians—miraculous escapes—account of his journal—anecdote of his modesty

In the year 1753 the people of Virginia were alarmed by a report that the French, aided by the Indians, were erecting a long line of military posts on the Ohio. This manœuvre, predicting no good to the ANCIENT DOMINION, was properly resented by Robert Dinwiddie, the governor, who wished immediately in the name of his king to forbid the measure. But how to convey a letter to the French commandant on the Ohio, *was the question.* For the whole country west of the Blue Mountains, was one immeasurable forest, from time immemorial the gloomy haunts of ravening beasts and of murderous savages. No voices had ever broke the awful silence of those dreary woods, save the hiss of rattlesnakes, the shrieks of panthers, the yells of Indians, and howling tempests. From such scenes, though beheld but by the distant eye of fancy, the hearts of youth are apt to shrink with terror, and to crouch more closely to their safer fire-sides. But in the firmer nerves of Washington, they do not appear to have made the least impression of the agueish sort. The moment he heard of the governor's wishes, he waited on him with—*a tender of his services.*

"Now Christ save my saoul, but ye're a braw lad!" said the good old Scotsman . . . *"and gin ye play your cards weel, my boy, ye shall hae nae cause to rue your bargain."* The governor took him to his palace that night, which was spent in preparing his letters and instructions. The next day, accom-

panied by an interpreter and a couple of servants, he set out on his journey, which being in the depth of winter, was as disagreeable and dangerous as Hercules himself could have desired. Drenching rains and drowning floods, and snow-covered mountains opposed his course, but opposed in vain. The generous ambition to serve his country, and to distinguish himself, carried him through all, and even at the most trying times, touched his heart with a joy unknown to the VAIN and TRIFLING. On his way home he was way-laid and shot at by an Indian, who, though not fifteen paces distant, happily missed his aim. The poor wretch was made prisoner; but Washington could not find in his heart to put him to death, though his own safety seemed to require the sacrifice. The next evening, in attempting to cross a river on a raft, he was within an ace of being drowned, and, the night following, of perishing in the ice: but from both these imminent deadly risks, there was a hand unseen that effected his escape.

About the middle of January he got back to Williamsburgh, and instantly waiting on the governor, presented him the fruits of his labours—the belts of wampum which he had brought from the Indian kings as pledges of their friendship—the French governor's letters—and last of all, his *journal* of the expedition. This it seems he had drawn up as a tub for the whale, that he might be spared the pain of much talking about *himself* and his *adventures*. For, like the king of Morven, *"though mighty deeds rolled from his soul of fire, yet his words were never heard."* The governor was much pleased with the Indian belts—more with the Frenchman's letter—but most of all with Washington's journal, which he proposed to have *printed* immediately. Washington begged hard that his excellency would spare him the mortification of seeing his journal sent out into the world in so mean a dress. He urged, that having been written in a wintry wilderness, by a traveller, young, illiterate, and often cold, wet, and weary, it needed a thousand amendments. *"Hoot awa, Major,"* replied his excellency, *"hoot awa, mon, what tauk ye aboot amendments; I am sure the pamphlet need na blush to be seen by his majesty himsel*—and in good troth I mean to send him a copy or twa of it. And besides, our Assembly will rise to-morrow or next day, and I wish each of the members to take a few copies home with them. So we must e'en straightway print the journal off hand as it is."

The journal, of course, was immediately printed. Every eye perused it, and every tongue was loud in its praise. Indeed it was not easy to err on the side of excess; for whoever with candour reads the journal, will readily pronounce it *an unique* in the history of juvenile productions. It discovers that vigor, and variety of talents, which take up, as it were, intuitively, the views belonging to any new subject that presents itself. It is the hasty production of a young man, born in the retreats of deepest solitude, in a time of profoundest peace, and brought up to the simple harmless employment of a surveyor, an employment which, more than any other, tends to tranquillize the mind. The verdure and music of the love-breathing spring; the bright fields and harvests of joy-inspiring summer, the faded leaves and mournful silence of autumn, with winter's solemn grandeur, were the scenes in which the youth of Washington was passed. In these he hears the roar of distant war—from these he is sent forth to mark the gathering storm. Instantly he breathes the whole spirit of his new engagement—*"Old things are done away, all things are become new"*—the chain and theodolite are forgotten—the surveyor is lost in the soldier—his shoulders are young, but they sustain the head of an old engineer—he marks the soil, the timber, the confluence of rivers, the sites for forts; in short, nothing connected with the defence of his country, escapes him. He penetrates the characters of the different people around him—the low sensuality of the Indian, ready, for a *dram,* to lift the tomahawk; the polished subtilties of the European, who can *"smile* and *smile"* and yet design the death of the traveller—these important truths present themselves intuitively to his mind, and shine with such lustre on the pages of his journal, as to command the admiration of every unprejudiced reader.

Among the gentlemen in Williamsburg, who had sense and virtue enough to appreciate the worth of Washington, one of the first was a Mr. Waller.—This gentleman, conversing on that subject with Mr. Robertson, speaker of the house of Burgesses, observed, that such services as those rendered by Major Washington, were much too important to be paid off by the light coin of common parlour puffs. *"This young man,"* said he, *"has deserved well of his country; and her Representatives in Ass[e]mbly ought to acknowledge the obligation."—"That's exactly my own opinion,"* replied Robertson, *"and if you will let me know when the major next visits us, I will make a motion to that effect."*

The next day, Washington, not having even dreamt of the honor intended him, entered the house, and going up stairs took his seat in the gallery. The eagle-eyed friendship of Mr. Waller quickly discovered him; and stepping to the chair, whispered it to Mr. Robertson, who instantly arose, and ordering silence, called out, "Gentlemen, it is proposed, that the thanks of this HOUSE be given to Major Washington, who now sits in the gallery, for the very gallant manner in which he executed the important trust lately reposed in him by his excellency governor Dinwiddie." In a moment, the HOUSE rose as one man, and turning towards Washington, saluted him with a general bow, and in very flattering terms expressed their high sense of his services.—Had an earthquake shaken the capitol to the centre, it could hardly have so completely confounded the major! He rose to make his acknowledgments, but, alas! his tongue had forgotten his office. Thrice he essayed to speak, but thrice, in spite of every effort, his utterance failed him, save faintly to articulate, *"Mr. Speaker! Mr. Speaker!"* To relieve him from his embarrassment, Mr. Robertson kindly called out, "Major Washington, Major Washington, sit down: your modesty alone is equal to your merit."

CHAPTER VI

The French and Indian war begins—Washington goes forth to meet the dangers of his country—aims a blow at fort Du Quesne—fails—gallant defence of Fort Necessity—retires from the service in disgust—pressed into it again by General Braddock—defeat and death of Braddock, and dreadful slaughter of his army

"WELL, WHAT IS TO COME, WILL COME!" said poor Paddy, when going to the gallows. Even so was come, as would seem, the time that *was* to come for *"kings to go forth to battle."* The truth is, numbers of *poor tax-ground,* and thence *uneducated* and *half-starved* wretches in *Britain* and *France,* were become diseased with a moral *cachexy* or *surcharge* of *bad humours,* such as gambling, swindling, horse stealing, highway-robbing, &c. which nothing but the saturnine pills and steel points of Mars could effectually carry off. Thus in all corrupted governments WAR is considered as a necessary evil. It was no doubt necessary *then.*

Such was the *remote cause*—the *proximate history* or how the *dance began,* we now proceed to relate.

We have just seen that the French, pouring down from the lakes of Canada, thick as autumnal geese, were dashing away on the Ohio, at an alarming rate—multiplying forts—holding TALKS—and strengthening their alliances with the Indians. And we have seen that Washington, with letters from governor Dinwiddie, had been out among the PARLEZVOUS, conjuring them by every thing venerable in treaties, or valuable in *peace,* to desist from such unwarrantable measures. But all to no purpose . . . for the French commandant, smiling at Washington as a *green horn,* and at Dinwiddie as an *old fool,* continued his operations as vigorously as though he knew not that the country in question made a part of the British empire.

Swift as the broad-winged packets could fly across the deep, the news was carried to England.—Its effect there was like that of a stone rudely hurled against a nest of *hornets*. Instantly, from centre to circumference, all is rage and bustle . . . the hive resounds with the maddening insects; dark tumbling from their cells they spread the hasty wing, and shrill whizzing through the air, they rush to find the foe. Just so in the *sea-ruling* island, from *queens-house* to *ale-house,* from *king* to *cockney,* all were fierce for fight. Even the red-nosed porters where they met, bending under their burdens, would stop, full-but in the streets, to talk of ENGLAND'S WRONGS; and, as they talked, their fiery snouts were seen to grow more fiery still, and more deformed. Then throwing their packs to the ground, and leaping into the attitude of boxers, with sturdy arms across, and rough black jaws stretched out, they bend forward to the *fancied fight!* The frog-eating foe, in shirtless ruffles and long lank queue, seems to give ground! then rising in their might, with fire striking eyes they press hard upon him, and coming, in hand and foot, with kick and cuff and many a hearty curse, they shew the GIGGLING CROWD, how, damn 'em! they would thump the French.

The news was brought to Britain's king just as he had dispatched his pudding; and sat, right royally amusing himself with a slice of Gloucester and a nip of ale. From the lips of the king down fell the luckless cheese, alas! not grac'd to comfort the stomach of the Lord's anointed; while crowned with snowy foam, his nut-brown ale stood untasted by his plate. Suddenly, as he heard the news, the monarch darkened in his place . . . and answering darkness shrouded all his court.

In silence he rolled his eyes of fire on the floor, and twirled his *terrible thumbs!* his pages shrunk from his presence; for who could stand before the king of thundering ships, when wrath, in gleams of lightning, flashed from his *"dark red eyes?"* Starting, at length, as from a trance, he swallowed his ale, the[n] clenching his fist, he gave the table a tremendous knock, and cursed the wooden-shoed nation by his God! Swift as he cursed, the dogs of war bounded from their kennels, keen for the chace, and snuffing the blood of Frenchmen on every gale, they raised a howl of death which reached these peaceful shores. Orders were immediately issued, by the British government, for the colonies to arm and unite in one confederacy. Virginia took the lead, and raised a regiment, to the second command in which she raised her favourite Washington. Colonel Fry, by right of seniority, commanded; but on his death, which happened soon after his appointment, Washington succeeded to the command.—With this little handful, he bravely pushed out into the wilderness, in quest of the enemy, and at a place called the little Meadows, came up with a party under one Jumonville, whom he killed, and took the whole party.

From his prisoners, he obtained undoubted intelligence, that the French troops on the Ohio, consisted of upwards of a thousand regulars, and many hundreds of Indians. But notwithstanding this disheartening advice, he still pressed on undauntedly against the enemy, and, at a place called the Great Meadows, built a fort, which he called Fort Necessity.

Soon as the lines of the entrenchments were marked off, and the men about to fall to work, Washington, seizing the hand of the first that was lifting his spade, cried out *"stop, my brave fellow! my hand must heave the first earth that is thrown up in defence of this country!"*

Leaving a small garrison behind him, he dashed on for Fort Duquesne, (Fort Pitt,) hoping by the reduction of that important post, to strike terror into the enemy, and break up their plans. But though this was a bold stroke of generalship, yet it appeared that he had not a force sufficient to effect it. For in the midst of his first day's march, he was met by a party of friendly Indians, who running up to him, with looks and gestures greatly agitated, cried out, *"Fly! fly! don't look behind you! your enemies are upon you, thick as the pigeons in the woods!"*

Washington called a council of his officers, who advised an immediate return to Fort Necessity, which they hardly recovered, before their sentinels fired an alarm, and running in, stated, that the woods were *alive with Frenchmen and Indians!*—It should have been observed, that the dreadful news, the day before, had produced so shameful a desertion among his troops in the course of the night, that, when the enemy attacked, which they did with 1500 men, Washington had but 300 to stand by him. But never did the true Virginian valour shine more gloriously than on this trying occasion—to see 300 young fellows—commanded by a smooth-faced boy—all unaccustomed to the terrors of war—far from home—and from all hope of help—shut up in a dreary wilderness—and surrounded by *five* times their number of savage foes, yet without sign of fear, preparing for mortal combat! Scarcely since the days of Leonidas and his three hundred deathless Spartans, had the sun beheld its equal. With hideous whoops and yells, the enemy came on like a host of tigers. The woods and rocks, and tall treetops, *filled with Indians,* were in one continued blaze and crash of fire-arms. Nor were our young warriors idle; but, animated by their youthful commander, plied their rifles with such spirit, that the little fort resembled a volcano in full blast, roaring and discharging thick sheets of liquid fire and of leaden deaths among their foes. For *nine* glorious hours, salamander-like, enveloped in smoke and flames, they sustained the attack of the enemy's whole force, and laid two hundred of them dead on the spot! Discouraged by such desperate resistance, the French general, the Count de Villiers, sent in a flag to Washington, highly extolling his gallantry, and offering him the most honourable terms. It was stipulated, that Washington and his little band of heroes, should march away with all the honours of war, and carry with them their military stores and baggage.

On their return to the bosom of their country, they were every where received with the praises which they had so well deserved. The Legislature voted the thanks of the Nation to Washington and his officers; with a pistole a-piece to each of his men, about 300.

In the course of the following winter, notice was given from the *mother country,* that American officers, acting with the British, should bear no command!! Hence the poorest shoat, if wearing the proud epaulette of a Briton, might command a Wolfe, if so unlucky as to be an American!!! Incensed at such an outrage on common justice, and the rights of his countrymen, Washington threw up his commission, and retired to his plantation, *Mount Vernon,* lately left him by his brother Lawrence.—Here, Cincinnatus-like, he betook him to his favourite plough;—but the season called for the sword; —and he was now risen too high to be overlooked in times like those when troubles and fears began to darken over all the land.

The report of his gallant but unsuccessful struggle with the French and Indians, soon reached England: and the ministry, thinking the colonies alone too weak to drive the enemy, hurried on General Braddock, with two heavy regiments, to their aid. This reinforcement arrived early in the spring of '55. Leaving them at the Capes on their way up to Bellehaven, (now ALEXANDRIA,) Braddock called at Williamsburg, to see Governor Dinwiddie, who attended him to Alexandria.

"Where is Colonel Washington?" said General Braddock; *"I long to see him."*

"He is retired from the service, Sir," replied the Governor.

"Retired! Sir!" continued the General, *"Colonel Washington retired! pray, Sir, what's the reason?"*

On hearing the cause, he broke into a passion against the order from the *war-office,* as a *shameful piece of partiality*—

extolled Colonel Washington as *"a young man of sense and spirit, who knew and asserted his rights as became a soldier and a British subject."*

He then wrote to Washington, whom he pressingly invited to join his army, and accept the rank of a volunteer aid-de-camp, in his own family. This invitation was cheerfully accepted by our young countryman, who waited on General Braddock soon as he heard of his arrival at Alexandria. About the same time, three companies of excellent Virginia marksmen, raised by order of the Legislature, arrived at the British camp.

It was in the month of June 1755, that the army, upwards of 2000 strong, left Alexandria, and with their faces to the west, began their march to the mournful ditty of *"over the hills and far away."* On the route, Washington was taken sick; and by the time they had reached the Little Meadows, had become so very ill, that Braddock, at the instance of the physicians, insisted most peremptorily that he should lie by until Colonel Dunbar with the rear of the army came up. With great reluctance he yielded to their wishes: but so great were his fears for the army, lest in those wild woods it should fall into some Indian snare, that the moment his fever left him, he got placed on his horse, and pursued, and overtook them the very evening before they fell into that ambuscade which he had all along dreaded. For the next morning, the 9th of July, when they were safely arrived within *seven* miles of Fort Duquesne! and so confident of success, that their general swore he would that night sup either in Fort Duquesne or in *hell,* behold, the Virginia Rangers discovered signs of the Indians!

Here Washington, with his usual modesty, observed to General Braddock what sort of an enemy he had now to deal with—an enemy who would not, like the Europeans, come forward to a fair contest in the field, but, concealed behind the rocks and trees, carry on a deadly warfare with their rifles.

He concluded with these words, *"I beg of your excellency the honor to allow me to lead on with the Virginia Riflemen, and fight them in their own way."*

Had it been decreed that this hapless army should have been saved, this was the counsel to have done it. But it would seem, alas! that Heaven had ordained their fall in that distant land; and there with their flesh to fatten the wolves and vultures on the hills of Monongahela. For General Braddock, who had all along treated the American officers with infinite contempt, rejected Washington's counsel, and swelling with most unmanly rage, replied, *"High times, by G—d! High times! when a young Buckskin can teach a British General how to fight!"* Instantly the pale, fever-worn cheeks of Washington turned fiery red—but smothering his feelings, he rode towards his men, biting his lip with grief and rage, to think how many brave fellows would draw short breath that day through the pride and obstinacy of one epauletted madman. Formed in heavy columns the troops continued to advance. A little beyond the Monongahela, was a narrow defile, through which lay their road, with moss-grown rocks on either side, and aged trees that spread an awful shade. Here, in perfect concealment, the French and Indians lay, waiting impatiently for this devoted army. Too soon, alas! the army came up, and entering the defile, moved along in silence, like sheep to the slaughter, little dreaming how close the bloody fates hovered around them. Thinking their prey now completely in their clutches, all at once, the Indians put up the most hideous yells, as if the woods were filled with ten thousand panthers. This they did, both as a terror to the British, and a signal to attack; for in the same moment they poured in a general fire, which instantly covered the ground with death in every hideous shape. Some were seen sinking pale and lifeless at once, giving up the ghost with only a hollow groan—others rolling on the earth, convulsed and shrieking in the last agonies, while life and life's warm blood together gushed in hissing torrents from their breasts. Such sights of their bleeding comrades, had the enemy but been in view, instead of depressing would but have inflamed British blood with fiercer thirst for vengeance. But, alas! to be thus entrapped in a dreary wild! to be thus pent up, and shot from behind rocks and trees, by an invisible enemy, was enough to dismay the stoutest hearts. Their native valour, however, and confidence in themselves, did not at once forsake them; but, animated by their officers, they stood their ground, and for a considerable time fought like heroes. But seeing no impression made by their fire, while that of the enemy, heavy as at first, with fatal flashes continued to cut down their ranks, they at length took a panic, and fell into great confusion. Happily, on the left, where lay the deadliest fire, Washington's rangers were posted; but not exposed like the British. For, on hearing the savage yells aforesaid, in a moment they flew each to his tree, like the Indians; and, like them, each levelled his rifle, and with as deadly aim. This through a kind Providence, saved Braddock's army; for exulting in their confusion, the savages, grimly painted, and yelling like furies, bursted from their coverts, eager to glut their hellish rage with a total massacre of the British. But, faithful to their friends, Washington's rangers stepped forth with joy to meet the assailants. Then rose a scene sufficient to fill the stoutest heart with horror. Burning alike for vengeance, both parties throw aside the slow-murdering rifles, and grasp their swift-fated tomahawks. Dreadfully above their heads gleams the brandished steel, as with full exerted limbs, and faces all inflamed with mortal hate, they level at each other their last decisive blows. Death rages through all their fast-thinning ranks—his bleeding victims are rolled together on every side. *Here* falls the brave Virginia Blue, under the stroke of his nimbler foe—and *there,* man on man, the Indians perish beneath the furious tomahawks, deep buried in the shattered brain. But who can tell the joy of Washington, when he saw this handful of his despised countrymen thus gallantly defending their British friends, and by dint of mortal steel driving back their bloodthirsty assailants. Happy check! for by this time, covered with wounds, Braddock had fallen—his aids and officers, to a man, killed or wounded—and his troops, in *hopeless, helpless* despair, flying backwards and forwards from the fire of the Indians, like flocks of crowding sheep from the presence of their butchers. Washington, alone, remained unhurt! Horse after horse had been killed under him. Showers of bullets had lifted his locks or pierced his regimentals. But still protected by Heaven; still supported by a strength not his own, he had continued to fly from quarter to quarter, where his presence was most needed, sometimes animating his rangers; sometimes striving, but in vain, to rally the regulars. 'Twas his lot to be close to the brave but imprudent Braddock when he fell, and assisted to place him in a tumbril, or little cart. As he was laid down, pale and near spent, with loss of blood, he faintly said to Washington—

"Well, Colonel, what's to be done now?"

"Retreat, Sir," replied Washington, *"retreat, by all means; for the Regulars won't fight, and the Rangers are nearly all killed!"*

"Poor fellows!" replied he, *"poor fellows!—Well, do as you will, Colonel, do as you will."*

The army then commenced its retreat, in a very rapid and disorderly manner, while Washington with his few surviving rangers, covered the rear.

Happily, the Indians did not pursue them far: but after firing a few random shots, returned in a body to fall upon the plunder; while Washington, with his frightened fugitives, continued their retreat, sadly remembering that more than one half of their *morning's gay companions* were left a prey to the ravening beasts of the desert. There, denied the common charities of the grave, they lay for many a year bleaching the lonely hills with their bones.

On reaching Fort Cumberland, where they met Colonel Dunbar, with the rear of the army, General Braddock died. He died in the arms of Washington, whose pardon he often begged for *having treated him so rudely that fatal morning—heartily wished,* he said, *he had but followed his advice*—frequently called his rangers *brave fellows! glorious fellows!* Often said, he should be *glad to live, if it was only to reward their gallantry!* I have more than once been told, but cannot vouch for the truth of it, that his sister, on hearing how obstinately Washington and his Blues had fought for her brother, was so affected that she shed tears: and sent them in from England handsome cockades, according to their number, and a pair of colours elegantly wrought by her own fair hands.

With respect to Washington, I cannot but mention here two very extraordinary speeches that were made about him, after Braddock's defeat, and which as things have turned out, look a good deal like prophecies. A famous Indian warrior, who acted a leading part in that bloody tragedy, was often heard to swear, that *"Washington was not born to be killed by a bullet! For,"* continued he, *"I had seventeen fair fires at him with my rifle, and after all could not bring him to the ground!"* And indeed whoever considers that a good rifle, levelled by a proper marksman, hardly ever misses its aim, will readily enough conclude with this unlettered savage, that there was some invisible hand, which turned aside his bullets.

The Rev'd. Mr. Davies, in a sermon occasioned by Braddock's defeat, has these remarkable words—*"I beg leave to point the attention of the public to that heroic youth, Colonel Washington, whom I cannot but hope Providence has preserved for some great service to this country!!"*

But though the American writers have pretty unanimously agreed that Washington was, under God, the saving Angel that stood up between Braddock's army and total destruction, yet did it profit him but little with his Sovereign. The British officers indeed admired him: but they had no idea of going any farther. *"To tell in Gath, and to publish in the streets of Askalon"* that a British army owed its safety to a young Buckskin, required a pitch of virtue and of courage above ordinary minds. Washington was therefore kept in the back ground; and General Braddock being dead, the command devolved upon Colonel Dunbar, whose conduct proved him to be one of those pusillanimous hirelings, *who flee when the wolf cometh.* To attempt, by some gallant effort, to recover what Braddock had lost,—or to hang upon the enemy and prevent, at least, those numerous *scalping parties,* which distracted with midnight murders and deluged the defenceless frontiers with blood, were brave and generous ideas, of which he seemed incapable. But, trembling under the general panic, he instantly ordered the tents to be struck, and pushing off under whip and spur of his fears, never halted until he had reached *Philadelphia;* where he went, as he called it, *into winter quarters,* (in the beginning of the *dog-days!*) leaving the whole frontiers of Maryland and Virginia exposed to the merciless tomahawk.

Such facts ought to be recorded for the benefit of young men, who, with no military qualifications but big limbs, can yet covet red coats and shoulder-knots.

Being thus shamefully deserted by Colonel Dunbar, Washington, with his thirty rangers, set out with sorrowful hearts to return home. But before he left Fort Cumberland, he dispatched an express, to inform Governor Dinwiddie, that *"General Braddock was slain—his army totally defeated—the remnant on their march to Philadelphia—and the whole frontier given up to the Indians!"* The consternation that was spread throughout the country by this news, was inexpressible. Heart-sickening terrors, as of a woman in labour, seized upon all families—and a frightened fancy found food for its fears in every thing around it—the blast whistling round the corners of their cabin, alarmed like the yell of murderous savages—the innocent death-bell—the croaking raven—the midnight howl of dogs—were all sure harbingers of fate. While, for dread of the Indians, the roads were filled with thousands of distracted parents, with their weeping little ones, flying from their homes.

The Governor instantly ordered a call of the Legislature, who, by the time Washington reached Williamsburgh, were assembled, and together with numbers of the citizens, went out and met him near the town.

The interview was tender. For the citizens were almost moved to tears, when they saw that of so many of their brave countrymen who went forth to battle, only this little handful remained! They were exceedingly rejoiced to see, alive and well, their beloved Washington. He had always been dear to them; but now doubly dear, in such times of danger. They mourned the misfortunes of their country, but laid no blame to him. On the contrary, it was universally believed, that, but for him the *ruin would have been complete. "Braddock,"* said they, *"lost the victory; but Washington saved the army."*

CHAPTER VII

Fatal effects of Braddock's defeat—Washington wishes to carry the war into the Indian country—government refuses—defensive war preferred—the frontiers desolated

GREAT was the joy at Fort Duquesne on the return of their troops from the slaughter of Braddock's army. The idea of victory, as appeared afterwards, had never once entered their heads—They had gone out just to *reconnoitre, and harrass the British in their approach!* How unbounded then must have been the joy of the garrison, on seeing their friends come back next morning, not sad and spiritless, as had been expected, but whooping and shouting for a glorious victory; and enriched with the artillery, ammunition, provisions, and baggage-waggons of a *British army cut to pieces!!*

The French commandant took care to make a proper use of his advantage; for soon as the days of savage feasting and drunkenness were over, he sent out deputations of his chiefs with *grand-talks* to several of the neighbouring tribes, who had not yet lifted the hatchet.

The tribes being assembled, and the calumet or pipe of friendship smoked around, the chiefs arose, and in all the pomp of Indian eloquence announced their great victory over *Long Knife* (the Virginians) and his white brothers, (the British)—then with a proud display of the numerous scalps and rich dresses which they had taken, they concluded with inviting the young men to unbury the tomahawk, and rush with them to drink the blood of their enemies.

This was enough—*"Grinning horribly, a ghastly smile,"* at such prospects of blood and plunder, the grim children of the desert, rose up at once to war. No time was lost in preparation.

A pouch of parched corn, and a bear-skin, with a rifle, tomahawk, and scalping knife, were their equipage. And in a few weeks after Braddock's defeat, an armament of at least 1400 of those blood-thirsty people were in full march over hills and mountains, to surprise and murder the Frontier Inhabitants.

Washington had all along foreseen the storm that would one day burst from Fort Duquesne. On his first trip through that country, *two* years before, he had marked the very spot, and pointed it out as, *"the key of the western world."* But Britain and America, (like the wild ass and her colts, though mule-stubborn in acting, yet snail-slow to act,) let slip the golden chance; till one Du Quesne, a French officer, with some troops, passing along that way in 1754, and struck, as Washington had been, with the situation, immediately built thereon a fort, which he called after his own name. It answered the fatal purposes which Washington had predicted. By means of the bold water courses on which it stood, it greatly favoured the conveyance both of *goods* and of *intelligence.* There the French laid up magazines for their Indian allies, and there they hoisted the dread signals of war.

Not having been able to prevail on his countrymen to occupy it before the enemy, Washington's whole ambition now was to take it from them. *"Send two thousand men,"*—said he, in numerous importunate letters to the Governor and Legislature, *"send two thousand men, and drain the fountain at once—the streams will fail of course."*

But, spite of this advice, the mad policy of a *defensive* war, prevailed in the Virginia Government and instead of raising 2000 men, they *voted to raise* about half that number! and then like hypocrites who make up in lip-service what they lack *in good works,* they dubbed him *Commander in Chief of all the troops raised or to be raised in Virginia,* with the privilege of *naming his own field officers!*

These vain honors served but to exalt him to a higher

sphere of misery—the misery of taking a wider survey of those misfortunes of his country which he could not remedy,—and to feel a deeper responsibility for those blunders of others, which he could not cure. He saw Fort Duquesne mustering her murderers, which he had no powers to prevent! He had a frontier of 360 miles to defend, and generally less than 700 men to defend it with! If he kept his troops embodied, the whole country would be left open to the savages—If he broke them down into small parties, they might be destroyed one after another, by a superior force—If he threw them into forts, they were sure to be starved; or laughed at by the enemy who could easily pass them in the night and surprise, destroy and murder the inhabitants with impunity. And though thus completely crippled by the stupidity or parsimony of the government, and incapacitated from doing any services for the country, yet great services were expected of him, and great blame bestowed for every failure. If no victories were gained over the enemy, he was blamed for *inactivity.* If the settlers were murdered, he was accused of neglect—and if he pointed out the errors of government, he was charged as *"officious"* and *"impertinent."* While young officers of the worthless sort, mere cork-drawers and songsters at great men's tables, were basely cutting in with a weak old governor's prejudices, to work him out, and to worm themselves into favour and rank.

But all these vexations and sorrows were but trifles in comparison of others which he was doomed to feel. Seeing no hopes of a force sufficient to attack Fort Duquesne, he formed a chain of garrisons along the frontier; and then, with a flying corps of the most active and daring young men, continued night and day, to scour the country in quest of the enemy's murdering parties. In this bold and dangerous employment, which lasted almost three years, he was often presented with sights of human destruction, sufficient to excite sympathy in hearts of flintiest stone.

On cautiously entering the hapless plantation with his men, they halt and listen awhile—but hear no voice of man—see no house, nor sign of habitation—all is void and silent. Marking the buzzards perched on the trees in the corn-fields, they approach and find, lying by his plough, the half-devoured carcass of a man. The hole in his breast shows that he had been shot, while the deep gashes in the forehead of his dead horses, point out the bursting strokes of the tomahawk. Amidst the ashes of the late dwelling, are seen, white as chalk, the bones of the mother and her children. But sometimes their raw and bloody skeletons, fed on by the hogs, are found in the yards or gardens where they were surprised.

"One day"—said he to an intimate; though it was but seldom that he mentioned those things, they gave him so much pain—"One day, as we drew near, through the woods, to a dwelling, suddenly we heard the discharge of a gun. Whereupon quickening our pace, and creeping up through the thick bushes to a fence, we saw what we had dreaded—a party of Indians, loaded with plunder, coming out of a house, which, by the smoke, appeared as if it were just set on fire. In a moment we gave the savages a shower of rifle balls, which killed every man of them but one, who attempted to run off, but in vain; for some of our swift-footed hunters gave chace, and soon overtook and demolished him with their tomahawks. On rushing into the house, and putting out the fire, we saw a mournful sight indeed—a young woman lying on the bed floated with blood—her forehead cleft with a hatchet—and on her breast two little children apparently twins, and about nine months old, bathing her bosom with the crimson currents flowing from their deeply gashed heads! I had often beheld the mangled remains of my murdered countrymen, but never before felt what I did on this occasion. To see these poor innocents—these little unoffending angels, just entered upon life, and, instead of fondest sympathy and tenderness, meeting their bloody deaths; and from hands of brothers too! filled my soul with the deepest horror of sin! but at the same time inspired a most adoring sense of that religion which announces the Redeemer, who shall, one day, do away man's malignant passions, and restore the children of God to primæval love and bliss. Without this hope, what man of feeling but would wish he had never been born!

"On tracing back into the corn-field the steps of the barbarians, we found a little boy, and beyond him his father, both weltering in blood. It appeared, from the print of his little feet in the furrows, that the child had been following his father's plough, and, seeing him shot down, had set off with all his might, to get to the house to his mother, but was overtaken, and destroyed!

"And, indeed, so great was the dread of the French and Indians, throughout the settlements, that it was distressing to call even on those families who yet survived, but, from sickness or other causes had not been able to get away. The poor creatures would run to meet us, like persons half-distracted with joy—and then with looks blank with terror, would tell that such or such a neighbour's family, perhaps the very night before, was murdered!—and that they heard their cries!—and saw the flames that devoured their houses!—and, also, that they themselves, after saying their prayers at night, never lay down to sleep, without first taking leave of one another as if they never expected to meet again in this world. But when we came to take our leave of these wretched families, my God! what were our feelings! to see the deep, silent grief of the men; and the looks of the poor women and children, as, falling upon their knees, with piercing screams, and eyes wild with terror, they seized our hands, or, hung to our clothes, intreating us for God's and mercy's sake not to leave them to be murdered! These things so bursted my heart with grief, that I solemnly declare to God, if I know myself, I would gladly offer my own life a sacrifice to the butchering enemy, if I could but thereby insure the safety of these my poor distressed countrymen."

Such were the scenes in which Washington was doomed to spend three years of a wretched life, rendered still more wretched by knowing so perfectly as he did, that the rapid charge of two thousand brave fellows upon Fort Duquesne, like the thundering shock of a two-and-forty pounder upon a water-spout, would have instantly dispersed the fatal meteor, and restored the golden hours of peace and safety. But to give colonel Washington 2000 men seemed to old governor Dinwiddie, like giving *the staff out of his own hand,* as he elegantly called it—and rather than do that, he would risk the desolation of the western country, by continuing a *defensive war,* and a mad dependence on a disorderly militia, who *would come and go as they pleased—get drunk and sleep when they pleased—whoop and halloo where they pleased—* and, in short, serve no other purpose on earth but to *disgrace* their officers, *deceive* the settlers, and *defraud* the public. Indeed so ruinous were these measures of governors Dinwiddie and Loudon, that in the short space of three years they completely broke up all the fine young settlements to the westward of Winchester, Fredericktown, and Carlisle, whereby numbers of poor souls *were* butchered! hundreds of rich plantations deserted! myriads of produce lost! and thousands of dollars sunk! and all for the sake of saving the paltry expense of raising in the first instance a force which would in ten weeks have taken Fort Duquesne, and completely broken up that den of thieves and murderers!

At length, in 1758, the government of Virginia devolved on general Forbes, who, to the infinite satisfaction of Washington, consented to second his views on Fort Duquesne. Washington earnestly recommended an early campaign, lest the Indian warriors who were to meet them in April at Winchester, should grow tired of waiting, and return home.

But the season was, unfortunately, so idled away, that marching orders were not given till the first of September, when, according to Washington's prediction, there was not a red man to be found in camp. The army then commenced its movements, but still as would seem, under the frown of Heaven.

For instead of sweeping along the old track, generally called *Braddock's road,* gen. Forbes was overpersuaded to take an entirely new route, every inch of which was to be cut through wilds and mountains covered with rocks and trees! In vain Washington remonstrated against this as a measure, *"which"* he said, *"if persisted in at this late season, would certainly ruin the undertaking."*—General Forbes was fixed.

In a letter to the *Speaker* of the House of Burgesses, Washington has these remarkable words—*"If this conduct of our leaders, do not flow from superior orders, it must flow from a weakness, too gross for me to name. Nothing now but a miracle can bring this campaign to a happy issue."* In a letter of a later date he says, *"well, all is lost! our enterprise is ruined! And we shall be stopped this winter at the Laurel Hills!"*

By the middle of November, after incredible exertions, the army, sure enough, reached the Laurel Hills, where Washington predicted it would *winter!* and *strange to tell!* General Forbes, with a caucus squad of his officers were actually in deep debate, whether they should spend the winter in that inhospitable wild, or tread back their mournful steps, to Winchester, when some prisoners brought the welcome news that the garrison of Fort Duquesne, for a long time past *unsupported by their countrymen,* and now *deserted by the Indians,* was so reduced, that they would surrender at sight of an enemy. General Forbes instantly changed his mind, and with a select detachment made a push for Fort Duquesne, the ruins of which he entered, without opposition, on the

28th of November, 1758. For, advertised of his approach, the French determined to quit it, and after having set fire to the buildings, got into their boats, and went down the river.

Having thus, after three years of labour and sorrow, attained his favourite wish—the reduction of Fort Duquesne and a total dispersion of the savages, Washington returned with joy to Williamsburgh, to take his seat in the legislature, to which he had been regularly chosen in his absence.

'Tis a thing well worth remark, because it happens but to few, that though he often failed of success, he never *once* lost the confidence of his country. *Early aware of the importance of character, to those who wished to be useful,* he omitted no honest act, thought no *pains,* no sacrifice of ease, too great to procure and preserve it. In the whole of that stupidly-managed war, as also in *another war* since that, which was not much better conducted, he always took care to keep the public well informed as to the part which he had acted, or wished to act, in the affair. Not content, *himself to know* that he had acted wisely or bravely, he took care that the public should know it also; in order that if at any time an uproar should be made, the saddle might be placed on the right horse. If the legislature, or governor Dinwiddie, or general Braddock, or any other superior, with whom he had public concern, and character at stake, made propositions which he disliked, he would modestly point out their *errors,* predict their *mischiefs,* and thus wash his hands of all blame: —which documents, through the channel of numerous letters to his friends, were always laid before the people. Hence, for the ruinous consequences of the weakness and obstinacy of Dinwiddie and Braddock, not a breath of censure was ever blown on him. On the contrary, in the *public* mind, he always *rose* as high, or higher, than the others sunk. It was universally believed, that had *he* governed, in place of Dinwiddie, the fatal Indian war would not have lasted a campaign.—And on the hills of Monongahela, had Washington commanded in place of Braddock, the French and Indians would have been handled very differently. Such were the sentiments with which the public were prepared to receive him, on his return into their welcoming bosom. Wherever he went, homage always waited upon him, though always uncourted. The grey-headed rose up to do him honour, when he came into their company; and the young men, with sighs, often wished for a fame like his. Happy was the fairest lady of the land, who, at the crowded ball, could get colonel Washington for her partner. And even at the house where prayer is wont to be made, the eyes of beauty would sometimes wander from the cold reading-preacher, to catch a livelier devotion from his *"mind-illumined face,"*—a face at once so dignified with virtue, and so sweetened with *grace,* that none could look on it without emotions very friendly to the heart: and sighs of sentiment too delicate for description, were often seen to heave the snowy bosoms of the noblest dames.

At the head of all these stood the accomplished Mrs. Martha Custis, the beautiful and wealthy widow of Mr. John Custis. Her *wealth* was equal, at least, to one hundred thousand dollars! But her beauty was a sum far larger still. It was not the shallow boast of a fine skin, which time so quickly tarnishes, nor of those short-lived roses, which sometimes wither almost as soon as blown. But it sprung from the HEART—from the *divine* and *benevolent affections,* which spontaneously gave to her *eyes,* her *looks,* her *voice* and her *manners,* such angel charms, that I could never *look* on her, without exclaiming with the poet, O!

> "She was nearest heaven of all on earth I knew;
> And all but adoration was her due."

For two such *kindred souls* to love, it was only necessary that they should meet. Their friendship commenced with the first hour of their acquaintance, and was soon matured into marriage, which took place about the 27th year of

Washington's life. His Lady was, I believe, six months younger.

But, that it is contrary to the rules of biography, to begin with the husband and end with the wife, I could relate of that MOST EXCELLENT LADY those things which the public would greatly delight to hear. However, gratitude to that bright saint, now in heaven, who was my noblest benefactress, while I preached in her parish, compels me to say, that her VIRTUES and CHARITIES were of that extensive and sublime sort, as fully to entitle her *hic jacet* to the following noble epitaph, a little altered, from one of the British Poets.

UNDERNEATH this marble hearse,
Lies the subject of all verse.
Custis' widow—great George's wife—
Death! ere thou robb'st another life,
Virtuous, fair, and good as SHE,
Christ shall launch a dart at thee.

CHAPTER VIII

Washington's mother has a very curious dream—it points to great coming troubles—a cloud rising in England—the causes of the revolutionary war

WHEN a man begins to make a noise in the world, his relatives (the Father, *sometimes,* but, always that tenderer parent, the *Mother,*) are sure to recollect certain *mighty odd dreams,* which they had of him *when he was a child.* What rare dreams, for example, had the mothers of "Macedonia's madman, and the Swede," while pregnant with those butchers of the human race! Mrs. Washington also had her dream, which an excellent old Lady of Fredericksburg assured me she had often heard her relate with great satisfaction; and, for the last time, but a few weeks before her death.

"I dreamt," said the Mother of Washington, "that I was sitting in the piazza of a large new house, into which we had but lately moved. George, at that time about five years old, was in the garden with his corn-stalk plough, busily running little furrows in the sand, in imitation of Negro Dick, a fine black boy, with whose ploughing George was so taken, that it was sometimes a hard matter to get him to his dinner. And so as I was sitting in the piazza at my work, I suddenly heard in my dream a kind of roaring noise on the *eastern* side of the house. On running out to see what was the matter, I beheld a dreadful sheet of fire bursting from the roof. The sight struck me with a horror which took away my strength, and threw me, almost senseless, to the ground. My husband and the servants, as I saw in my dream, soon came up; but, like myself, were so terrified at the sight, that they could make no attempt to extinguish the flames. In this most distressing state, the image of my little son came, I thought, to my mind more dear and tender than ever, and turning towards the garden where he was engaged with his little cornstalk plough, I screamed out twice with all my might, *George! George!*—In a moment, as I thought, he threw down his mimic plough, and ran to me saying, *"High! Ma! what makes you call so angry! 'an't I a good boy—don't I always run to you soon as I hear you call?"* I could make no reply, but just threw up my arms towards the flame. He looked up and saw the house all on fire: but instead of bursting out a crying, as might have been expected from a child, he instantly *brightened* up and seemed ready to fly to extinguish it. But first looking at me with great tenderness, he said, *"Oh, Ma! don't be afraid: God Almighty will help us, and we shall soon put it out."*—His looks and words revived our spirits in so wonderful a manner, that we all instantly set about to assist him. A ladder was presently brought, on which, as I saw in my dream, he ran up with the nimbleness of a squirrel; and the servants supplied him with water, which he threw on the fire from an *American gourd.* But that growing weaker, the flame appeared to gain ground, breaking forth and roaring most dreadfully, which so frightened the servants, that many of them, like persons in despair, began to leave him. But he, still undaunted, continued to ply it with water, animating the servants at the same time, both by his words and actions. For a long time the contest appeared very doubtful; but at length a venerable old man, with a tall cap and iron rod in his hand, like a lightning rod, reached out to him a curious little trough, like a *wooden shoe!* On receiving this, he redoubled his exertions, and soon extinguished the fire. Our joy on the occasion was unbounded. But he, on the contrary, showing no more of transport now than of terror before, looked rather sad at sight of the great harm that had been done. Then I saw in my dream that after some time spent as in deep thought, he called out with much joy, *"Well, Ma! now if you and the family will but consent, we can make a far better roof than this ever was;* a roof of such a *quality,* that, if well *kept together,* it will last for ever; but if you take it apart, you will make the house ten thousand times worse than it was before."

This, though certainly a very curious dream, needs no Daniel to interpret it; especially if we take Mrs. Washington's *new house,* for the young Colony Government—the fire on its east side, for North's civil war—the gourd which Washington first employed, for the American 3 and 6 months inlistments —the old man with his cap and iron rod, for Doctor Franklin —the *shoe-like* vessel which he reached to Washington, for the Sabot or wooden-shoed nation, the French, whom Franklin courted a long time for America—and the new roof proposed by Washington, for a staunch honest Republic —that *"equal government,"* which, by guarding alike the welfare of all, ought by all to be so heartily beloved as to *endure for ever.*

Had it been appointed unto any man to quaff unmingled happiness in this life, George Washington had been that man. For where is that pleasurable ingredient with which his cup was not full and overflowing?

Crowned with honours—laden with riches—blest with health—and, in the *joyous prime* of 27, sharing each *rural* sweet in the society of a charming woman who doated on him, he surely bid fair to spend his days and nights of life in ceaseless pleasure!—But ah!—as sings the sweet bard of Zion,

> OUR days, alas! our mortal days,
> Are short and wretched too!
> *"Evil* and *few!"* the Patriarch says,
> And well the Patriarch knew!
> 'Tis but, at best, a narrow bound,
> That Heaven allots to men;
> And pains and sins run through the round,
> Of three-score years and ten!

From this, the universal lot, not Washington himself could obtain exemption. For in the midst of his favourite labours, of the plough and pruning-hook, covering his extensive farms with all the varied delights of delicious fruits and golden grain, of lowing herds and snowy flocks, he was suddenly called on by his *country,* to turn his plough-share into the sword, and go forth to meet a torrent of evils which threatened her. The fountain of those evils, whence at length flowed the great civil war, which for ever separated Britain and her children, I proceed now briefly to state.

After the reduction of Canada, the British officers who commanded on that expedition, came to Boston and New-York, on a visit to their American brethren in arms, who had served with them in that war. Soon as their arrival was announced, the Americans flew to meet and welcome them. They were paraded through the streets as the saviours of the land—the doors of all were thrown open to receive them—and every day, during their stay, was spent in feasting and public dinners, which, for sake of their beloved guests, were made as splendid as possible, though always through the aid of obliging neighbours. The rooms glittered with *borrowed plate*—wines of every vintage sparkled on the crowded sideboards—while the long-extended tables were covered with finest fish and flesh, succeeded by the richest desserts. The British officers were equally charmed and astonished at such elegant hospitality; and, on their return to England, gave a full loose to their feelings. They painted the colonial wealth in the colourings of romance, and spoke of the Americans as a people, who, in comparison of the British, lived like kings.

Thus, American hospitality, by a strange perversion had like to have poisoned American Liberty! For, from that time, the British ministry began to look upon the Americans with an evil eye, and to devise ways and means to make us *"bear a part of their burdens!"* But what did they mean by this? Did they mean to acknowledge us as Sons of Britons; equally free and independent with our brethren in England? and, like them, allowed a representation in Parliament, who should freely vote our money to the common cause?

Oh no! an idea so truly British and honourable, was not at all in their thoughts. We were not to be treated as *brothers*, but as *slaves!* over whom an unconditional right was claimed to tax and take our property at pleasure!!!

Reader, if you be a Briton, be a Briton still—preserve the characteristic calm and candor of a Briton. I am not about to say one word against your nation. No! I know them too well: and thank God, I can say, *after several years of residence among them*, I believe them to be as *Honest, Charitable*, and *Magnanimous* a people as any on God's earth. I am about to speak of the MINISTRY only, who certainly, at that time, were a most ambitious and intriguing junto, that by *bad means* had *gotten* power, and by *worse* were endeavouring to extend it, even to the destruction of both *American and British Liberty*, as the excellent Mr. Pitt charged them.—No Englishmen can desire fuller evidence than this one infernal claim made against us by lord North—*"taxation without representation!!"* As a plea for such despotic doings, NORTH and his creatures set out with boldly trumpeting the wonderful things they had done for America. *"They, it seems, first discovered the country!—they settled it—they always had defended it—it was their blood—their treasure—their ships, and sailors, and soldiers, who created the British colonies!!"*

O dear!—and what then?—why, to be sure, after having done such mighty things for the Americans, they had as clear a right to their gold and silver, as a butcher has to the hair and hides of his cattle!

This language was actually carried into *Parliament!* where a Mr. Charles Townsend, to enforce the stamp act, cried out, *"Who are these Americans? Are they not our children, planted by our care, nourished by our indulgence, and protected by our arms?"*

At this, the brave Colonel Barré, with cheeks all inflamed with virtuous indignation, thus broke forth on the insolent speechifier. *"They planted by your care! No, sir: your oppres-*

sions planted them in America. They fled from your tyranny to a then uncultivated and inhospitable country, where they exposed themselves to all the evils which a wilderness, filled with blood-thirsty savages, could threaten. And yet, actuated by true English love of liberty, they thought all these evils light in comparison of what they suffered in their own country, and from you, who ought to have been their friends.

"They nourished by your indulgence! No, sir! they grew by your neglect. As soon as you began to indulge them, that boasted indulgence was to send them hungry packs of your own creatures, to spy out their liberties!—to misrepresent their actions!—and to prey upon their substance!—Yes, sir, you sent them men, whose behaviour has often caused the blood of those Sons of Liberty to recoil within them—men promoted by you to the highest seats of justice, in that country, who, to my knowledge, had good cause to dread a court of justice in their own!—They protected by your arms!—No, sir! They have nobly taken up arms in your defence; have exerted a most heroic valour, amidst their daily labours, for the defence of a country whose frontier was drenched in blood while its interior parts gave up all their savings to our emolument!"

All this was very true. For the Americans had not only planted, but in a great measure protected themselves. In the French and Indian war, from '55 to '63, they lost nearly 30,000 of their stoutest young men! And by regular returns it appears that Massachusetts alone expended about 500,000*l.* sterling in that time!!! Nor only so, but they had never hesitated for a moment to furnish to the last man and shilling whatever Britain had required.

But, alas! what signifies *right* against *might!* When a king wants money for his own pride, or for his hungry relations, and when his ministers want stakes for their gaming tables, or diamond necklaces for their strumpets, they *will* have it, though plundered colonies should lack bread and spelling books for their children. For in the year '63, when the lamp of God was burning with peculiar brightness in our land, and both Britain and her colonies enjoyed a measure of blessings seldom indulged to the most favoured nations—When, at the very mention of Old-England, our hearts leaped for joy, as at the name of a great and venerable mother, and that mother felt an equal transport at thoughts of us, her flourishing colonies—When all the produce of these vast and fertile regions was poured into her beloved lap, and she, *in return*, not allowing us the trouble to make even a *hob-nail,* heaped our families with all the necessaries and elegancies of her ingenious artists—When, though far separated by an ocean's roar, we were yet so *united* by love and mutual helpfulness, that the souls of Columbus, Raleigh, and Smith, looking down from heaven, with joy beheld the consummation of all their labours and wishes! At that happy period, Lord North brought in a bill to tax the colonies, without allowing us a voice in their councils!! The colonies were thunderstruck: and Britain herself, groaning through all her island *"gave signs of woe that all was lost!"*

Doctor Franklin, who was then in England as a colony agent, on hearing that this most iniquitous bill had actually passed both houses, and was ratified by the king, wrote to a friend in America in these words—"The sun of our liberty is set—you must all now light up the double candles of Industry and Economy—but, above all things, *encourage the young people to marry and raise up children as fast as they can."*

Meaning, that America, yet too weak to resist the chains which a wicked ministry were forging for her, should instantly fly to *heaven-ordered marriage,* for heroic youth, to snap the ignominious bonds from their own and their father's arms.

But the sons of Columbia, though few in number, had too long enjoyed the sweets of Liberty and Property, to part with them so tamely, because a king and his minions had ordered it. No! blessed be God, their conduct was such as to strike the world with this glorious truth, that *a brave people, who know their rights, are not to be enslaved.*

For, soon as it was told in America, that the stamp-act had passed, the people rose up against it as one man—the old grudges between churchmen and dissenters, were instantly forgotten—every man looked to his fellow as to a brother for aid against the coming slavery—their looks on each other were as lightnings in a parched forest—the sacred fire kindled and ran from end to end of the continent. In every colony, the people rushed into patriotic societies—reminded each other of their rights—denounced the stamp-act as a most audacious infringement,—burnt in effigy the promoters of it—tore down the houses of those bastard Americans who had received the stamps to sell—and menaced loudly a nonintercourse with Britain, if the act was not *immediately repealed!*

This spirited behaviour filled all England with amazement. Every man there, no matter what his principles or politics, felt it to the very quick. The manufacturers and merchants trembled—the tories raved—the whigs rejoiced, and with the great Pitt and Burke at their head, publickly applauded the Americans, and denounced the stamp-act as entirely contrary to the spirit of British freedom. In short the cry against it was so loud both in England and America, that the ministry, covered with shame, were obliged to give way, and abandon the project.

The cloud, which had hung so dark over the two countries, being thus happily scattered, many began to cherish the hope that we should have a clear sky again, and that the former golden days would soon return. But alas! those golden days were gone to return no more! Government had shown the cloven foot—and America had taken a fright which nothing but whole years of kindliest treatment could ever do away. But, unfortunately, the ministry were in no humour to show that kindness. Long accustomed to speak of the

Americans as a pack of *"convicts, whom, by transportation, they had kindly saved from the gallows,"* instead of giving them credit for their late spirited behaviour, they considered it as the height of audacity: and though from necessity they had yielded to their demands, they were determined to have revenge on the first opportunity. That opportunity was too soon afforded.

It should have been noticed, that with the duty on stamped paper, similar duties had been laid on glass, tea, &c. &c. all of which had been repealed with the stamp-act, except that on *tea.* This the ministry had artfully retained: partly to cover the shame of their defeat, but chiefly in hopes of *familiarizing* the Americans to *taxing.* For though lord North was never, that I know of, charged with being a wizzard, yet did he not lack sense to know that if he could but prevail on the young Mammoth to take down a tax, though no bigger than a *Gnat,* he should soon bring him to swallow a *Camel!* But, glory to God! the Americans had too much of British blood, to allow an *unconstitutional* tax in *any shape or size.* Independent and coy as the birds of their forests, they would not suffer a stranger's hand even to *touch* the sacred nest of their rights. Soon therefore as the ministry began in 1773 to order a *"collection of the taxes on tea,"* the colonies took fire again, and the old flame of '64 was completely rekindled throughout the continent. But still in the very storm and tempests of their rage, they never lost sight of the respect due their mother country. Their numerous letters and petitions to the KING, to the PARLIAMENT, and to the PEOPLE of Britain, all, all breathe the full spirit of dutiful children, and of loving brothers. In terms the most modest and pathetic, they state the extreme injustice and barbarity of such measures—their total inconsistency with the spirit of the *British Constitution*—their positive inadmissibility into America—or, in that event, the certainty of a civil war, with all its fatal effects on the two countries.

Tempered with meekness, and pointed with truth, their arguments reach the hearts of the British patriots, who all fly in eager myriads to extinguish the kindling flames of civil war. Foremost of this noble band is seen the venerable form of Chatham. Though worn with years and infirmities, he quits his bed, and, muffled up in flannels and furs, crawls to the House of Lords, to give his last advice, and yet avert, if possible, the impending ruin. He rises to speak. A solemn silence prevails, while the looks of the crowded audience are bending forward upon him, to catch the accents of his magic tongue. His eyes are upon the ground, but his thoughts are not there—they are travelling like sun-beams over all the earth. Britain and America, with all their population and interests, lie open before his vast mind, with all the varied evils of the threatened war. In Britain he beholds a fearful pause in the pulse of industry and joy—the loom is still—the anvil resounds no more . . . while the harbours, late alive with bustling business and cheerful songs, now crowded with silent dismantled ships, present a scene of national mourning. In the colonies, he sees the plains, lately crowned with joyful harvests, now covered with armed bands of Britons and Americans rushing to murderous battle . . . while in Europe, the proud Spaniard, the sarcastic Gaul, and broad grinning Hollander, with shrugs and sneers enjoy the coming fray, as a welcome prelude to the downfal of their hated rival. He next paints the Americans as native sons of Britain . . . and, at once, enthusiastic lovers of *liberty* and of their *mother country* . . . ready, as her *children,* to *give* her *every thing;* but, as her *slaves, nothing.* Though harshly treated, they still love her, and wish for nothing so much as a hearty *reconciliation,* and a glad return of all the former friendships and blessings. At thought of this most desirable of all events, the parent soul of the great orator is stirred within him; his aged frame trembles with strong feeling, which heaves his labouring bosom, and swells his changeful face. At length his powerful words break forth.

"For God's sake, then, my lords, let the way be instantly opened for reconciliation; I say instantly, or it will be too late for ever. The Americans tell you, and remember it is the language of the whole continent . . . they tell you, they will *never submit* to be taxed without their own consent . . . They insist on a repeal of your laws . . . they do not ask it as a favour, they claim it as a *right;* they *demand it.* And I tell you the acts must be repealed . . . they *will* be repealed, you *cannot* enforce them. But bare repeal will not satisfy this enlightened and spirited people. What! satisfy them by repealing a bit of paper . . . by repealing a piece of parchment! No! you must declare you have *no right to tax* them—then they may trust you—then they will confide in you . . . There are, my lords, three millions of whigs in America. Three millions of whigs, with arms in their hands, are a *formidable body!* There are, I trust, double that number of whigs in England. And I hope the whigs in both countries will join and make a common cause. They are united by the strongest ties of sentiment and interest; and will therefore, I hope, fly to support their brethren. In this most alarming and distracted state of our affairs, though borne down by a cruel disease, I have crawled to this house, my lords, to give you my best advice, which is, to beseech his majesty that orders may instantly be dispatched to General Gage to remove the troops from Boston—their presence is a source of perpetual irritation and suspicion to those people. How can they trust you, with the bayonet at their breasts? they have all the reason in the world to believe that you mean their death or slavery. Let us then set to this business in earnest—there is no time to be lost—every moment is big with danger. Nay, while I am now speaking, the decisive blow may be struck, and millions involved in the dreadful consequences! The very first drop of blood that is drawn will make a wound perhaps never to be healed—a wound of such rancorous malignity, as will, in all probability, mortify the whole body, and hasten, both on

England and America, that dissolution to which all nations are destined."

Here was a speech, sufficient, one would have thought, to stop the career of the maddest politicians—but neither this, nor the advice of Lord Camden, nor the numerous and pathetic addresses from London, Liverpool, and Jamaica, could produce the least change in the ministry. *"Let the Americans,"* said Lord Gower with a sneer, *"sit talking about their natural rights! their divine rights! and such stuff! we will send them over a few regiments of grenadiers to help their consultations!"* Thus high-toned was the language of ministry, and thus stoutly bent on the submission of the Americans. Indeed, in some instances, they would not honour them so far as to give their "humble petitions" a reading, but consigned them to what the whig opposition pleasantly called, *"the committee of oblivion."*

The tea-tax was, of course, at any rate to be collected. But as there could be no tax without tea, nor tea unless it was sent, several ships of that obnoxious weed were purposely pushed off for America. Lord Fairfax happened to be at Mount Vernon when Washington received advice from a friend in London that the tea ships were about to sail—*"Well, my Lord,"* said he, *"and so the ships, with the gunpowder tea, are, it seems, on their way to America!"*

"Well but, colonel, why do you call it gunpowder tea?"

"Why, I am afraid, my Lord," replied Washington, *"it will prove inflammable, and produce an explosion that shall shake both countries."*

The event corresponded with Washington's prediction. Looked on as sent to insult and enslave them, the ships were every where received with the heartiest curses of the people, who quickly boarded them—in some places furiously tumbling their fragrant cargoes into the flashing deep—in others, sternly ordering the captains to depart, under penalty of being instantly tucked up to the yard arms.

On the arrival of this news in England, the countenance of the minister was dark with fury: and he proceeded, without delay, to mix up for the colonies a cup of fiery indignation, of which Boston, it seems, was to have the largest dose. As that most undutiful child had always led off the dance in outrage and rebellion against the parent state, it was determined that she should pay the piper for *old and new*—that her purse should answer for all the tea that had been destroyed—that her luxuriant trade, which had made her so wanton, should be taken from her—and that, spite of her high looks and proud stomach, she should sit on the stool of repentance, until his gracious majesty, George III. should be pleased to pronounce her *pardon!!*

On the receipt of this intelligence at Boston, the passions of the people flew up, five hundred degrees above blood-heat! throughout the continent the fever raged with equal fury. The colonies all extolled Boston for the firmness with which she had asserted her *chartered rights*—liberal contributions were made for her relief—and this ministerial attack on her liberties, was considered as an attack on the liberties of the whole, which were now thought to be in such danger, as loudly to call for a general congress from all the colonies, to deliberate on their common interest. This most unkingly body sat down for the first time, in Philadelphia, September 5th, 1774. They began with publishing *a bill of rights,* wherein, "they repeated their loyalty and love to the mother country, together with an earnest wish for a *constitutional* dependence on her. But, at the same time, they begged leave to assure, that though she, in her excessive fondness, might suffer herself to be bound and insulted by North and Bute, and other Philistine lords, yet they, for their parts, were resolved, like true sons of British Sampsons, to rise and fight to the last locks of their heads. They asserted, and begged leave to do it pretty roundly too, as it was now high time to speak plain, that by the *immutable laws of nature*—by the *principles of the British constitution—and by their several charters,* they had a right to liberty, the liberty of British subjects—that their ever-honoured *fathers,* at the time of their emigration to this country, were entitled to all the rights of freemen—and since, by such emigration, they had neither forfeited nor surrendered these rights—that they, their children, were determined, at the risk of every thing short of their *eternal salvation,* to defend and to transmit them entire to their innocent and beloved offspring."

Millions of choice spirits in England, Scotland, and Ireland, cried out, *"that's well said! and may God's arms strike with our American brothers!"* This was coming to the point, and produced the effect that might have been expected. For, instantly, all exportation of arms and ammunition to America was prohibited—large reinforcements were sent to the king's troops at Boston—and every step was taken to compel the colonies to submission. This filled up the measure of American hatred to the ministry, and called forth the most vigorous preparations for war. Every ounce of gunpowder was husbanded like so much gold-dust: Powder-mills and musquet-manufactories were erected in most of the colonies; while others, as not liking this slow way of doing things, laid violent hands at once upon all the king's arms and ammunition that came in their way.

The hell-fraught cloud of civil war was now ready to burst: and April the 19th, 1775, was the fatal day marked out by mysterious heaven, for tearing away the stout infant colonies from the long-loved paps of the old mother country. Early that morning, general Gage, whose force in Boston was augmented to 10,000 men, sent a detachment of 1000 to destroy some military stores which the Americans had collected in the town of Concord, near Lexington. On coming to the place, they found the town militia assembled on the green near the road. *"Throw down your arms, and disperse, you rebels,"* was the cry of the British officer, (Pitcairn) which was immediately followed by a general discharge of the soldiers; whereby eight of the Americans were killed, and several wounded. The provincials retired. But finding that the British still continued their fire, they returned it with good interest; and soon strewed the green with the dead and wounded. Such fierce discharges of musquetry, produced the effect that might have been expected in a land of freemen, who saw their gallant brothers suddenly engaged in the strife of death. Never before had the bosoms of the swains experienced such a tumult of heroic passions. Then throwing aside the implements of husbandry, and leaving their teams in the half finished furrows, they flew to their houses, snatched up their arms, and bursting from their wild shrieking wives and children, hasted to the glorious field where LIBERTY, heaven-born goddess, was to be bought for blood. Pouring in now from every quarter, were seen crowds of sturdy peasants, with *flushed cheeks* and *flaming eyes,* eager for battle! Even age itself forgot its wonted infirmities: and hands, long palsied with years, threw aside the cushioned crutch, and grasped the deadly firelock. Fast as they came up, their ready muskets began to pour the long red streams of fiery vengeance. The enemy fell back appalled! The shouting farmers, swift-closing on their rear, followed their steps with death, while the British, as fast as they could load, wheeling on their pursuers, returned the deadly platoons. Like some tremendous whirlwind, whose roaring sweep all at once darkens the day, riding the air in tempest, so sudden and terrible, amidst clouds of dust, and smoke, and flame, the flight of Britain's warriors thundered along the road. But their flight was not in safety. Every step of their retreat was stained with trickling crimson—every hedge or fence by which they passed, took large toll of hostile carcasses. They would, in all probability, have been cut off to a man, had not general Gage, *luckily recollected,* that, *born of Britons,* these Yankees might possess some of the family valour, and therefore sent 1000 men to support the detachment. This reinforcement met the poor fellows, faint with fear and fatigue, and brought them safely off to Boston.

In this their first field, the American farmers gleaned of the British about sixty-three, in slain, and two hundred and eighty wounded and prisoners. The fire of civil discord now broke out a roaring flame, and, with equal ardour, both parties hastened to clap on the *"kettle of war."*

National prejudices ought to be scouted from the face of the earth. Colonel Grant actually said in parliament, that, *"with five regiments he could march through all America!!!"* Oh! had that profound philosopher but beheld the SCRUB RACE above, he might have learned *two things* . . . 1st. that he was never born to be a prophet. And 2nd. that it is not to *this* or *that* country exclusively, that we are to look for brave men, but in *every* country where the people are accustomed to breathe the proud air of liberty, and to rejoice in the sweet fruits of their labours as all *their own.*

Soon as the battle of Lexington was told to the astonished ministry in England, a grand caucus of lords was held, to consider the best *ways* and *means* to bring the rebels to their senses. "One spoke after this manner, and another after that." Presently up rose Lord George Germaine, and with all Moloc in his looks, hurled the curses of Amalek against the Americans. *"Vengeance!* gentlemen!" he cried, "vengeance! your insulted island—your wounded honour—your murdered countrymen—all cry *havoc!* and bid slip the dogs of war. Gods! can we sit debating here, when rank rebellion lords it over our colonies, and the tongues of rebel curs are red in the blood of our bravest soldiers slain. No! let our swift-avenging armies fly across the ocean, and lighting like a tornado on the rebel continent, from end to end, with fire and sword sweep both town and country before them."

Here the celebrated Mr. Wilkes, in the spirit of a TRUE BRITON, roared out, "Aye that's right! that's right! Lord

George! that's exactly up to our old English proverb—*the greater the coward, the crueller the devil!"*

"Coward! Sir!" replied Lord George, black with rage, *"Coward! what do you mean by that, sir?"*

"I mean, sir," returned Mr. Wilkes, *"that the hero who could not stand fire on the plains of Minden, does well to advise fire and sword in the woods of America."*

Upon this, the unlovely names of *liar* and *scoundrel* were exchanged with a freedom which showed that in the quarrel with America, the passions of the two parties knew no bounds. Happily for America, this spirit of Mr. Wilkes was not peculiar to himself. Thousands of enlightened and virtuous whigs breathed it with equal ardour. The gallant Duke of Buckingham, on hearing how bravely the Americans had behaved at Lexington, exclaimed, *"Well, thank God! there are yet some veins in the world that beat high with British blood!"*

Lord Effingham, also, being called on to go against the Americans, returned his sword to the king, saying, *"he had received it, on oath, to maintain the cause of justice, not of oppression!!"*

But though the right heads in England were numerous, they were not sufficiently so to direct the wrong heads there. A feeble minister, and his puny lordlings, still held the reins; and though, compared with the great nation which they governed, they seemed but as monkeys on the back of a mammoth, yet they had, too long, the fatal art so to blindfold and goad the noble animal, as to make her *run riot* over her own children, and crush thousands of them into their bloody graves.

On this day, June 12, 1775, general Gage issued his proclamation of rebellion, with threats of heaviest vengeance against the rebels; extending however in the king's name, the golden sceptre of mercy to all true penitents, Samuel Adams, and John Hancock, excepted. These gentlemen, by their extraordinary zeal in the cause of liberty, had so mortally offended the ministry, that nothing short of their lives could make atonement. Orders were sent privately to General Gage, to seize and hang them in Boston, or to send them over in irons to be hung in England. But God gave his Angels charge of them, so that not a hair of their heads was hurt.

The British, 10,000 strong, were still in Boston, where, ever since the affair of Concord, they had been surrounded by an army of 20,000 provincials, all so eager to try the city by *storm,* that it was with the greatest difficulty their officers could restrain them.

How adorable the goodness of God for ordering that the ministerial attack on our liberties, should fall on the *populous* and high-toned New-Englanders! The heroic spirit with which they repelled it, should, to eternity, endear them to their *southern brothers.*

CHAPTER IX

Battle of Bunker's-hill—of Sullivan's Island—Declaration of Independence—Defeat of the Americans on Long-Island—Howe looks big—times squally

———And fame of Bunker's hill endure,
Till time itself shall be no more.

THIS hill of fame still lifts his yellow brow, half hid in sedge, on the plain of *Charlestown*—a lovely port north of Boston, to which it is united by an elegant bridge. To confine the British as closely as possible to Boston, the American generals, on the night of June 16, dispatched 1500 men to throw up an entrenchment on Bunker's-hill. The party did not begin their work till about 12 o'clock; but pushed it with such spirit, that, by day-break, they had surrounded themselves with a tolerably decent ditch—without embrasures indeed, because they had no cannon to stare through them; nor even a bayonet to bristle over its ridges.

Soon as the rosy morn appeared, they were discovered by the British men of war, which quickly saluted them with their great guns and mortars. But regardless of shells and shot, the dauntless Yankees still drank their *Switchel** and plied their work.

Finding that his ships of war, with all their thunders, had not been able to dislodge them: Gage ordered to their aid 3000 men with a train of artillery, under command of Generals Howe and Pigot. By twelve o'clock they were all safely landed on the Charlestown side, near Bunker's-hill, the destined place of storm. An interesting scene is now about

* *A mild moralizing malmsey, made of molasses and water, which the prudent Yankees drink, to the great benefit of their health and senses, while their southern neighbours are be-fooling and be-poisoning themselves with grog.*

to open—for not only the British and American armies from the neighbouring heights, are eagerly looking on, but all the surrounding country, timely alarmed, are running together, in terror, to behold the coming fight. Among the crowding spectators are seen thousands of tender females, with panting bosoms and watery eyes, fixed upon the fields below, anxiously waiting the fate of their Brothers, Fathers, and Husbands. After a hurried moment spent in forming, the British troops began to advance in heavy columns, with all the martial pomp of flying colours and rattling drums. At the same time, by order of Gage, the beautiful port of Charlestown, of 300 fine buildings, with a tall steepled church, was wrapped in flames, roaring like distant thunder, and tost on eddying winds in fiery billows to the clouds—while far and wide the adjoining plains are covered with British soldiers in crimson regimentals and shining arms, moving on to the attack with incessant discharges of muskets and great guns. Close, on the brow of the hill, appears the little fort, dimly seen through smoke, and waved over by one solitary flag, and very unlike to stand the shock of so powerful an armament. But the Americans are all wound up to the height of Liberty's enthusiasm; and, lying close behind their works, with fowling-pieces loaded with ball and buck-shot, wait impatiently for the approaching enemy. Their brave countrymen, Putnam and Warren, are in the fort, constantly reminding them of that glorious inheritance, Liberty, which they received from their gallant fathers; and now owe to their own dear children.—*"Don't throw away a single shot, my brave fellows,"* said old Putnam, *"don't throw away a single shot, but take good aim; nor touch a trigger, till you can see the whites of their eyes."*

This steady reserve of fire, even after the British had come up within pistol-shot, led them to hope that the Americans did not *mean to resist!* and many of their friends on the heights had near given up all for lost. But soon as the enemy were advanced within the fatal distance marked, all at once a thousand triggers were drawn, and a sheet of fire, wide as the whole front of the breast-work, bursted upon them with most ruinous effect. The British instantly came to a halt—still keeping up their fire—but altogether at random and ineffectual, like men in a panic. While full exposed, within point-blank shot, ranks on ranks they fell before the American marksmen, as the heavy-eared corn before the devouring hail-storm, when with whirlwind rage it smites the trembling earth, and rushes on, smoking and roaring through the desolated fields. The enemy still maintained their ground like Britons, though all in front was nothing but one wide destructive flash; and nought around but heaps of their shrieking, dying comrades. But in a few minutes the slaughter became so general, that they could stand it no longer, but broke and fled in the utmost disorder, to the shore side; and some even took refuge in their boats! Their officers with some difficulty brought them back to a second charge, when the Americans, waiting till they were come up within a few rods of the fort, recommenced their fire, with a mortality which broke and drove them again. Some of the officers attempted to bring them *on a third time:* but others cried out, that *"it was no better than murder!"* It is probable they would hardly have made another effort, had not the generals Clinton and Burgoyne, spectators of their defeat, hastened over from Boston with fresh troops to their aid.

The Americans, being nearly destitute of ammunition, and attacked by such superior force, were obliged to retreat, which they did in tolerable order, but not till they had given the enemy, as they mounted the works, their last cartridges, and to some of them the buts of their guns—for want of bayonets. The British, 'tis true, by such great advantage of numbers and weapons, gained the day, but sung no *te deum.* To have given 1350 men, killed and wounded, for a poor ditch of 12 hours labour, seemed to them a bargain hardly worth thanking God for.

Among the slain of the enemy was Major Pitcairn, author

of the murders at Lexington a few weeks before! And travellers often turn aside to drop a tear on the tomb where Warren sleeps.

During the autumn and winter of 1775, Washington could effect nothing against the British, but to hold them close confined in Boston, where the scurvy got in among them, and proved very fatal. To remedy this evil, immense quantities of live stock and vegetables were shipped from Britain—5,000 fat oxen—14,000 sheep—12,000 hogs, with 22,000 pounds sterling worth of sour-crout!!! And nearly the same amount in hay, oats and beans, for a *single regiment of cavalry!!* *"Blessed are the meek!"* for they shall save a world of expense.

In consequence of some disturbances, this year in South-Carolina, in *favour* of the ministry, Sir Peter Parker was dispatched with nine ships of war, with a large land force, commanded by Clinton and Cornwallis, to make an attempt on Charleston, the capital. Before the ships could be brought to pay their respects to the town, they must, it seems, pass a little *fort* on Sullivan's Island. This, however, being defended only by raw militia, was hardly looked on as an obstacle. Happily for America, the command of the fort had been committed to general Moultrie; for the chief in command, gen. Charles Lee, though otherwise brave, was ever in the *frights* at the thought of a British man-of-war; and, for a *general,* much too free in lending his fears to others. For, while Moultrie was showing him the *fort,* and in the language of a *fiery patriot,* was boasting what handsome resistance he hoped it would make; Lee, with infinite scorn replied *"Pshaw! a mere slaughter house! a mere slaughter house! a British man of war will knock it about your ears in half an hour!"*—He even proposed to *abandon* the fort!—The courage of *one* man saved Charleston, and perhaps the State; that fortunate man, was John Rutledge, Esq. governor of South-Carolina. He insisted that the fort should be defended to the *last extremity.* Moultrie was called in. *"Well, general*

Moultrie," said gov. Rutledge, "*what do you think of giving up the fort?*" Moultrie could scarcely suppress his indignation. "*No man, sir,*" said he to Lee, "*can have a higher opinion of the British ships and seamen than I have. But there are others who love the smell of gunpowder as well as they do; and give us but plenty of powder and ball, sir, and let them come on as soon as they please.*" His courage was quickly put to the test; for about 10 o'clock, on the 28th of June, in the glorious 1776, Sir Peter Parker, with seven tall ships formed his line, and bearing down within point-blank shot of the fort, let go his anchors and began a tremendous fire. At every thundering blast he fondly hoped to see the militia take to the sands like frightened rats from an old barn on fire. But, widely different from his hopes, the militia stood their ground, firm as the Black-jacks of their land, and levelling their four-and-twenty pounders with good aim, bored the old hearts of oak through and through at every fire. Their third broad-side carried away the springs on the cables of the commodore's ship, which immediately swung around right stern upon the guns of the fort—"*Hurra! my sons of thunder,*" was instantly the cry along the American battery, "*look handsomely to the commodore! now, my boys, for your best respects to the commodore!*" Little did the commodore thank them for *such respects;* for in a short time he had 60 of his brave crew lying lifeless on his decks, and his cock-pit stowed with the wounded. At one period of the action, the quarter-deck was cleared of every soul, except Sir Peter himself. Nor was he entirely excused; for an honest cannon-ball, by way of broad hint that it was out of character for a *Briton* to fight against *liberty,* rudely snatched away the bag of his silk breeches. Thus, Sir Peter had the honour to be the first and I believe the only Sans Culotte ever heard of in American natural history!!

The Americans stood the fire like SALAMANDERS, for the neighbouring shores were lined with thousands of their dearest relatives, anxiously looking on! The British tars, poor fellows! had no sisters, mothers, nor wives, spectators of their strife, but fought, notwithstanding, with their wonted heroism. Long accustomed to mastery in battles with the French, and greatly out-numbering the fort both in men and guns, they counted on *certain victory;* and tho' dreadfully handled, yet scorned to yield. Immense were the exertions on both sides; and while the powder of the fort lasted, the conflict was awfully grand—From ships to fort, and from fort to ships again, all below seemed one stream of solid fire; all above, one vast mountain of smoke darkening the day, while unintermitted bursts of thunder deafened all ears, and far around shook both land and sea.

The heroes in the fort won immortal honour. One brave fellow, a Serjeant Jasper, observing the flag staff shot away, jumped down from the fort on the beach, in the hottest fury of the battle, and snatching up the flag, returned it to its place, streaming defiance, with a—*"Hurra, my boys, Liberty and America for ever."* Governor Rutledge rewarded him with a sword. Another Serjeant, M'Donald, while roaring away with his 24 pounder, was terribly shattered by a cannon ball. When about to expire, he lifted up his dying eyes and said—*"My brave countrymen, I die, but don't let the cause of Liberty die with me."* Now louder and louder still, peal on peal, the American thunder burst forth with earth-trembling crashes; and the British ships after a long and gallant struggle, hauled off with a good fortnight's worth of work for surgeons, carpenters, and riggers.

Sir Peter was so dumb-founded by this *drubbing,* that it took him full eight-and-forty hours to recover his stomach for his beef and pudding. So wonderfully had it let him down, that even his *black pilots* grew impudent upon him. For as he was going out over the bar he called to Cudjo (a black fellow, a Pilot who was sounding the depth of the water.)—*"Cudjo!* (says he) *what water have you got there?"*

"What water, massa? what water? why salt water, be sure, sir!—sea water alway salt water, an't he massa?"

"You black rascal, I knew it was salt water, I only wanted to know how much water you have there?"

"How much water here, massa! how much water here! God bless me, massa! where I going get quart pot for measure him?"

This was right down impudence; and Cudjo richly deserved a rope's end for it; but Sir Peter, a good natured man, was so tickled with the idea of measuring the *Atlantic* ocean with a *quart pot,* that he broke into a hearty laugh, and ordered Cudjo a *stiff drink of grog.*

'Twas the celebrated Samuel Chase, the Demosthenes of Maryland, who first taught the startled vaults of Congress-hall to re-echo the name of Independence. After enumerating many a glaring instance of *ministerial* violation of American rights—on all of which George the Third, the *expected father of his people,* had looked with a *most unfatherly calmness*—his countenance became like the dark stormy cloud edg'd with lightning; then swinging his arm in the air, with a tremendous stamp and voice of thunder, that made the hollow dome resound, he swore—"By the G— of Heaven he owed no allegiance *to the king of England!"*

Many in Congress trembled at hearing such a speech; and, on mention of *Independence,* felt the pang which nature feels when soul and body are parting. But fearing that *"true friendship could never grow again, where wounds of deadly hate had pierced so deep,"* they at length resolved to part. The gentlemen appointed by Congress to frame the declaration of Independence, were THOMAS JEFFERSON, JOHN ADAMS, DR. FRANKLIN, R. SHEARMAN[1] and R. R. LIVINGSTON. On hearing their nomination to a task so high and arduous, they met; and after some conversation on the subject, parted, under the agreement that each of their number should draft

[1] "R. SHEARMAN" is Roger Sherman (1721–1793) of Connecticut.

his own declaration, and read it next day, in rotation to the rest. At the fixed hour next day, they met—but *"who should read first,"* was the question. Mr. Jefferson was fixed on, and, after much importunity, consented to read his *form,* which had the honour to give such complete satisfaction, that none other was read.

A few days after this, Lord Howe came upon the coast with a *forest* of men of war and transports, shading far and wide the frightened ocean, and bearing nearly 40,000 men, British, Hessians, and Waldeckers. Supposing that this had intimidated the American commander, Lord Howe wrote a letter to him, directed—*"George Washington, Esq."* This he refused to receive! looking on it as an insult to *Congress,* under whom he had the honour to bear the commission of *Commander in Chief,* and should have been addressed as such. General Howe, then sent an officer (Colonel Patterson) to converse with him on the subject of *reconciliation. . . .* Having heard what he had to say, Washington replied, *"by what has yet appeared, sir, you have no power but to grant* pardons; *but we, who have committed no faults, want no pardons; for we are only fighting for our rights as the descendants of Englishmen."*

The unfortunate defeat of Long-Island, now took place, on August 28th, which though the *hottest* day in the *year,* had like to have been the *freezing point* in the American affairs. For, on this day, the British with an infinite superiority of force, after having defeated the Americans with great loss, were investing the slender remains of their army, and had actually broke ground within six hundred yards of the little redoubt that feebly covered their front. Soon as it was dark, Washington ordered the troops to convey their baggage and artillery to the water side, whence it was transported over a broad ferry all night long, with amazing silence and order. Providentially a thick fog continued next morning till ten o'clock; when that passed away, and the sun broke out, the

British were equally surprised and enraged to see the rear guard with the last of the baggage, in their boats, and out of all danger.

Lord Howe, supposing that such a run of misfortunes must have put Congress into a good humour to think about *peace,* signified a willingness to have a *grand talk* on the subject. Congress sent Dr. Franklin, Mr. Adams, and Mr. Rutledge, each with his belt of wampum. But finding that his lordship was still harping on the old string, *pardons! pardons!* they took up their hats, and very *erectly* stalked off.

Towards the close of this trying campaign, it is a fact, that Washington had not 3000 men: and even these were so destitute of *necessaries,* that nothing but their love and veneration for *him* kept them together. And with this handful he had to oppose a victorious army, of nearly forty thousand veterans!! But Jehovah, the God of Hosts, was with him: and oft' times, in the ear of the slumbering hero, his voice was heard, *"fear not, for I am with thee; be not dismayed, for I am thy God."*—Hence, under all the disheartening circumstances of this campaign, Washington not only kept up his own spirits, but cheered those of his drooping comrades. Hearing his officers one day talk about the gloominess of the American affairs, he humourously clasped his neck with his hands, and said with a smile, *"I really cannot believe yet, that my neck was ever made for a halter!"*

For four months, during the summer and fall of 1776, the Americans were obliged to retreat before the enemy, who completely over-ran the Jerseys, filling every town and hamlet with their victorious troops. . . . During their pursuit through the Jerseys, the behaviour of the Hessians towards the country people was barbarous in the extreme. To make them fight the better, it seems they had been told that the Americans, against whom they were warring, were not (like the Europeans) *Christians* and *gentlemen,* but *mere savages,* a race of Cannibals, who would not only tomahawk a poor Hessian, and haul off his hide for a *drum's head,* but would just as lieve barbacue and eat him as they would a pig. *"Vat! Vat!* cried the Waldeckers, with eyes staring wild and big as billiard balls, *"Vat! eat Hessian man up like vun hock! Oh mine Got and Vader! vot peoples ever bin heard of eat Christian man before! Vy! shure des Mericans mush be de deble."*

This was Hessian logic: and it inspired them with the utmost abhorrence of the Americans, to whom they thought the *worst* treatment much too good . . . they burnt houses—destroyed furniture—killed the stock—*abused the women!*—and spread consternation and ruin along all their march.

To save their families from such horrid tragedies, the Americans flocked in, by thousands, to general Howe, to take the oath of allegiance. And the best judges were of opinion, that this alarming apostacy would soon become *general* throughout the two great states of Pennsylvania and New Jersey! And indeed no wonder; for to most people it appeared that the cause of liberty was a *gone cause.* But, still, firm as the iron rudder-bands that maintain the course of the ship in her trembling flight over raging seas, so firmly did Washington cleave to his countrymen, and cover their retreat.

They had been obliged to retreat from Long-Island to New-York, from New-York, over the Hudson, to New-Jersey, and now, over the Delaware, to Pennsylvania. "My God! general Washington, how long shall we retreat?" said general Reed, "where shall we stop?" "Why sir," replied Washington, "if we can do no better, we'll retreat over every river in America; and last of all over the mountains, whence we shall never lack opportunities to annoy, and finally, I hope, to expel the enemies of our country."

But, God be thanked, our toils and trials were not to be pushed to such sad extremities; for general Howe, having driven the Americans to the *western side* of the Delaware, stationed 4000 men in Trenton, Bordentown, and Burlington, on its *eastern bank,* and then returned with the main army to eat their winter puddings in Brunswick and New-York.—Here, Washington, with joy, first discovered an opportunity to make a blow. Not doubting, but that such a long run of success had taught the enemy to think very *highly of themselves,* and as *meanly* of the *Americans;* and suspecting, too, that at Christmas, which was close at hand, instead of watching and praying like *good christians,* they would, very likely, be drinking and hopping like fools, he determined then and there if possible to make a smash among them. To this end he broke his little remnant of an army into three divisions; two of which he committed to generals Ewing and Cadwallader to attack at Bordentown and Burlington . . . the third he meant to lead in person to the heavier charge on Trenton. Every thing being in readiness by Christmas night, soon as it was dark they struck their tents and moved off in high spirits, once more to try their fortune against a long victorious enemy. But alas! the enthusiasm of the gallant Cadwallader and Ewing was soon arrested; for on arriving at the river, they found it so filled with ice, as to preclude all possibility of crossing. Thus, to their inexpressible grief, was blasted the ardent wish to aid their *beloved* chief in this his last bold attempt to save America. Ignorant of the failure of *two-thirds* of his plan, Washington and his little *forlorn hope,* pressed on through the darksome night, pelted by an incessant storm of hail and snow. On approaching the river, nine miles above Trenton, they heard the unwelcome roar of ice, loud crashing along the angry flood. But the object before them was too *vast* to allow one thought about difficulties. The troops were instantly embarked, and after five hours of infinite toil and danger, landed, some of them *frost-bitten,* on the same shores with the enemy. Forming the line they renewed their march. *Pale,* and slowly moving along the neighbouring hills was seen, (by Fancy's eye) the weeping GENIUS of LIBERTY. Driven from the rest of the world, she had fled to the wild woods of America, as to an assured asylum of rest.—Here she fondly hoped, through long unfailing time, to see her children pursuing their cheerful toils, *unstarved* and *uncrushed* by the INHUMAN FEW. But alas! the *inhuman few,* with fleets and armies, had pursued her flight! Her *sons* had gathered around her, but they had failed—some, on their *bloody beds:* others, dispersed; all desponding. *One little band alone* remained! and, now, resolved to bleed or to defend, were in rapid march to face *her foes. Pale* and in tears, with eyes often lifted to Heaven, she moved along with her children to witness perhaps the last conflict.

The Sun had just tipt with gold the adjacent hills, when snowy Trenton, with the wide-tented fields of the foe, hove in sight. To the young in arms this was an awful scene, and nature called a short-liv'd terror to their hearts. But not unseen of Washington was their fear. He marked the sudden paleness of their cheeks, when first they beheld the enemy, and quick, with half-stifled sighs, turned on him their wistful looks. As the big lion of Zara, calling his brindled sons to battle against the mighty rhinoceros, if he mark their falling manes and crouching to his side, instantly puts on all his terrors—his eyes roll in blood—he shakes the forest with his deepening roar, till, kindled by their father's fire, the maddening cubs swell with answering rage, and spring undaunted on the Monster. Thus stately and terrible rode *Columbia's first and greatest son,* along the front of his halted troops. The eager wish for battle flushed over his burning face, as, rising on his stirrups, he waved his sword towards the hostile camp, and exclaimed, *"there! my brave friends! there are the enemies of your country! and now, all I ask of you, is, just to remember what you are about to fight for. March!"* His looks and voice rekindled all their fire, and drove them undaunted to the charge. The enemy saw their danger when it was too late! but, as if resolved to tax their courage, to pay for their carelessness, they roused the thunder of their drums and flew to arms. But before they could form, the Americans led on by

Washington, advanced upon them in a stream of lightning, which soon decided the contest. Col. Rhal, a brave German who commanded them, fell by the musket of the intrepid captain (now general) Frelinghuysen, of New-Jersey. The ghosts of forty of his *countrymen* accompanied him; and very nearly one thousand were made prisoners. Five hundred British horse effected their escape to Bordenton. Could Ewing and Cadwallader have crossed the river, agreeably to Washington's plan, the enemy's whole line of cantonments would have been completely swept!!

To rouse his desponding countrymen, Washington immediately marched down to Philadelphia, and made triumphal entry with all his prisoners, preceded by their cannon and colours, and waggons bristling with muskets and bayonets. The poor tories could scarcely believe their own eyes. The whigs, many of them wept for joy.

To do away from the minds of the Hessians, their ill-grounded dread of the Americans, Washington took great care, from the moment they fell into his hands, to have them treated with the utmost tenderness and generosity. He contrived that the wealthy Dutch farmers should come in from the country and converse with them. They seemed very agreeably surprised at such friendly attentions. The Dutchmen at length proposed to them to quit the British service and go and turn farmers. . . . At this the Hessians paused a little, and said something about *parting with their country*.

"Your country!" said the farmers, "Poor fellows! where is your country? You have no country. To support his *pomps* and *pleasures,* your prince has torn you from your country, and sold you like slaves (for 30*l.* a-head) to fight against us, who never troubled you. Then leave the vile employment and come live with us. Our lands are rich; come help us to cultivate them. Our tables are covered with fat meats, and with milk and honey; come sit down and eat with us like brothers. Our daughters are young and beautiful and good;

then shew yourselves *worthy,* and you shall have our daughters; and we will give you of our lands and cattle, that you may work and become rich and happy as we are. You were told that General Washington and the Americans were savages, and would devour you! But from the moment you threw down your arms, have they not been as kind to you as you had any right to expect?"

"O yes!" cried they, "and a thousand times more kind than we deserved. We were told the Americans would show us no pity, and so we were cruel to them. But we are sorry for it now, since they have been so good to us; and now we love the Americans, and will never fight against them any more!"

Such was the effect of Washington's policy; the *divine policy of doing good for evil.* It melted down his iron enemies into golden friends. It caused the Hessian soldiers to join with the American farmers! . . . not only so, but to write such letters to their countrymen, that they were constantly breaking loose from the British to run over to the Americans . . . insomuch that in a little time the British would hardly trust a Hessian to stand sentinel!

Though this victory was gained on the 26th of December, yet we find Washington again, on the 1st of January, across the angry Delaware, with his country's flag bold-waving over the heights of Trenton. Lord Cornwallis advanced in great force to attack him. The Americans retreated through the town, and crossing the Sanpink (a creek that runs along its eastern side) planted their cannon near the ford, to defend its passage. The British army following, close in their rear, entered the town about 4 o'clock; and a heavy cannonade commenced between the two armies, which were separated only by the Sanpink and its narrow valley. "Now, sir!" said sir William Erskine to Cornwallis, "now is the time to make sure of Washington."

"Oh no!" replied Cornwallis, "our troops have marched a good way to-day, and are tired. And the old fox can't make his escape; for with the help of the Delaware, now filled with ice, we have completely surrounded him. To-morrow morning, fresh and fasting, we'll fall upon him, and take him and his ragamuffins all at once!"

"Ah! my Lord!" returned sir William, "if Washington be the soldier that I *fear he is,* you'll not see him *there to-morrow morning!"*

Night coming on, the artillery ceased to roar; and lighting up their fires, both armies proceeded to supper and to sleep. About midnight, having *renewed all the fires,* Washington put his little army in motion, and passing along the enemy's rear, hasted to surprise a large body of their troops at Princeton. Soon as it was day, Cornwallis was greatly mortified to find there was no American army on the banks of the Sanpink. *"That's exactly what I feared,"* said sir William. Just as they were in deep thought on the matter, they heard the roar of Washington's cannon at Princeton. *"There,"* continued sir William, *"There is Washington now, cutting up our troops!"* And so it was; for on arriving at Princeton, about sun-rise, Washington met three British regiments, who had just struck their tents, and were coming on in high spirits to attack him at Trenton. To it, in a moment, both parties fell like heroes. At the first onset the Americans gave way; but sensible that all was at stake, Washington snatched a standard, and advancing on the enemy, called to his countrymen to follow: his countrymen heard and rushed on to the charge. Then flash and clash went the muskets and bayonets.—Here the servants of George, and there the sons of liberty, wrapped in clouds and flames, together plung'd to mutual wounds and death.

> "God save the king!" the British heroes cry'd,
> "And God for Washington!" Columbia's sons reply'd.

The name of Washington imparted its usual animation to his troops. The enemy gave way in all quarters, and were pursued four miles. The victors returned with 400 prisoners;

the bayonet had stopped 120 on the field. But they fell not alone. The gallant Mercer, and 63 of his brave countrymen, sleep with them. But the strife of the heroes was but for a moment; and they have forgotten their wounds. Together now, they feast in Paradise, and when meet their eyes of love, their joys are no[t] dashed by the remembrance of the past.

The British officers gave Washington full credit for such fine strokes of generalship, and began to look thoughtful whenever his name was mentioned.

The enemy now (January 15th) drew in all their forces to winter-quarters at Brunswick, where Washington continued to thin their numbers by cutting off their foraging parties; so that every load of hay, or dish of turnips they got, was at the price of blood.

Thus gloriously, in ten days, was turned the tide of victory in favour of America, by him whom Heaven, in mercy not to America alone, but to Britain, and to the world, had raised up to found here a wide empire of liberty and virtue. The character of Washington was exalted to the highest pitch, even throughout *Europe,* where he was generally styled the American Fabius, from the famous Roman general of that name, who opposed Hannibal with success. A distinction to which he was justly entitled, from the invincible firmness with which he rejected every finesse of the British generals; as also, from that admirable judgment with which he suited the defence of the nation to the genius and abilities of the people, and to the natural advantages of the country, thereby not allowing the enemy to profit by their great superiority of *numbers, discipline,* and *artillery,* and constantly cutting them off by skirmishes and surprise.

The ministerial plan for this year (1777) was to reduce the Americans, by cutting off all communications between the northern and southern states! To effect this General Howe, with 20,000 men, was to go round from New-York to the Head of Elk, and thence march on, due north, through Philadelphia; while general Burgoyne with 10,000 men, setting out from Canada, was to pass along down the lakes, and thence due south to meet his brother Howe; the straight line, formed by the junction of these two gentlemen, was to possess such virtues, that it was supposed no American could be found hardy enough to set foot over it!!

Accordingly, July 23, general Howe left Sandy-Hook, sailed up the Chesapeake, and landed at the mouth of *Elk-River,* marched on, with but little interruption, except at Brandywine, to Philadelphia—Into this elegant city, on the 26th of September, 1777, he entered in triumph; fondly supposing, that, in America, as in Europe, the capture of the city was the same thing as the reduction of the country. But instead of finding himself master of this great continent, whose rattlesnakes alone in the hand of heaven, could scourge his presumption; it was with no small difficulty he could keep possession of the little village of Germantown. For, on the morning of the 4th of October, Washington made an attack on him with such judgment and fury, that his troops gave way in every quarter. *"The tumult, disorder* and *despair* in the *British army,* says Washington, *were unparalleled."* But, in the very moment of the most decisive and glorious victory, when some of the provincial regiments had more prisoners than men, the Americans, through the mistake of a *drunken* officer, began to *retreat!!* Washington's grief and mortification were inexpressible.

But while he was annoying the enemy by land, he did not lose sight of their fleet, which was now forcing its way up the Delaware, to keep open to the army a channel of supplies. They arrived, without molestation, within 8 miles of Philadelphia, at a marsh called Mud-Island. On this poor harmless spot, the fittest, however, that nature in this peaceful land of Friends could furnish, Washington had ordered a Fort to be thrown up, the command of which, with 230 men, he assigned to lieutenant-colonel Samuel Smith. On the eastern or

Jersey side of the river, at a place called Red-bank, he ordered a strong redoubt, the command of which, with 205 men, was given to Colonel Greene. These, with some chevaux-de-frise sunk in the river, and a few gallies, formed all the barrier that Washington could present against the British navy. The strength of this barrier was soon put to a fiery trial. Great preparations were made to attack the Americans, at the same instant, both by land and water. Count Donop, with a host of Hessians, was sent over to be in readiness to attack Red-Bank, while the tide of flood, groaning under their enormous weight, brought up the men of war. The morning was still, and the heavens overcast with sad clouds, as of nature sympathizing with her children, and ready to drop showers of celestial pity on their strifes. No sooner had the ships floated up within three cables length of the fort, than they began a most tremendous cannonade: while cannon-balls and fire-tailed bombs, like comets, fell upon it thick as hail. The gallant Smith and his myrmidons stood the shock to a miracle, and like men fighting under the eye of their Washington, drove the two-and-thirty pounders through them with such spirit and success, that in a little time, the Augusta, a heavy 64 gun ship, took fire, and blew up, the horrible balloon of many of the crew. Another ship, called the Merlin, or *Black-Bird,* soon got on the wing, blew up likewise, and went off in thunder to join the Augusta.

At the same moment, Col. Donop, with his Hessians, made a gallant attack on the fort at Red-Bank. After a few well directed fires, Greene and his men artfully retired from the *out-works.* The enemy now supposing the day their *own,* rushed on in vast numbers along a large opening in the fort, and within twenty steps of a masked battery, of 18 pounders, loaded with grape-shot and spike-nails. All at once hell itself seemed to open before their affrighted view. But their pains and their terrors were but for a moment. Together down they sunk by hundreds, into the sweet slumbers of death, scarcely sensible of the fatal blow that reft their lives.

Heaps on heaps the slaughter'd Hessians lie:
Brave Greene beholds them with a tearful eye.
Far now from home, and from their native shore,
They sleep in death, and hear of wars no more.

Poor Donop was mortally wounded, and taken prisoner. The attentions of the American officers, and particularly the kind condolence of the Godlike Washington, quite overcame him: and his last moments were steeped in tears of regret, for having left his native land, to fight a distant people, who had never injured him.

On hearing of his misfortune, Washington sent an officer to condole with him. The officer was conducted to his apartment, and delivered the message. The wounded Count appeared much affected—a tear swelled in his eye—and he said to the officer, *"Present to general Washington the thanks of an unfortunate brother soldier—tell him I expect to rise no more—but, if I should, the first exertion of my strength shall be, to return to him my thanks in person."* The officer sent, was colonel Daniel Clymer, of Berks, Pennsylvania. *"See here, Colonel,"* said the dying count, *"see in me the vanity of all human pride! I have shone in all the* courts of Europe, *and now I am dying here, on the banks of the Delaware, in the house of an obscure Quaker!"*

After six weeks of infinite fatigue, with great loss of men and money, the British forced a passage large enough for their provision ships to Philadelphia, where general Howe and his officers held their balls this winter; while 16 miles distant, the great Washington, well pleased with his campaign, retired and hutted it at Valley Forge.

While such ill success attended this part of the ministerial plan, viz. to choke the colonies by a *military noose,* so tightly drawn from Chesapeake to Champlain, as to stop all circulation between the northern and southern states; a worse fate frowned on their attempt in the north—General Burgoyne, with 10,000 veterans, besides a host of Canadians and Indians, issuing forth from Canada in June '77, came pouring along down the lakes, like the thundering Niagara, with an impetuosity that swept every thing before it. The hatchets of the Indians were drunk with American blood. No age, no sex, could soften them. "The widow's wail, the virgin's shriek, and infant's trembling cry," was music in their ears. In cold blood they struck their cruel tomahawks into the defenceless head of a Miss M'Rea, a beautiful girl, who was that very day to have been married! Such acts of inhumanity called forth the fiercest indignation of the Americans, and inspired that *desperate* resolution of which the human heart is capable, but which no human force can conquer. The New Englanders, who were nearest to these infernal scenes, turned out *en masse*. Washington hurried on Gates and Arnold with their furious legions; and to these he joined the immortal Morgan with his dreadful phalanx, 1000 riflemen, whose triggers were never touched in vain, but could throw a ball a hundred yards at a squirrel's head, and never miss.

The first check given to Burgoyne's career, was at Bennington. Hearing that the Americans had laid up large provisions in that town, he detached a Colonel Baum, with 600 Germans, to surprise it; and, at the same time, posted Colonel Breyman in the neighbourhood, with an equal number, to support him if necessary. Finding the place too well guarded either for surprise or storm, Baum fortified himself at a little distance, and sent back for Breyman. The American commander, the brave general Starke, thinking these enemies fully enough, at least not wishing for any more, sallied out, and with great fury attacked Baum's intrenchments. At the first onset, the Canadians and British marksmen took to their heels, and left the poor Germans in the lurch. After a gallant resistance, Baum was mortally wounded, and his brave countrymen killed or taken to a man. In the mean time Breyman, who had not heard a syllable of all this, arrived at the place of action, where, instead of the cheering huzzas of joyful friends, he was saluted, on all hands, with the deadly whizzing of rifle bullets. After receiving a few close and scorching fires, the Germans hastily betook themselves to flight. The neighbouring woods, with night's sable curtains, enabled the fugitives to save themselves, for that time at least.—The enemy lost in these two engagements not less than 1000 men, killed, wounded, and prisoners.

About the same time all their forts on the lakes were surprised—Colonel St. Leger was defeated at Fort-Stanwix—the Indians began to desert—Arnold and Morgan were coming up like mountain-storms,—and the militia from all quarters were pouring in. Burgoyne began to be alarmed, and wrote to New-York for aid; but finding that Clinton could give him none, and that the salvation of his army depended on themselves, he gallantly determined, on the 7th of October, 1777, to stake his all on the cast of a *general battle.*

His army, in high spirits, was formed within a mile of the American camp. Burgoyne, with the flower of the British troops, composed the centre—brigadier-general Frazer commanded the left—the Germans, headed by major-generals Philips and Reidesdel, and Col. Breyman formed the right. With a fine train of artillery, flying colours, and full roll of martial music, from wing to wing the towering heroes moved. On the other hand, *fired* with the love of *liberty,* the Americans poured out by thousands, eager for the glorious contest. Their *dear* country's flag waves over their heads; the thoughts of the warriors are on their *children,* and on the *chains* now forging for their tender hands. The avenging passions rise, and the battle moves. Morgan brought on the action. In a large buckwheat field, which lay between the two armies, he had concealed his famous regiment of riflemen. The enemies, chiefly Canadians and Indians, advance, suspecting no harm. They were suffered to come up within point-blank shot, when they received a general fire, which strewed the field with their dead bodies. Morgan pursued: but was soon met by a heavy reinforcement from the British, who quickly drove him, in turn.

Arnold then moved on to support Morgan, and, in a short time, with nine heavy regiments was closely engaged with the whole of the British army, both parties fighting as if each was determined never to yield: while the incessant crash of muskets and roar of artillery appeared both to sight and sound as if two wrathful clouds had come down on the plain, rushing together, in hideous battle with all their thunders and lightnings. The weight, however, of the American fire, was directed against the enemy's centre, extending along the left wing: and though it was some time sustained with the greatest firmness, yet at length it prevailed and threw the British into confusion. But the gallant Frazer flying to their assistance, soon restored their order and renewed the fight. Severely galled still by Morgan's rifles on the flank, and hard pressed at the same time, in front by Arnold, they gave way a second time: and a second time Frazer's presence revived their valour, and rekindled the battle in all its rage.

Here Arnold did an act unworthy of the glory of the well fought battle. He ordered up twelve of his best riflemen, and pointing to Frazer, who on horseback, with brandished sword was gallantly animating his men, he said, *"Mark that officer! —Himself is a host—let me not see him long!"*

The riflemen flew to their places, and in a few moments the hero was cut down.[2] With him fell the courage of the left wing, who being now fiercely charged, gave way, and retreated to their camp. But scarcely had they entered it, when the Americans, with Arnold at their head, stormed it with inconceivable fury; rushing, with trailed arms through a heavy discharge of musquetry and grape shot. The British fought with equal desperation, for their all was at stake, and the

[2] "I beg you to change Arnold, in the affair of killing Genl Frazer, to Morgan as it stood at first. Persons are now living who have heard Morgan tell it 1000 times, sorrowg." (Weems to Carey, July 11, 1816; Skeel, I, 66.) Morgan figured as the culprit in the 7th edition (1808), Arnold in the 8th (1809) and in subsequent editions. Here as in other instances Weems's publisher seems to have paid little attention to his author's requests.

Americans like a whelming flood, were bursting over their intrenchments, and, hand to hand, with arguments of bloody steel, were pleading the cause of ages yet unborn. Hoarse as a mastiff of true British breed, Lord Balcarras was heard from rank to rank, loud-animating his troops; while on the other hand, fierce as the hungry tiger of Bengal, the impetuous Arnold precipitated his heroes on the stubborn foe. High in air, the encountering banners blazed! *there* bold waving the lion-painted standard of Britain, and *here* the streaming pride of Columbia's lovely stripes—while thick below, ten thousand eager warriors close the darkening files, all bristled with vengeful steel. No firing is heard; but shrill and terrible, from rank to rank, resounds the clash of bayonets—frequent and sad the groans of the dying. Pairs on pairs, Britons and Americans, with each his bayonet in his brother's breast, fall forward together *faint-shrieking* in death, and mingle their smoking blood.

Many were the widows, many the orphans that were made that day. Long did the daughters of Columbia mourn their fallen brothers! and often did the lovely maids of Caledonia roll their soft blue eyes of sorrow along the sky-bound sea, to meet the sails of their returning lovers.

But alas! their lovers shall return no more. Far distant, on the banks of the roaring Hudson they lie, pale and helpless on the fields of death. Glassy now and dim are those eyes which once beamed with friendship or which flamed in war. Their last thoughts are towards the maids of their love; and the big tear glistens in their eye, as they heave the parting groan.

Then was seen the faded form of Ocean's Queen, far-famed Britannia, sitting alone and tearful on her western cliffs. With downcast look her faithful lion lay roaring at her feet; while torn and scattered on the rock were seen her many trophies of ancient fame. Silent, in dishevelled locks, the goddess sat, absorbed in grief, when the gale of the west came blackening along the wave, laden with the roar of murderous battle.

At once she rose—a livid horror spread her cheeks—distraction glared on her eyeballs, hard strained towards the place whence came the groans of her children! the groans of her children fast sinking in a distant land—thrice she essayed to *curse* the destroyers of her race; but thrice she remembered that *they too were her sons.* Then wild shrieking with a mother's anguish, she rent the air with her cries, and the hated name of NORTH resounded through all her caves.

But still in all its rage the battle burned, and both parties fought with an obstinacy, never exceeded. But, in that moment of danger and of glory, the impetuous Arnold, who led the Americans, was dangerously wounded, and forced to retire; and several regiments of British infantry pouring in to the assistance of their gallant comrades, the Americans, after many hard struggles, were finally repulsed.

In another quarter, where the strength of the Germans fought, the Americans, led on by Morgan, carried the intrenchments sword in hand. The face of Morgan was like the full moon in a stormy night, when she looks down red and fiery on the raging deep, amidst foundering wrecks and cries of drowning seamen; while his voice, like thunder on the hills, was heard, loud-shouting his heroes to the bloody charge. The tall regiments of Hesse Cassel fell or fled before them, leaving their baggage, tents, and artillery in the hands of the victors.

This was a bloody day to both armies: but so peculiarly disheartening to the British, that they were obliged to retreat that night to Saratoga, where in a few days, (on the 13th of October, 1777), they surrendered to the Americans, under Gates, by whom they were treated with a generosity that perfectly astonished them. For, when the British were marched out to lay down their arms, there was not an American to be seen! They had all nobly retired for a moment, as if unwilling to give the pain, *even to their enemies,* of being spectators of so humiliating a scene! Worthy countrymen of Washington!

this deed of yours shall outlive the stars; and the blest sun himself, *smiling,* shall proclaim, that in the wide travel of his beams, he never looked upon its like before.

Thus, gloriously for America, ended the campaign of '77. That of '78 began as auspiciously. In May, Silas Dean arrived from France, with the welcome news of a *treaty* with that powerful people, and a letter from Louis XVI, to Congress, whom he styled—*very dear great friends and allies.*

Soon as it was known by the British ambassador at Paris, Lord Stormont, that the king of France had taken part with the Americans, he waited on the French minister, De Vergennes; and with great agitation mentioned the report, asking if it was *possible* it could be true,

"Very possible, my Lord," replied the smooth Frenchman.

"Well, I'm astonished at it, sir," continued Stormont, "exceedingly astonished. America, sir, is our daughter! and it was extremely indelicate of the French king thus to decoy her from our embraces, and make a w—e of her!"

"Why as to that matter, my Lord," quoth Vergennes, with the true Gallic shrug, "there is no great harm done. For the king of France is very willing to marry your daughter, and make an honest woman of her."

CHAPTER X

Lord North, coming to his senses, sends commissioners to America—Clinton evacuates Philadelphia—Washington pursues him—battle of Monmouth—Arnold's apostacy—André apprehended—executed—his character

THE news of the total loss of Burgoyne and his army soon reached Parliament, where it produced a consternation never before known in that house. The Ministry, utterly confounded, could not open their lips; while the Whig minority, with great severity lashed their obstinacy and ignorance. Lord North, beginning now to find, as the great Chatham had foretold, that *"three millions of Whigs, with arms in their hands, were not to be enslaved,"* became very anxious to *conciliate!* Commissioners were sent over with offers to *repeal* the *obnoxious taxes!* and also with promises of *great favours* which Lord North would confer on America, if she would but make up the dispute with the mother country. The better to dispose her towards these offers, elegant presents were to be made to her best friends, (such as Washington, the President of Congress, &c. &c.) to speak a good word for Lord North's *favours!!* But, observe, *Independence* was to be *out of the question!*

Doctor Franklin used laughingly to say, that "Lord North and his great favours, put him in mind of an old bawd, and her attempts upon a young virgin, to whom she promised every thing but Innocence. While in robbing her of innocence, the old hag knew well enough that she was robbing the poor girl of that without which she would soon, in spite of her fine gowns and necklaces, become a miserable outcast and slave."

Finding that Lord North, in the multitude of his favours, had entirely forgotten the only one which they valued, i. e. the *Independence of their country,* the committee of Congress broke off all farther converse with the ministerial commissioners, who proceeded immediately to try the efficacy of their *presents.* To Washington, 'tis said, a *viceroyship,* with tons of gold, was to have been tendered. But, to the honour of the commissioners be it said, not one of their number was graceless enough to breathe the polluted wish into his ear. They had, however, the hardihood to throw out a bait of 10,000 guineas to the President of Congress, Gen. Read. His answer is worthy of lasting remembrance. *"Gentlemen,"* said he, *"I am poor, very poor; but your king is not rich enough to buy me!"*

On the 18th of June, the British army, now under the command of Clinton, evacuated Philadelphia for New-York. The figure they made on the road had something of the air of the *sublime;* for their baggage, loaded horses, and carriages, formed a line not less than twelve miles in length. General Washington, whose eye, like that of the sacred dragon, was always open and fixed upon the enemies of America, immediately crossed the Delaware after them—pushed on detached corps to obstruct their advance—gall their flanks—and fall on their rear, while he himself moved on with the main body of the army. By the 27th, Clinton had advanced as far as Monmouth, and Washington's troops were close on his flank and rear. Next morning General Lee, with 5000 men, was ordered to begin the attack; Washington moving on briskly to support him. But, as he advanced, to his infinite astonishment he met Lee retreating, and the enemy pursuing. *"For God's sake, General Lee,"* said Washington with great warmth, *"what's* the cause of this *ill-tim'd prudence."*

"No man, sir," replied Lee, quite convulsed with rage, *"can boast* a larger portion of that rascally virtue than your *Excellency!!"*

Dashing along by the madman, Washington rode up to his troops, who at sight of him rent the air with *"God save great Washington!"*

"My brave fellows," said he, *"can you* fight?"

They answered with 3 *cheers! "Then face about, my heroes, and charge."*—This order was executed with infinite spirit. The enemy, finding themselves now warmly opposed in front, made an attempt to turn his left flank, but were gallantly attacked and driven back. They then made a rapid push to the right, but the brave Greene, with a choice body of troops and artillery, repulsed them with considerable slaughter. At the same instant, Wayne advanced with his legion, and poured in so severe and well directed a fire, that the enemy were glad to regain their defiles. Morgan's rifles distinguished themselves that day. Washington and his heroes lay upon their arms all night, resolved to fall on the enemy the moment they should attempt their retreat next morning. But during the night they moved off in *silence,* and got such a start that Washington thought it dangerous, in such hot weather, to make a push after them. The Americans lost 58 killed—140 wounded. The British had 249 killed, and the wounded in proportion. Numbers, on both sides, died of the extreme *heat,* and by drinking *cold water.*

In September 1780, an attempt was made to take off our Washington, and by means which I can hardly believe the old British lion was ever well pleased with.

I allude to the affair of Arnold's treason. That which makes rogues of thousands, I me[a]n *Extravagance,* was the ruin of this great soldier. Though extremely brave, he was of that vulgar sort, who having no taste for the *pleasures* of the *mind,* think of nothing but high living, dress, and show. To rent large houses in Philadelphia—to entertain French Ambassadors—to give balls and concerts, and grand dinners and suppers, required more money than he could honestly command. And, alas! such is the stuff whereof spendthrifts are made, that to fatten his *Prodigality* Arnold consented to starve his *Honesty;* and provided he might but figure as a gorgeous Governor, he was content to retail, by the billet and the gill, wood and rum unfairly drawn from the commissary's store!

Colonel Melcher, the barrack master, mentioned the matter to Congress, who desired him to issue to General Arnold no more than his proper *rations.* He had scarcely got home when Arnold's servant appeared with an order for another large supply of *Rum, Hickory wood, &c. &c.*

"Inform your master," said Melcher, *"that he can't have so much."*

Arnold immediately came down, and in great passion asked Colonel Melcher, if it was true he had protested his bill.

"Yes, sir!"

"And how durst you do it!"

"By order of Congress, sir."

At this, Arnold, half choked with rage, replied, *"D—n the Rascals! I'll remember them for it. Sampson like I'll shake the pillars of their Liberty-temple about their ears!"*

On the evacuation of Philadelphia by the British, Gen. Arnold had been appointed temporary governor of that city, where he behaved like a desperado, who sticks at nothing to stop the deadly leaks of his prodigality, and to keep himself from sinking. Among other bold strokes, he seized and sold large quantities of American property, pretending it was British. Complaints were made to Congress, who, unwilling to expose the man who had fought so gallantly for Liberty, treated him with great gentleness; and for the same reason, Washington, after a mild reproof, gave him the command of West Point, with a large body of troops.

The history of Arnold's embarrassments and his quarrel with his countrymen, soon got down to New-York to the British commander, who well knowing the ticklish situation of a *proud* man, caught on the horns of *poverty,* sends him up a major André, with money in his pocket. The major, by means yet unknown to the public, got near enough to Arnold to *probe* him, and, alas! found him, both in principle and purse, hollow as an exhausted receiver, and very willing to be filled up with English guineas. English guineas, to the tune of ten thousand, with the rank and pay of Brigadier General, are offered him; and Arnold agrees, Oh! shocking to humanity! Arnold agrees to sacrifice Washington.

The outlines of the project, were, it seems, that Arnold should make such a disposition of the troops at West Point, as to enable sir Henry Clinton, so completely to surprise them, that they must inevitably, either lay down their arms or be cut to pieces—with *General Washington among them!!* The victorious British were then, both by land and water, to rush upon the feeble and dispirited residue of the American army, in the neighbourhood, utterly unable to resist, when there would follow such a slaughter of men, and such a sweeping of *artillery, ammunition, stores,* &c. &c. as would completely break down the spirit of the nation, and reduce them to unconditional submission to the *Ministry!*

To be certified of this delightful truth, André, during Washington's absence from West Point, comes ashore from a sloop of war, with a surtout over his regimentals, spends a day and night with Arnold; sees with his own eyes, the dear train laid, the matches lighted, and every thing in readiness, a few nights hence, to send the *old Virginia farmer* and his *republic* a-packing.

Every thing being settled to satisfaction, André wishes to set off to carry the glorious news to Gen. Clinton; but, behold! by a fine stroke of Providential interference, he cannot get on board the ship!! Arnold gives him a horse and a pass to go to New-York by land. Under the name of Anderson he passes, in safety, all the guards. Now, like an uncaged bird, and light as the air he breathes, he sweeps along the road. His fame brightens before him—stars and garters, coaches and castles, dance before his delighted fancy—even his long-loved reluctant Delia (Miss Seward) is *all his own—she joins in the nation's gratitude*—softly she rolls her eyes of love, and brightening in all her beauty, sinks on his enraptured breast! In the midst of these *too, too happy thoughts,* he is met by three young militia men. Though not on duty, they challenge him; he answers by the name of Anderson, shews his pass and bounds away. Here the guardian genius of Columbia burst into tears—she saw the fall of her hero, and her country's liberties crushed for ever. Dry thine eyes, blest saint, thy Washington is not fallen yet—the thick bosses of Jehovah's buckler are before the chief, and the shafts of his enemies shall yet fall to the earth, accurst—For, scarce had André passed the young militia-men, before one of them tells his comrades, that *"he does not like his looks,"* and insists that he shall be called back and questioned again. His answers prove him a spy. He would have fled, but they level their musquets. Trembling and pale, he offers them an elegant gold-watch to let him go; no! he presses on them a purse bloated with guineas; no! he promises each of them a handsome pension for life—*but all in vain.* The *power* that guarded Washington was wroth with André. On searching him they find in his boot, and in Arnold's own *hand-writing,* a plan of the whole conspiracy! Sons of the generous soul, why should I tell how major André died? The place where his gallows stood is overgrown with weeds—but smiling angels often visit the spot, for it was *bathed with the tears of his foes.*

His candour, on his examination, in some sort expiated his crime. It melted the angel soul of Washington: and the tears of the hero were mingled with the ink that signed the death-warrant of the hapless youth. The names of the young men who arrested poor André, were, JOHN PAULDING, DAVID WILLIAMS, and ISAAC VAN VERT. They were at cards under a large poplar that grew by the road, where the major was to pass. Congress bestowed a silver medal, and settled on each of them $200 annually for life.

American writers have recorded a thousand handsome things of unfortunate André. They have made him scholar, soldier, gentleman, poet, painter, musician, and, in short, EVERY THING that talents and taste can make a man. The following anecdote will show that he was much greater still.

"Some short time before that fatal affair which brought him to his end, (said my informant Mr. Drewy, a painter, now living at Newbern,) a foraging party from New-York made an inroad into our settlement near that city. The neighbours soon got together to oppose them; and, though not above fifteen years old, I turned out with my friends. In company was another boy, in age and size nearly about my own speed. We had counted on a *fine chace;* but the British were not to be driven so easily as we had expected. Standing their ground not only put us to flight, but captured several of our party; *myself* and the *other boy* among them. They presently set out with us for New-York; and, all the way, as we were going, my heart ached to think how my poor mother and sisters would take on when night came, and I did not return. Soon as they brought me in sight of the prison, I was struck with horror. The gloomy walls, and frightful guards at the doors, and wretched crowds at the iron windows, together with the thoughts of being locked up there in dark dungeons with disease and death, so overcame me, that I bursted into tears. Instantly a richly dressed officer stepped up, and taking me by the hand, with a look of great tenderness, said, *"My dear boy! what makes you cry?"* I told him I could not help it when I compared my present sad prospect with the happy one I enjoyed in the morning with my mother and sisters at home. *"Well, well, my dear child,* (said he) *don't cry, don't cry, any more."* Then turning to the jailer ordered him to stop till he should come back. Though but a boy, yet I was deeply struck with the wonderful difference betwixt *this man* and the rest around me. He appeared to me like a *brother; they like brutes.* I asked the jailer who he was. *"Why, that's major*

André, (said he angrily) *the adjutant-general of the army; and you may thank your stars that he saw you, for I suppose he is gone to the general to beg you off,* as *he has done many of your d——d rebel countrymen."* In a short time he returned; and with great joy in his countenance called out—*"Well, my sons, I've good news, good news for you! The General has given you to me, to dispose of as I choose; and now you are at liberty! So run home to your fond parents, and be good boys; mind what they tell you: say your prayers; love one another, and God Almighty will bless you."*

And yet André perished, on a gallows, while Arnold, after living to old age, died in his bed!! Shall we hence infer with Brutus, that *"Virtue is but an empty name?"* and that André had been good in vain? God forbid! Goodness and happiness are twins. Heaven hath *joined them together,* and Hell cannot *put them asunder.* For proof, we need go no further than to André himself—to André *in prison!* Even in that *last* and *gloomiest* scene of his life, we see the power which virtue has to illuminate the *dark,* to enliven *the sad,* and to raise her votaries above the terrors of death. In the first moment of his capture, when vulgar minds are thinking of nothing but *self-preservation,* he is thinking of nothing but *duty* and *generosity.* Regardless of himself, he is only anxious for Arnold. Having by letter advised that wretched man of his *danger,* and giving him time to escape, he then gallantly asserts his own real character, and avows himself *"the Adjutant General of the British army."*

The truth is, he had been sent by Gen. Clinton, on a dirty piece of business he was not fit for; and of which he was so heartily ashamed, that he appears to have been willing to atone for it with his life. Hence to the questions put at his trial, he answered with a candour which at once surprised and melted the *Court Martial*—he answered, with the candour of a mind which feared its *own* condemnation more than that of any human tribunal.—He heard his sentence of death with perfect indifference; and at the place of execution behaved like one who had fulfilled the high duties of son, brother, and man, with constant attention to a happy immortality. Thus giving the friends of virtue abundant cause to exclaim:

> "Far more true peace the dying André felt,
> Than Arnold ever knew in prosp'rous guilt."

He, poor wretch, survived! but only to live a life, at once hated and despised—*hated* by the British General, whom he had shown capable of *assassinating* the man he could not *conquer*—*hated* by the British *army,* whom he had robbed of one of its brightest ornaments—and hated by the *officers,* who could not bear to see what they called *"a d—mn'd traitor,"* not only introduced into their company, but placed over their heads! In short, Arnold was an *eye-sore* to every man of honour in England, where he was often most grossly insulted.

Soon after his flight to England with the slender remains of the British army, he went down to Southampton, where the broken hearted Mother and Sisters of the unfortunate André lived. And so little was he acquainted with the human heart, that he called to *see them!* On hearing his name announced by the servant, they burst into tears, and sent him word, that *"they did not wish to see him."*

The moment he received Major André's letter, the terrified Arnold made his escape to New-York.

British historians have wondered that he left his wife in the power of Washington. But Arnold knew in whom he trusted; and the generous man behaved exactly as Arnold had foreseen; for he immediately sent him his clothes and baggage, and wrote a polite letter of condolence to his lady, offering her a conveyance to her husband, or to her friends in Pennsylvania.

Washington now waged the war with various success. On the *one* hand, his hero of Saratoga (Gates) was defeated with great loss, at Camden; on the *other,* the British lost, on the

King's-Mountain, the brave Colonel Ferguson, with all his army, 1,400 men. Colonel Ferguson and his men were supposed by the British, the most *exquisite marksmen* alive. And indeed to hear their *bravadoes,* one would suppose, that give them but guns of a proper calibre, and they would think it a light affair to snuff the moon or drive the centre of the fixed stars. But the *American Rifle-boys* soon let them into a truer way of thinking. For in a few rounds they pink'd the brave Col. and put 300 of his exquisite marksmen asleep; which struck such a *wholesome* panic into the survivors, that they threw down their shooting-irons, and like thrifty gentlemen, called out right lustily for quarters.

Of the Americans there fell but few; but among these was one, whose fame *"Time with his own eternal lips shall sing."* I mean the brave Col. Williams. He it was, whose burning words first kindled the young farmers at their ploughs, and led them to the King's Mountain, to measure their youthful rifles with Ferguson's heroes. On receiving the ball which opened in his breast the crimson sluice of life, he was borne by his aids, into the *rear;* where he was scarcely laid down, fainting with loss of blood, before a voice was heard, loud exclaiming, *"Hurra! My Boys! the day is our own! the day is our own! they are crying for quarters!!"* Instantly he started, as from the beginning sleep of death, and opening his heavy eyes, eagerly called out, *"My God! who are crying for quarters?"—"The British! The British!"* replied the powder-blackened rifleman. At this, one last beam of joy lighted in a smile on his dying face: then faintly whispering, *God be praised!* he bowed his head in everlasting peace.

Joy follow thee, my brother, to HIS BLEST PRESENCE who sent thee a pillar of fire to blast the mad efforts of men fighting *against themselves!* On earth thy fame shall never fail. Children *yet unborn* shall lisp the name of Williams. Their cherub lips shall often talk of him whose patriot eye beheld them, afar off, smiling on the breast, and with a parent's ardor hasted to ward from their guiltless heads the curses of monarchy.

After the defeat of Gates, Washington sent on his favorite Greene to head the southern army against the victorious Cornwallis and Tarleton. With Greene he joined the famous Morgan, whose riflemen had done such signal service during the war.

To draw Cornwallis's attention from a blow meditated against the British post at Ninety-Six, Greene detached Morgan to Paulet's river, near the neighbourhood of Cornwallis and Tarleton. Immediately the pride of Tarleton rose. He begged of his friend, lord Rawdon, to obtain for him the permission of the commander in chief to go and attack Morgan. *"By Heaven, my lord,* (said he) *I would not desire a finer feather in my cap than Col. Morgan, Such a prisoner would make my fortune." "Ah, Ben,* (replied Rawdon, very coolly) *you had better let the old waggoner alone."* As no refusal could satisfy, permission at length was granted him; and he instantly set out. At parting, he said to lord Rawdon with a smile, *"My lord, if you will be so obliging as to wait dinner, the day after to-morrow, till four o'clock, Col. Morgan shall be one of your Lordship's guests." "Very well, Ben,* (said the other) *we shall wait; but remember, Morgan was brought up under Washington."*—There followed Tarleton to battle about 1000 choice infantry and 250 horse, with two field pieces. To oppose this formidable force, Morgan had but 500 militia, 300 regulars, and 75 horse. His militia were *but* militia; but his regulars were the famous MARYLAND LINE led by Howard; men who would have done honour to the plains of Austerlitz. The intrepid Desaix, who turned the tide of war in the bloody strife of Marengo, was only equal to Washington, Col. of the horse. Morgan had no wish to fight; but Tarleton compelled him; for about two hours before day on the 17th of January, '81, some of Washington's cavalry came galloping into camp with news that the British were but eight miles off, and would be up by day break. Instantly Morgan called a *council of war,* composed but of Howard, Washington, and himself. "Well, gentlemen, (said he) what's to be done? shall we fight or fly? shall we leave our friends to our enemies, and burning our meal and bacon, so hardly got, turn out again into the starving woods; or shall we stand by both, and fight like men?"

"No burning! no flying, (replied they) but let's stand, and fight like men!"

"Well then, my brave fellows, (said Morgan) wake up the troops, and prepare for action."

The ground on which this very memorable battle was fought, was an open pine barren. The militia were drawn up about two hundred yards in front of the regulars, and the horse some small distance in the *rear.* Just after day-break, the British came in sight, and halting within a quarter of a mile of the militia, began to prepare for battle. The sun had just risen, as the enemy, with loud shouts, advanced to the charge. The militia, hardly waiting to give them a distant fire, broke and fled for their horses, which were tied at some distance on the wings of the Maryland line. Tarleton's cavalry pushed hard after the fugitives, and, coming up with them just as they had reached their horses, began to cut them down. Unable to bear that sight, Col. Washington, with his corps, dashed on to their rescue.[1] As if certain of victory, Tarleton's men were all *scattered in the chase!* . . . Washington's on the contrary, sensible of the *fearful odds* against them, advanced close and compact as the Spartan phalanx. Then sudden and terrible the charge was made! Like men fighting, life in hand, all at once they rose high on their stirrups! while in streams of lightning their swords came down, and heads and arms, and caps, and carcasses, distained with spouting gore, rolled

[1] This sudden introduction of another Washington is a little confusing. The colonel was William Washington (1752–1810), who was not related to George Washington.

fearfully all around. Mournfully from all sides the cries of the wounded were heard, and the hollow groans of the dying.

Agonizing with rage and grief, Tarleton beheld the flight of his *boasted victory,* and the slaughter of *his bravest troops.* He flew to reanimate them—he encouraged—he threatened—he stormed and raved; but all in vain; no time was given to rally: for like the heavy ship under crowded canvass, bursting through the waves, so strong and resistless Washington's squadron went on, hewing down and overthrowing every thing in their way. Confounded by such a fatal charge, the British cavalry could not stand it, but broke and fled in the utmost precipitation; while, bending forward over their horses, and waving their blood-stained swords, the loud shouting Americans pursued. The woods resounded with the noise of their flight.

As when a mammoth suddenly dashes in among a thousand buffaloes, feeding at large on the vast plains of Missouri; all at once the innumerous herd, with wildly rolling eyes, and hideous bellowings, break forth into flight, while close at their heels, the roaring monster follows—earth trembles as they fly. Such was the noise in the chase of Tarleton, when the swords of Washington's cavalry pursued his troops from Cowpens' famous fields. It was like a peal of thunder, loud roaring at first, but gradually dying on the ear as it rolls away along the distant air.

By this time the British infantry were come up; and, having crossed a little valley, just as they ascended the hill, they found themselves within twenty steps of Howard and his regulars, who received them with a right soldierly welcome, and taking good aim, poured in a general and deadly fire—a slaughter so entirely unexpected, threw the enemy into confusion. Seeing this wonderful change in the battle, the militia recovered their spirits, and began to form on the right of the regulars. Morgan, waving his sword, instantly rode up to them, and with a voice of thunder roared out,

"Hurra! my brave fellows, form, form! Old Morgan was never beat in his life . . . one fire more, my heroes, and the day is our own!" With answering shouts, both regulars and militia then advanced upon the enemy, and following their fire with the bayonet, instantly decided the conflict. The ground was covered with the dead; the tops of the aged pines shook with the ascending ghosts. With feeble cries and groans, at once they rose, like flocks of snow-white swans when the cold blasts strikes them on the lakes of Canada, and sends them on wide-spread wings, far to the south to seek a happier clime.

Washington pursued Tarleton 20 miles! and during the race was often so near him, that he could easily have killed him with a pistol shot. But having strictly forbidden his men to fire a pistol that day, he thought it would never do to break his *own orders*. However there was one of his men who broke them. At one time Washington was 30 or 40 yards ahead of his men—Tarleton observing this, suddenly wheeled with a couple of his dragoons to cut him off. Washington, with more *courage* than *prudence* perhaps, dashed on, and rising on his stirrups made a blow at Tarleton, with such force, that it beat down his guard and mutilated one or two of his fingers. In this unprotected state, one of the British dragoons was aiming a stroke which must have killed him. But, the good genii, who guard the name of *Washington,* prevailed, for in that critical moment a mere dwarf of a Frenchman rushed up, and, with a pistol ball, shivered the arm of the Briton. The other dragoon attempted to wheel off, but was cut down. Tarleton made his escape.

Tarleton was brave, but not generous. He could not bear to hear another's praise. When some ladies in Charleston were speaking very handsomely of Washington, he replied, with a scornful air, that, *"he should be very glad to get a sight of Col. Washington, he had heard much talk of him,* (he said) *but had never seen him yet." "Why sir,* (rejoined one of the ladies) *if you had looked behind you at the battle of the Cowpens, you might very easily have enjoyed that pleasure.*"

While in the neighbourhood of Halifax, North-Carolina, Tarleton dined in a large company. The elegant and witty Mrs. Wiley Jones happened to be of the party. The ladies, who chiefly were whigs, were frequently praising the brave Col. Washington. Tarleton with looks considerably angry, replied, "that he was very much surprised that the Americans should think so highly of Col. Washington; for, from what he could learn, he was quite an illiterate fellow, and could hardly write his own name." "That may be very true, (replied Mrs. Jones) but I believe, sir, you can testify that he knows how to make his mark." Poor Tarleton looked at his crippled finger, and bit his lips with rage.

Washington continued the war against the British till '81; when Cornwallis pushed into Virginia, and fortified himself at York-Town. But the eye of Washington was upon him; and with an address, which, the British historians say, was never equalled, he concerted a plan that ended in his total destruction. He artfully wrote letters to Greene, informing, that, "*in order to relieve Virginia, he was determined immediately to attack New-York.*" These letters were so disposed as to fall into the right hands. Clinton took the alarm. But while Clinton was in daily expectation of a visit from him, Washington and his army, now across the Delaware, were in full stretch to the south, darkening the day with their clouds of rolling dust. Cornwallis saw that the day of his fall was at hand. He had done all that a *brave*, would to God we could add, a *humane* man could do, but all in vain. On the last of September, Washington sat down before York, with 100 pieces of heavy artillery. On the 7th of October this dreadful train began to thunder; and the British works sunk before them. Lord Cornwallis, unwilling to expose his army to the destruction of a general assault, agreed on the 17th to surrender. This was justly considered as the close of war; which having been *begun* with *supplication,* Washington piously ordered to be finished with *thanksgiving.*

In the siege of Cornwallis, the behaviour of the Americans, was, as usual, generous and noble. The amiable Col. Scammel, adjutant-general, of the American army, and uncommonly beloved by them, was badly wounded, and taken prisoner by some British dragoons, who barbarously trotted him on before them, *three miles,* into town, where he presently died of fever and loss of blood. Great was the mourning for Scammel. In a few nights, Washington gave orders to storm two of the enemy's redoubts, which were carried almost in an instant. The British called for quarters: A voice of death was heard, *"Remember poor Scammel!"—"Remember, gentlemen, you are Americans!"* was rejoined by the commander, and instantly the points of the American bayonets were thrown up towards *heaven!*

The conduct of the French also, was such as to entitle them to equal praise.

For when the British marched out to lay down their arms, the French officers were seen to shed tears—they condoled with the British, and tendered them their purses!—Glorious proof, that God never intended men to be, as some *wickedly* term it, *natural enemies.*

On hearing in Congress the fall of Cornwallis, the door-keeper swoon'd with joy—on hearing the same news announced in Parliament, Lord North fell back in his chair, and bursted into tears! On receipt of the above news, congress broke forth into songs of praise to God: Parliament into execrations against their Prime Minister—Congress hastened to the temple to pay their vows to the *Most High;* Parliament bustle to St. James's with a petition to the King for a change of men and measures. The King was graciously pleased to hear the voice of their prayer. Men and measures were changed, and a decree was passed that whoever should advise war and a farther widening of the breach between Britain and

America, should be denounced an equal enemy to both. Then full leafed and green the olive branch of peace was held out to the nations: and the eyes of millions on both sides the water were lifted in transport to the lovely sign. The stern features of war were relaxed; and gladdening smiles began again to brighten over the *"human face divine."* But Washington beheld the lovely sign with doubt. Long accustomed unerringly to predict what Britain would do, from what he knew she had *power* to do, he had *nothing* to *hope,* but, *every* thing to *fear.* America, without *cash* or *credit!*—her officers, without a dollar in pocket, strolling about camp in long beards and dirty shirts—her soldiers often without a crust in their knapsacks or a dram in their canteens—and her citizens *every where* sick and tired of war!—Great Britain, on the other hand, every where victorious over the fleets of her enemies—completely mistress of the watery world, and, Judas-like, bag bearer of its commerce and cash! with such resources, with all these trumps in her hands, will she *play quits,* and make a draw game of it? Impossible! but if she should, "it must be the work of that Providence who ruleth in the armies of Heaven and Earth, and whose hand has been visibly displayed in every step of our progress to Independence." "Nothing," continued Washington, "can remove my doubts but an order from the ministry to remove their fleets and armies."

That welcome order, at length, was given! and the British troops, sprucely powdered and perfumed, in eager thousands hied on board their ships.

> *"All hands unmoor!"* the stamping boatswain cry'd:
> *"All hands unmoor!"* the joyous crews replied.

Then all in a moment they fly to work. Some, seizing the ready handspikes, vault high upon the windlasses, thence coming down all at once with the hearty Yo-heave-O, they shake the sounding decks and tear from their dark oozy beds the ponderous anchors. Others, with halyards hard strained through the creaking blocks, sway aloft the wide-extended yards, and spread their canvas to the gale, which, with increasing freshness, bears the broad-winged ships in foam and thunder through the waves. Great was the joy of the multitude, for they were hastening to revisit their *native land,* and to meet those eyes of love which create a heaven in the virtuous breast. But the souls of some were sad. These were the *reflecting few,* whose thoughts were on the past, and on the *better hopes* of *former days!* To *them,* the flowing bowl, the lively joke, the hearty laugh and song, gave no delight; nor yet the blue fields of ocean brightly shining round, with all her young billows wantoning before the playful breeze. Their country ruined and themselves repulsed, how could they rejoice! Then slowly retiring from the noisy crew, by themselves apart they sat on the lofty stern, high above the burning track which the ships left behind them in their rapid flight. *There,* deep in thought they sat with eyes sad fixed on the lessening shores, and ruminated even to melancholy. The dismal war returns upon their thoughts, with the pleasant days of '76, then bright with hope, but now, alas! all darkened in despair. " 'Twas then," said they, "we first approached these coasts, shaded far and wide with our navies nodding tall and stately over the heaving surge. From their crowded decks looked forth myriads of blooming warriors, eagerly gazing on the lovely shores, the farms, and flocks, and domes, fondly thought *their own,* with all the beauteous maids, the easy purchase of a bloodless strife! But ah, vain hope! Washington met us in his strength. His people poured around him as the brindled sons of the desert around their sire when he lifts his terrible voice, and calls them from their dens, to aid him in war against the mighty rhinoceros. The battle raged along a thousand fields—a thousand streams ran purple with British gore. And now of all our blooming warriors, alas! how few remain! Pierced by the fatal rifle, far the greater part now press their bloody beds. There, each on his couch of honour, lie those who were once the flower of our host. There lies the gallant Frazer, the dauntless Ferguson, the accomplished Donop, and that pride of youth, the generous André, with thousands equally brave and good. But, O! ye dear partners of this cruel strife, though fallen you are not forgotten! Often, with tears do we see you still, as when you rejoiced with us at the feast, or fought by our sides in battle. But vain was all our valour; for God fought for Washington. Hence our choicest troops are fallen before him; and we, the sad remains of war, are now returning, inglorious, to our native shores. Land of the graves of Heroes, farewell! Ghosts of the noble dead! chide not the steps of our departure! you are left; but it is in a land of brothers who often mourned the death which their valour gave. But now the unnatural strife is past, and peace returns. And O! that with peace may return that spirit which once warmed the hearts of Americans towards their British brethren, when the sight of our tall ships was wont to spread joy along their shores; and when the planter, viewing his cotton-covered fields, rejoiced that he was preparing employment and bread for thousands of our poor!!"

The hostile fleets and armies thus withdrawn; and the Independence of his country acknowledged, Washington proceeded, at the command of Congress, to disband the army! To this event, though of all others the dearest to his heart, he had ever looked forward with trembling anxiety. Loving his soldiers as his children, how could he tell them the painful truth which the poverty of his country had imposed on him? How could he tell them, that after all that they had done and suffered with him, they must now ground their arms, and return home, many of them without a decent suit on their backs, or a penny in their pockets?

But he was saved the pain of making this communication; for they soon received it from another quarter, and with circumstances calculated to kindle the fiercest indignation against their country. Letters were industriously circulated through the army, painting in the strongest colours, their own unparalleled sufferings, and the Ingratitude of Congress.

"Confiding in her honor," said the writer, "did you not cheerfully enlist in the service of your country, and for her dear sake encounter all the evils of a soldier's life? Have you not beaten the ice-bound road full many a wintry day, without a shoe to your bleeding feet; and wasted the long bitter night, without a tent, to shelter your heads from the pelting storm? Have you not borne the brunt of many a bloody fight, and from the hands of hard struggling foes torn the glorious prize, YOUR COUNTRY'S INDEPENDENCE? And now after all, after wasting in her service the flower of your days—with bodies broken under arms, and bones filled with the pains and aches of a seven year's war, will you suffer yourselves to be sent home in rags to your families, to spend the sad remains of life in poverty and scorn?—No! my brothers in arms, I trust you will not. I trust you bear no such coward minds. I trust that after having fought so bravely for the rights of others, you will now fight as bravely for your own rights. And now is the accepted time and golden hour of redress, while you have weapons in your hands, the strength of an army to support you, and a beloved General at your head, ready to lead you to that justice which you owe yourselves, and which you have so long but vainly expected from an ungrateful country."

These letters produced, as might have been expected, a most alarming effect. Rage, like a fire in secret, began to burn throughout the camp. Washington soon perceived it. He discovered it in his soldiers as gathered into groupes they stood and talked of their grievances, while with furious looks and gestures they stamped on the earth, and hurled their curses against Congress. Gladdening at such success of his first letters, the writer instantly sent around a second set, still more artful and inflammatory than the first: the passions of the army now rose to a height that threatened instantaneous explosion. But still their eyes, beaming reverence and love, were turned towards their honoured chief, to whom they had ever looked as to a father.

Often had they marked his tears, as, visiting their encampments, he beheld them suffering and sinking under fevers and fluxes, for want of clothes and provisions. Often, had they hushed their complaints, trusting to his promises that Congress would still remember them. But behold! his promises and their hopes are all alike abortive!

And will not Washington, the friend of Justice, and father of his army, avenge them on a government which has thus basely defrauded them and deceived him? There needed but a glance of his approbation to set the whole army in motion. Instantly with fixed bayonets they would have hurled the hated Congress from their seats, and placed their beloved Washington on the throne of St. Tammany. Here, no doubt, the tempter flashed the dangerous diadem before the eyes of our Countryman: but religion at the same time, pointed him to the GREAT LOVER OF ORDER, holding up that crown in comparison of which the diadems of kings are but dross. Animated with such hopes he had long cherished that ardent philanthropy which sighs for Liberty to all countries, and especially to his own. For Liberty he had fought and conquered, and now considered it with all its blessings as at hand. "*Yet a little while, and* America shall become the glory of the earth—a nation of Brothers, enjoying the golden reign of equal laws, and rejoicing under their own vine and fig-tree, and no tyrant to make them afraid. And shall these glorious prospects be darkened? shall they be darkened by WASHINGTON! shall he, ever the friend of his country, become her bitterest enemy, by fixing upon her again the iron yoke of monarchy? shall he! the Father of his army, become their assassin, by establishing a government that shall swallow up their liberties for ever?"

The idea filled his soul with horror. Instead, therefore, of tamely yielding to the wishes of his army to their *own ruin,* he bravely opposes them to their true *good:* and instead of drinking in, with traitorous smile, the hosannas that would make him King, he darkens his brow of Parental displeasure at their impiety. He flies to extinguish their *rising rebellion;* he addresses letters to the officers of the army, desiring them to meet him at an appointed time and place. Happily for America, the voice of Washington still sounded in their ear as the voice of a father. His officers, to a man, all gathered around him; while, with a countenance inspiring veneration and love, he arose and addressed the eager-listening chiefs. He began with reminding them of the great argument for which they had first drawn their swords, i.e. THE LIBERTIES OF THEIR COUNTRY. He applauded that noble spirit with which they had submitted to so many privations—combated so many dangers—and overcome so many difficulties. And now, said he, after having thus waded, like Israel of old, through a *Red Sea* of blood, and withstood the thundering *Sinais* of British fury—after having crushed the fiery serpents of Indian rifles, and trampled down those insidious Amalekites, the tories—after having travelled through a howling *wilderness* of war, and, with the *ark* of your country's liberties in camp, safely arrived on the borders of Canaan, and in sight of the glorious end of all your labours, will you now give yourselves up the dupes of a *"British emissary,"* and for the sordid *flesh-pots* of a few months' pay, rush into civil war, and fall back to a worse than Egyptian bondage? No! my brave countrymen, I trust you will not. I trust, that an army so famed throughout the world for patriotism, will yet maintain its reputation. I trust, that your behaviour on this last, this most trying occasion, will fill up the measure of your heroism, and stamp the American character with never-dying fame. You have achieved miracles, but a greater miracle still remains to be achieved. We have had the glory to conquer our enemies;

now for the greater glory to conquer ourselves. Other armies, after subduing the enemies of their country, have themselves, for *power* and plunder, become her tyrants, and trampled her liberties under foot; be it our nobler ambition, after sufferings unparalleled for our needy country, to return cheerful, though pennyless, to our homes, and patiently wait the rewards which her gratitude will, one day, assuredly betsow. In the mean time, beating our swords into ploughshares, and our bayonets into reaping hooks, let us, as peaceful citizens, cultivate those fields from which, as victorious soldiers, we lately drove the enemy. Thence, as from the noblest of theatres, you shall display a spectacle of patriotism never seen before—you shall teach the delighted world, that men are capable of finding a heaven in noble actions—and you will give occasion to posterity to say, when speaking of your present behaviour, had this day been wanting, the triumph of our fathers' virtues would have been incomplete."

As he spoke, his cheeks, naturally pale, were reddened over with virtue's pure vermillion; while his eyes of cœrulean blue were kindled up with those indescribable fires which fancy lends to an angel orator, animating poor mortals to the sublime of god-like deeds. His words were not in vain. From lips of wisdom, and long-tried love, like his, such counsel wrought as though an oracle had spoke. Instantly a committee of the whole was formed, with general Knox at their head, who, in thirty minutes, reported the following resolutions, which were *unanimously* adopted:

"Resolved—that having engaged in the war from motives of the purest love and zeal for the rights of man, no circumstance of distress or danger shall ever induce us to sully the glory we have acquired at the price of our blood, and eight years' faithful service."

"Resolved—that we continue to have an unshaken confidence in the justice of congress and our country."

"Resolved—that we view with abhorrence, and reject with

disdain, the infamous proposition contained in a late anonymous address to the officers of the army."

The officers then hasted back to their troops, who had been impatiently expecting them; and related Washington's speech. They also stated, as his firm conviction, that "the claims of every soldier would be liquidated, his accounts accurately ascertained, and adequate funds provided for the payment of them, as soon as the circumstances of the nation would permit."

The soldiers listened to this communication with attention, and heard the close of it without a murmur. *"They had no great opinion,* they said, *of congress; but having gone such lengths for duty and old George, they supposed they might as well now go a little farther, and make thorough work of it. A little pay would, to be sure, have been very welcome; and it was a poor military chest that could not afford a single dollar, especially as some of them had hundreds of miles to their homes. But surely the people won't let us starve for a meal's victuals by the way, especially after we have been so long fighting their battles. So, in God's name, we'll even shoulder our knapsacks, whenever our old general shall say the word.*

The next day the breaking up of the army began, which was conducted in the following manner. The troops after breakfast were ordered under arms. On receiving notice that they were ready to move, Washington with his aids, rode out on the plains of their encampment, where he sat on his horse awaiting their arrival. The troops got in motion, and with fifes and muffled drums playing the mournful air of *Roslin Castle,* marched up for the last time, into his presence. Every countenance was shrowded in sorrow. At a signal given, they grounded their arms; then waving their hats, and faintly crying out *"God save great Washington,"* through watery eyes they gave him a long adieu, and wheeled off in files for their native homes. With pensive looks his eye pursued them as they retired, wide spreading over the fields. But when he saw those brave troops who had so long obeyed him, and who had just given such an evidence of their affection, when he saw them slowly descending behind the distant hills, shortly to disappear for ever, then nature stirred all the father within him, and gave him up to tears. But he wept not *"as those without hope."* He rejoiced in the remembrance of HIM who treasures up the toils of the virtuous, and will one day, bestow that reward which *"this world cannot give."*

But the whole army was not disbanded at once. Shortly after this he went down to New-York to finish what remained of his duty as commander in chief, and to prepare to return home. On the last day that he was there, it being known that he meant to set out for Virginia at one o'clock, all his officers, who happened to be in town, assembled at Francis's tavern, where he lodged, to bid him a last farewell. About half after twelve the general entered the room, where an elegant collation was spread, but none tasted it. Conversation was attempted, but it failed. As the clock struck one, the general went to the side-board, and filling out some wine, turned to his officers, and begged they would join him in a glass. Then, with a look of sorrow and a faultering voice, he said, *"Well my brave brothers in arms, we part—perhaps to meet in this life no more. And now I pray God to take you all in his holy keeping, and render your latter days as prosperous as the past have been glorious."*

Soon as they had drunk, he beckoned to general Knox, who approached and pressed his hand in tears of delicious silence. The officers all followed his example, while their manly cheeks, swollen with grief, bespoke sensations too strong for utterance. This tender scene being over, he moved towards the door, followed by his officers. By this time the street from the hotel to the river was filled with light infantry, and thousands of citizens, who all attended him in silence to the water-side, where he was to take boat. Here another pleasing proof of esteem was given him. Instead of the common ferry boat, a barge magnificently decorated, was ready to receive him, with the American jack and colours flying, and manned with thirteen sea-captains, all in elegant blue uniforms. On stepping aboard the barge, he turned towards the people, who stood in vast crowds on the shore, and, waving his hat, bade them a silent adieu, which they in like solemn manner returned, all waving their hats, and without speaking a word. Having received their *honoured freight,* the sons of Neptune, ready with well-poised oars, leap forward to the coxswain's call; then, all at once falling back, with sudden stroke they flash their bending blades into the yielding flood. Swift at their stroke the barge sprung from the shore, and, under the music of echoing row-locks, flew through the waves, followed by the eager gaze of the pensive thousands. The sighing multitude then turned away from the shore with feelings whose source they did not, perhaps, understand. But some, on returning to their homes, spoke to their listening children of what they had seen, and of the honours which belong to such virtue as Washington's.

He lodged that night at Elizabethtown, 15 miles from New-York. The next morning, elate with thoughts of home, he ascended his chariot, and with bounding steeds drove on his way through the lovely country of New-Jersey. This, no doubt, was the pleasantest ride by far that he had known since the dark days of '75. For though joyless winter was spread abroad with her cold clouds, and winds shrill whistling over the flowerless fields, yet to his patriot eye the face of nature shone brighter than in latter years, when clad in springtide green and gold—for it was covered over with the bright mantle of *peace.* His shoulders were freed from the burden of *public cares,* and his heart from the anxieties of *supreme command*—with a father's joy he could look around on the thick settled-country, with all their *little ones,* and flocks, and herds, now no longer exposed to danger.

"Happy farmers! the long winter of war is past and gone—the spring time of PEACE is returned; and the voice of her dove is heard in our land. Restore your wasted farms—spread abroad the fertilizing manure, and prepare again to crown your war-worn fields with joyful crops."

"Happy children! now pour forth again in safety to your schools—treasure up the golden knowledge, and make yourselves the future glory and guardians of your country."

"Happy citizens! hasten to rebuild the ruined temples of your God—and lift your glad songs to HIM the great ruler of war, who aided your feeble arms, and trampled down the mighty enemy beneath your feet."

But often, amidst these happy thoughts, the swift wheeled chariot would bring him in view of fields on which his bleeding memory could not look without a tear.—*"There the battling armies met in thunder—the stormy strife was short; but yonder mournful hillocks point the place where many of our brave heroes sleep: perhaps some good angel has whispered that their fall was not in vain."*

On his journey homewards, he stopped for a moment at Philadelphia, to do an act, which to a mind proudly honest like his, must have been a sublime treat. He stopped to present to the comptroller-general an account of all the public monies which he had spent. Though this account was in his own hand writing, and accompanied with the proper vouchers, yet it will hardly be credited by European statesmen and generals, that, in the course of an eight years' war, he had spent only 12,497*l.* 8*s.* 9*d.* sterling!!

From Philadelphia he hastened on to Annapolis, where congress was then in session, that he might return to that honourable body the commission with which they had entrusted him.

Having always disliked parade, he wished to make his resignation in writing; but congress, it seems, willed otherwise. To see a man voluntarily giving up *power,* was a spectacle not to be met with every day. And that they might have the pleasure of seeing him in this last, and perhaps greatest, act of his public life, they expressed a wish to receive his resignation from his own hand at a full *audience.* The next day, the 23d of December, 1783, was appointed for the purpose. At an early hour the house was crowded. The members of congress, with the grandees of the land, filled the floors; the ladies sparkled in the galleries. At eleven o'clock, Washington was ushered into the house, and conducted to a seat which had been prepared for him, covered with red velvet. After a becoming pause, and information given by the president, that the United States in congress assembled were ready to receive his communication, he arose, and with great brevity and modesty observed, that he had presented himself before them, to resign into their hands with satisfaction the commission which, eight years before, he had accepted with diffidence. He begged to mingle his sincerest congratulations with them, for the glorious result of their united struggles—took no part of the praise to himself, but ascribed all to the blessing of Heaven on the exertions of the nation. Then fervently commending his dearest country to the protection of Almighty God, he bade them an affectionate farewell; and taking leave of all the employments of public life, surrendered up his commission!

Seldom has there been exhibited so charming a display of the power which pre-eminent virtue possesses over the human heart, as on this occasion. Short and simple as was the speech of Washington, yet it seems to have carried back every trembling imagination to the fearful days of '75, when the British fleets and armies were thundering on our coasts, and when nothing was talked of but slavery, confiscation, and executions. And now they saw before them the man to whom they all looked for safety in that gloomy time, and who had completely answered their fond hopes—had stood by them uncorruptible and unshaken—had anticipated their mighty enemy in all his plans—had met him at every point—had thwarted, defeated and blasted all his hopes—and, victory after victory won, had at length laid his strong legions in dust or in chains, and had secured to his country a glorious independence, with the fairest chance of being one of the most respectable and happy nations of the earth—and, in consequence of all this, had so completely won the hearts of his army and his nation, that he could perhaps have made himself their *master*—at all events, a Cæsar or a Cromwell would, at the hazard of a million of lives, made the sacrilegious attempt. Yet they now saw this man scorning to abuse his power to the degradation of his country,—but, on the contrary, treating her with the most sacred respect—dutifully bowing before her *delegated presence,* the congress—cheerfully returning the commission she had entrusted him with—piously laying down his extensive powers at her feet—and modestly falling back into the humble condition of the rest of her children. The sight of their great countryman, already so beloved, and now acting so generous, so godlike a part, produced an effect beyond the power of words to express. Their feelings of admiration and affection were too delicious, too big, *for utterance*. Every countenance was swollen with sentiment, and a flood of tears gushed from every eye, which, though a silent, was perhaps the richest offering of veneration and esteem ever paid to a human being.

Having discharged this last great debt to his country, the next morning, early, he ascended his chariot, and listened with joy to the rattling wheels, now running off his last day's journey to Mount Vernon. Ah! could gloomy tyrants but feel what Washington felt that day, when, sweeping along the road, with grateful heart, he revolved the mighty work which he had finished—*his country saved, and his conscience clear;* they would tear off the accursed purple, and starting from their blood-stained thrones, like Washington seek true happiness in making others happy.

O WASHINGTON! thrice glorious name,
What due rewards can man decree?
Empires are far below thy aim,
And sceptres have no charms for thee;
Duty alone has thy regard,
In her thou seek'st thy great reward.

CHAPTER XI

Washington again on his farm—sketch of his conduct there—suggests the importance of inland navigation—companies forming—urges a reform of the old constitution—appointed president of the United States—great difficulties to encounter—gloriously surmounts them

To be happy in every situation is an argument of wisdom seldom attained by man. It proves that the heart is set on that which alone can ever completely satisfy it, i.e. the imitation of God in benevolent and useful life. This was the happy case with Washington. To establish in his country the golden reign of liberty was his grand wish. In the accomplishment of this he seeks his happiness. He abhors war; but, if war be necessary, to this end he bravely encounters it. His ruling passion must be obeyed. He beats his ploughshare into a sword, and exchanges the peace and pleasures of his farm for the din and dangers of the camp. Having won the great prize for which he contended, he returns to his plough. His military habits are laid by with the same ease as he would throw off an old coat. The camp, with all its parade and noise, is forgotten. He awakes, in his silent chambers at Mount Vernon, without sighing for the sprightly drums and fifes that used to salute him every morning. Happy among his domestics, he does not regret the shining ranks, that, with ported arms used to pay him homage. The *useful citizen* is the high character he wishes to act—his sword turned into a ploughshare is his favourite instrument, and his beloved farm his stage. Agriculture had been always his delight. To breathe the *pure healthful* air of a *farm,* perfumed with odorous flowers, and enriched with golden harvests, and with numerous flocks and herds, appeared to him a life nearest connected with individual and national happiness. To this great object he turns all his attention, bends all his exertions. He writes to the most skilful farmers, not only in America but in *England* (for Washington was incapable of bearing malice against a people who had made friends with his country); he writes, I say, to the ablest farmers in America and England, for instructions how best to cultivate and improve his lands—what grains, what grasses, what manures would best suit his soils; what shrubs are fittest for fences, and what animals for labour.

But, to a soul large and benevolent like his, to beautify his own farm, and to enrich his own family, seemed like doing nothing. To see the whole nation engaged in glorious toils, filling themselves with plenty, and inundating the sea-ports with food and raiment for the poor and needy of distant nations—this was his godlike ambition. But, knowing that his beloved countrymen could not long enjoy the honor and advantage of such glorious toils, unless they could easily convey their swelling harvests to their *own markets,* he hastened to rouse them to a proper sense of the infinite importance of forming canals and cuts between all the fine rivers that run through the United States. To give the greater weight to his counsel, he had first ascended the *sources* of those great rivers—ascertained the distance between them—the obstacles in the way of navigation—and the probable expense of removing them.

Agreeable to his wishes, two wealthy companies were soon formed to extend the navigation of James River and Potomac, the noblest rivers in Virginia. Struck with the exceeding benefit which both themselves and their country would speedily derive from a plan which he had not only suggested, but had taken such pains and expense to recommend, they pressed him to accept one hundred and fifty shares of the company's stock, amounting to near 40,000 dollars! But he instantly refused it, saying, "what will the world think if they should hear that I have taken 40,000 dollars for this affair? Will they not be apt to suspect, on my next proposition, that money is my motive? Thus, for the sake of money, which indeed I never coveted from my country, I may lose the power to do her some service, which may be worth more than all money!!"

But, while engaged in this goodly work, he was suddenly alarmed by the appearance of an evil, which threatened to put an end to all his well-meant labours for ever—this was, the *beginning dissolution* of the federal government!! The framers of that fair but flimsy fabric, having put it together according to the square and compass of equal rights and mutual interests, thought they had done enough. The good sense and virtue of the nation, it was supposed, would form a foundation of rock whereon it would safely rest, in spite of all commotions, foreign or domestic.

"But, alas!" said Washington, "experience has shown that men, unless constrained, will seldom do what is for their own good. With joy I once beheld my country feeling the liveliest sense of her rights, and maintaining them with a spirit apportioned to their worth. With joy I have seen all the wise of Europe looking on her with admiration, and all the good with hope, that her fair example would regenerate the old world, and restore the blessings of equal government to long oppressed HUMANITY. But alas! in place of maintaining this glorious attitude, America is herself rushing into disorder and dissolution. We have powers sufficient for self-defence and glory: but those powers are not exerted. For fear congress should abuse it, the people will not trust their power with congress. Foreigners insult and injure us with impunity, for congress has no power to chastise them.—Ambitious men stir up factions; congress possesses no power to scourge them. Public creditors call for their money; congress has no power to collect it. In short, we cannot long subsist as a nation,

without lodging somewhere a power that may command the full energies of the nation for defence from all its enemies, and for supply of all its wants. The people will soon be tired of such a government—they will sigh for a change—and many of them already begin to talk of *monarchy*, without horror!!"

In this, as in all cases of apprehended danger, his pen knew no rest. The leading characters of the nation were roused; and a CONVENTION was formed of deputies from the several states, to revise and amend the general government. Of this convention Washington was unanimously chosen president. —Their session commenced in Philadelphia, May, 1787, and ended in October. The fruit of their six months labour was the present excellent CONSTITUTION, which was no sooner adopted, than the eyes of the whole nation were fixed on him as the president.

Being now in his 57th year, and wedded to his farm and family, he had no wish to come forward again to the cares and dangers of public life. Ease was now become almost as necessary as dear to him. His reputation was already at the highest; and as to money, in the service of his country he had always refused it. These things considered, together with his acknowledged modesty and disinterestedness, we can hardly doubt the correctness of the declaration he made, when he said, that, *"the call to the magistracy was the most unwelcome he had ever heard."*

However, as soon as it was officially notified to him, in the spring of 1789, that he was unanimously elected president of the United States, and that congress, then sitting in New-York, was impatient to see him in the chair, he set out for that city. Then all along the roads where he passed, were seen the most charming proofs of that enthusiasm with which the hearts of all delighted to honour him. If it was only said, *"General Washington is coming,"* it was enough. The inhabitants all hastened from their houses to the highways, to get a sight of their great countryman; while the people of the towns, hearing of his approach, sallied out, horse and foot, to meet him. In eager throngs, men, women, and children pressed upon his steps, as waves in crowding ridges pursue the course of a ship through the ocean. And as a new succession of waves is ever ready to take the place of those which had just ended their chase in playful foam, so it was with the ever-gathering crowds that followed their Washington.

"On reaching the western banks of Schuylkill," said a gentleman who was present, "I was astonished at the concourse of people that overspread the country, apparently from Gray's ferry to the city. Indeed one would have thought that the whole population of Philadelphia was come out to meet him. And to see so many thousands of people on foot, on horseback, and in coaches, all voluntarily waiting upon and moving along with *one* man, struck me with strangely agreeable sensations. Surely, thought I, there must be a divinity in goodness, that mankind should thus delight to honour it."

His reception at Trenton was more than flattering. It was planned, they said, by the ladies, and indeed bore marks that it could have been done only by them. The reader must remember, that it was near this place that the fair sex in '76 suffered such cruel indignities from the enemy; and also that it was here that Providence in the same year enabled Washington so severely to chastise them for it. The women are not apt to forget their benefactors. Hearing that Washington was on his way to Trenton, they instantly held a caucus among themselves, to devise ways and means to display their gratitude to him. Under their direction, the bridge over the Sanpink (a narrow creek running through Trenton, from whose opposite banks Washington and the British once fought) was decorated with a triumphal arch, with this inscription in large figures:

DECEMBER 26, 1776.

THE HERO WHO DEFENDED THE MOTHERS, WILL ALSO PROTECT THE DAUGHTERS.

He approached the bridge on its south side, amidst the heartiest shouts of congratulating thousands, while on the north side were drawn up several hundreds of little girls, dressed in snow-white robes, with temples adorned with garlands, and baskets of flowers on their arms. Just behind them stood long rows of young virgins, whose fair faces, of sweetest red, and white, highly animated by the occasion, looked quite angelic—and, back of them, in crowds stood their venerable mothers. As Washington slowly drove off the bridge, the female voices all began, sweet as the first wakings of the Eolian harp, and thus they rolled the song:

Welcome, mighty chief! once more
Welcome to this grateful shore
Now no mercenary foe
Aims again the fatal blow,
Aims at thee the fatal blow.
Virgins fair, and matrons grave,
(These thy conquering arm did save!)
Build for thee triumphal bowers.
Strew, ye fair, his way with flowers;
Strew your hero's way with flowers.

While singing the last lines, they strewed the way with flowers before him.

Some have said that they could see in his altered looks, that he remembered the far different scenes of '76; for that they saw him wipe a tear. No doubt 'twas the sweet tear of gratitude to him who had brought him to see this happy day.

At New-York the behaviour of the citizens was equally expressive of the general veneration and esteem. The ships in the harbour were all dressed in their flags and streamers;

and the wharves where he landed richly decorated. At the water's edge he was received by an immense concourse of the joyful citizens, and amidst the mingled thunder of guns and acclamations, was conducted to his lodgings. Such honours would have intoxicated most men; but to a mind, like his, habitually conversant with the far sublimer subjects of the Christian philosophy, they must have looked quite puerile. Indeed, it appears from a note made in his Journal that very evening, that he regarded all these marks of public favour rather as calls to humility than pride. "The display of boats on this occasion," says he, "with vocal and instrumental music on board, the decorations of the ships, the roar of cannon, and the loud acclamations of the people, as I passed along the wharves, gave me as much pain as pleasure, contemplating the probable reverse of this scene after all my endeavours to [do] good."

It was on the 23d of April, 1789, that he arrived in New-York: and on the 30th, after taking the oath, as president of the United States, to *preserve, protect and defend the constitution,* he entered upon the duties of his office.

As things then stood, even his bitterest enemies, if he had any, might have said *"happy man be his dole!"* for he came to the helm in a perilous and fearful season. Like, *chaos, "in the olden time,"* our government was *"without form and void, and darkness dwelt upon the face of the deep."* Enemies innumerable threatened the country, both from within and without, abroad and at home—the people of *three continents* at daggers drawn with the young republic of America!

The pirates of Morocco laying their uncircumcised hands on our rich commerce in the Mediterranean!

The British grumbling and threatening war.

The Spaniards shutting up the Mississippi!

The Kentuckians in great wrath! threatening to break the union, and join the Spaniards!

The Indian nations, from Canada to Georgia, unburying the tomahawk!

North-Carolina and Rhode-Island blowing on the confederacy! strong parties in other states against it!—and an alarming insurrection in Massachusetts! While, to combat all these enemies, the United-States had but 600 regular troops!! and, though eighty millions of dollars in debt, they had not one cent in the treasury!!! Here, certainly, if ever, was the time *to try a man's soul.* But Washington despaired not. Glowing with the love of his country, and persuaded that his country still enjoyed an opportunity to be great and happy, he resolved, whatever it might cost him, that nothing should be wanting on his part to fill up the measure of her glory. *But first of all,* in his *inaugural speech,* he called upon Congress and his countrymen, to look up to God for his blessing; next as to *themselves,* to be most industrious, honourable, and *united,* as became men responsible to ages yet unborn, for all the blessings of a republican government, *now,* and perhaps for the *last time,* at stake on *their wisdom and virtue;*—then as to himself. *"I feel,"* said he, *"my incompetency of political skill and abilities. Integrity and firmness are all I can promise. These, I know will never forsake me, although I may be deserted, by all men: and of the consolations to be derived from these, under no circumstances can the world ever deprive me."*—And last of all, as in a crazy ship at sea, tost by furious winds, no pilot can save without the aid of able seamen, Washington prudently rallied around him the wisest of all his countrymen.

Mr. Jefferson, secretary of foreign affairs.
Col. Hamilton, secretary of the treasury.
General Knox, secretary of war.
Edmund Randolph, attorney-general.
John Jay, chief justice.

John Rutledge, James Wilson, John Cushing, Robert Harrison, John Blair,	associate judges.

These judicious preparations being made for the storm, (Heaven's blessing invoked, and the ablest pilots embarked with him,) Washington then seized the helm, with a gallant *hard-a-lee,* luffed up his ship at once to the gale, hoping yet to shoot the hideous gulphs that threatened all around.

His first attention was turned to the call of *Humanity,* i. e. to satisfy and make peace with the Indians. This was soon done; partly by *presents,* and by establishing in their country, houses of *fair trade,* which, by preventing *frauds,* prevent those grudges that lead to *private* murders, and thence to public disturbances and wars. Some of the Indian tribes, despising these friendly efforts of Washington, were obliged to be drubbed into peace, which service was done for them by General Wayne, in 1794—but not until many lives had been lost in *preceding defeats;* owing chiefly, it was said, to the very intemperate passions and potations of some of their officers. However, after the first shock, the loss of these poor souls was not much lamented. Tall young fellows, who could easily get their half dollar a day at the healthful and glorious labours of the plough, to go and enlist and rust among the lice and itch of a camp, for *four dollars a month,* were certainly not worth their country's crying about.

Washington's friendly overtures to Spain were equally fortunate. Believing that he desired nothing but what was perfectly *just,* and what both God and man would support him in, she presently agreed to *negotiate*—the navigation of the Mississippi was given up—the Kentuckians were satisfied —and Spain and the United States lived on good terms all the rest of his days.

Washington then tried his hands with the British. But alas! he soon found that they were not made of such pliable stuff as the Indians and Spaniards. Nor had he the British alone to complain of. He presently found it as hard to please his *own countrymen,* in the matter of a treaty, as to please *them.*

For whether it was that the two nations still retained a most unchristian recollection of what they had suffered from one another during the past war—or whether, more unchristianly still, they felt the odious spirit of *rivals,* and sickened at each other's prosperity—or whether each nation thought that the ships of the other were navigated by *their seamen;* but so it was that the prejudices of the two people, though sprung from the same progenitors, ran so high as to render it extremely difficult for Washington to settle matters between them. But it was at length happily effected, without the horrors of another war. Though the *treaty* which brought about this desirable event was entirely execrated by great numbers of sensible and honest men no doubt, yet Washington, led, as he says, by duty and humanity, ratified it.

If the signing of the treaty displayed his *firmness,* the operation of it has, perhaps, shewn his *wisdom.* For, surely, since that time, no country like this ever so progressed in the public and private blessings of industry, wealth, population, and morals. Whether greater, or, indeed, equal blessings would have resulted from a bloody war with England, at that time, let others determine.

But scarcely had Washington got clear of his embarrassments with Britain, before still worse were thrown in his way by France.

The cause was this—"The French army, as Doctor Franklin observes, having served apprenticeship to LIBERTY, in America, on going back to France, set up for themselves." Throughout the kingdom, *wherever they went,* they could talk of nothing but the Americans. "Ah, happy people!" said they, "neither oppressing nor oppressed, they mingle together as one great family of brothers; where every man is free, every man labours for himself, and wipes, with joy, the sweat from his brow, because 'tis the earnest of plenteous food and clothing, education, and delights, for his children!"

The people every where listened with eagerness to these descriptions of American happiness, and sighed to think of their own wretchedness. The smothered fire soon broke out, the press teemed with papers and pamphlets on the RIGHTS OF MAN—the TRUE ENDS OF GOVERNMENT,—and the BLESSINGS OF LIBERTY. The eyes of the great nation were presently opened to a sight of her degraded and wretched state. Then suddenly springing up, like a mighty giantess from the hated bed of violation and dishonour, she began a course of vengeance as terrible as it had been long delayed. The unfortunate king and queen were quickly brought low.—The heads of her tyrants every where bounded on the floors of the guillotine, while in every place dogs licked the blood of nobles, and the bodies of great lords were scattered like dung over the face of the earth.

Fearing that, if France, were suffered to go on at this rate, there would not, in a little time, be a CROWN left in Europe, the crowned heads all confederated to stop her. The whole surrounding world, both by land and water, was in commotion; and tremendous fleets and armies poured in from every side, to overwhelm her. With unanimity and valour equal to their danger, the war-loving Gauls rushed forth in crowding millions to meet their foes. The mighty armies joined in battle, appearing, to the terrified eye, as if the whole human race were rushing together for mutual destruction. But not content with setting the eastern world on fire, the furious combatants like Milton's warring SPIRITS tearing up and flinging mountains and islands at each other) flew to America to seize and drag her into their war.

Flaming on this errand, Mr. Genet lighted on our continent as an envoy from France. He was received with joy as a brother republican. The people every where welcomed him as the representative of a beloved nation, to whom, under God, they owed their liberties. Grand dinners were given—sparkling bumpers were filled, and standing up round the vast convivial board, with joined hands and cheeks glowing with friendship and the generous juice, they rent the air with—*"health and fraternity to the sister republics of France and America."*

Washington joined in the general hospitality to the stranger. He extolled the valour, and congratulated the victories of his brave countrymen. *"Born, sir, said he, in the land of Liberty, for whose sake I have spent my best years of life in war, I cannot but feel a trembling anxiety whenever I see an oppressed people drawing their swords and rearing aloft the sacred banners of freedom."*

Enraptured at finding in America such a cordial spirit towards his country, Mr. Genet instantly set himself to call it into the fullest exertion. And by artfully ringing the changes on *British cruelty,* and *French generosity,* to the Americans, he so far succeeded as to prevail on some persons in Charleston to commence the equipment of privateers against the British.—Dazzled by the lustre of a *false gratitude* to one nation, they lost sight of their *horrid injustice* to another; and during the profoundest peace between England and America, when the American planters, by their flour, rice, and cotton, were making money almost as fast as if they had mints upon their estates; and, on the other hand, the British artizans were driving on their manufactures day and night for the Americans—in this sacred season and state of things, certain persons in Charleston, began to equip privateers against England.

Grieved that *his countrymen should be capable* of such an outrage against *justice,* against *humanity,* and every thing sacred among men; and equally grieved to see them so far forget, so far *belittle themselves* as to become willing cat's paws of one nation, to tear another to pieces, he instantly issued his *proclamation,* stating it as the *"duty and therefore the interest of the United States to preserve the strictest neutrality between the belligerents, and prohibiting the citizens of the United States, from all manner of interference in the unhappy contest."*

This so enraged Mr. Genet, that he threatened to appeal from the president to the people! i. e. in plain English to try to overthrow the government of the United States!!

But, thank God, the American people were too wise and virtuous to hear these things without feeling and expressing a suitable indignation. They rallied around their beloved president; and soon gave this most inconsiderate stranger to understand, that he had insulted the sacred person of their father.

Washington bore this insult with his usual good temper! but at the same time took such prudent measures with the French government, that Mr. Genet was quickly recalled.

Having at length attained the acme of all his wishes—having lived to see a general and efficient government adopted, and for eight years in successful operation, exalting his country from the brink of infamy and ruin to the highest ground of prosperity and honour, both at home and abroad: *abroad,* peace with the Indians—with Britain—with Spain—and, some slight heart-burnings excepted, peace with France; and with all the world: at *home,* her shining ploughshares laying open the best treasures of the earth—her ships flying over every sea—distant nations feeding on her bread, and manufacturing her staples—her revenue rapidly increasing with her *credit, religion, learning, arts,* and whatever tends to national glory and happiness, he determined to lay down that load of public care which he had borne so long, and which, now in his 66th year he found was growing too heavy for him. But feeling towards his countrymen the solicitude of a father for his children, over whom he had long watched, but was about to leave to themselves; and fearing, on the *one hand,* that they might go astray, and, hoping, on the other, that from his long labours of love, he might be permitted to impart the counsels of his long experience, he drew up for them a *farewell address,* which the filial piety of the nation has since called *"his Legacy."*

As this little piece, about the length of an ordinary sermon, may do as much good to the people of America as any sermon ever preached, that DIVINE ONE on the mount excepted, I shall offer no apology for laying it before them, especially as I well know that they will all read it with the feelings of children reading the last letter of a once-loved father now in his grave. And who knows but it may check for a while that fatal flame of discord which has destroyed all the once GLORIOUS REPUBLICS of ANTIQUITY, and here now at length in the United States has caught upon the last republic that's left on the face of the earth?

WASHINGTON'S LAST WORDS

To the People of the United States.

September, 1796.

FRIENDS AND FELLOW-CITIZENS,

"THE period for a new election of a citizen, to administer the executive government of the United States, being not far distant—and the time actually arrived when your thoughts must be employed in designating the person who is to be clothed with that important trust—it appears to me proper, especially as it may conduce to a more distinct expression of the public voice, that I should now apprize you of the resolution I have formed, to decline being considered among the number of those out of whom a choice is to be made.

"I beg you, at the same time, to do me the justice to be assured, that this resolution has not been taken without a strict regard to all the considerations appertaining to the relation which binds a dutiful citizen to his country; and that, in withdrawing the tender of service, which silence in my situation might imply, I am influenced by no diminution of zeal for your future interest, no deficiency of grateful respect for your past kindness; but am supported by a full conviction, that the step is compatible with both.

"The acceptance of, and continuance hitherto in the office to which your suffrages have twice called me, have been a uniform sacrifice of inclination to the opinion of duty, and to a deference for what appeared to be your desire. I constantly hoped, that it would have been much earlier in my power, consistently with motives which I was not at liberty to disregard, to return to that retirement from which I had been reluctantly drawn. The strength of my inclination to do this, previous to the last election, had even led to the preparation of an address to declare it to you: but mature reflection on the then perplexed and critical posture of our affairs with foreign nations, and the unanimous advice of persons entitled to my confidence, impelled me to abandon the idea.

"I rejoice that the state of your concerns, external as well as internal, no longer renders the pursuit of inclination incompatible with the sentiment of duty or propriety; and am persuaded, whatever partiality may be retained for my services, that, in the present circumstances of our country, you will not disapprove my determination to retire.

"The impressions with which I first undertook the arduous trust, were explained on the proper occasion. In the discharge of this trust, I will only say, that I have, with good intentions, contributed towards the organization and administration of the government, the best exertions of which a very fallible judgment was capable. Not unconscious, in the outset, of the inferiority of my qualifications, experience in my own eyes, perhaps still more in the eyes of others, has strengthened the motives to diffidence of myself: and every day the increasing weight of years admonishes me more and more that the shade of retirement is as necessary to me as it will be welcome. Satisfied that if any circumstances have given peculiar value to my services, they were temporary, I have the consolation to believe, that while choice and prudence invite me to q[illegible] the political scene, patriotism does not forbid it.

"In looking forward to the moment which is intended to terminate the career of my public life, my feelings do not permit me to suspend the deep acknowledgment of that debt of gratitude which I owe to my beloved country, for the many honours it has conferred upon me; still more for the stedfast confidence with which it has supported me; and for the opportunities I have thence enjoyed of manifesting my inviolable attachment, by services faithful and persevering, though in usefulness unequal to my zeal. If benefits have resulted to our country from these services, let it always be remembered to your praise, and as an instructive example in our annals, that, under circumstances, in which the passions, agitated in every direction, were liable to mislead—amidst appearances sometimes dubious—vicissitudes of fortune often discouraging—in situations in which not unfrequently want of success has countenanced the spirit of criticism—the constancy of your support was the essential prop of the efforts, and a guarantee of the plans by which they were effected. Profoundly penetrated with this idea, I shall carry it with me to my grave, as a strong incitement to unceasing vows that Heaven may continue to you the choicest tokens of its beneficence; that your union and brotherly affection may be perpetual; that the free constitution, which is the work of your hands, may be sacredly maintained; that its administration in every department may be stamped with wisdom and virtue; that, in fine, the happiness of the people of these states, under the auspices of Heaven, may be made complete, by so careful a preservation and so prudent a use of liberty, as will acquire to them the glory of recommending it to the applause, the affection, and the adoption of every nation which is yet a stranger to it.

"Here, perhaps, I ought to stop. But a solicitude for your welfare, which cannot end but with my life, and the appre-

r, natural to that solicitude, urge me, on
e the present, to offer to your solemn con-
nd to recommend to your frequent review, some
, which are the result of much reflection, of no
erable observation, and which appear to me all-
i. tant to the permanency of your felicity as a people. These will be offered to you with the more freedom, as you can only see in them the disinterested warnings of a parting friend, who can possibly have no personal motive to bias his counsel. Nor can I forget, as an encouragement to it, your indulgent reception of my sentiments on a former and not dissimilar occasion.

"Interwoven as is the love of liberty with every ligament of your hearts, no recommendation of mine is necessary to fortify or confirm the attachment.

"The unity of government, which constitutes you one people, is also now dear to you. It is justly so; for it is a main pillar in the edifice of your real independence, the support of your tranquillity at home, your peace abroad; of your safety; of your prosperity; of that very liberty which you so highly prize. But as it is easy to foresee, that from different causes, and from different quarters, much pains will be taken, many artifices employed, to weaken in your minds the conviction of this truth; as this is the point in your political fortress, against which the batteries of internal and external enemies will be most constantly and actively (though often covertly and insidiously) directed, it is of *infinite moment,* that you should properly estimate the *immense* value of your *national union,* to your collective and individual happiness; that you should cherish a cordial, habitual, and immoveable attachment to it; accustoming yourselves to think and speak of it as of the palladium of your political safety and prosperity; watching for its preservation with jealous anxiety; discountenancing whatever may suggest even a suspicion that it can in any event be abandoned; and indignantly frowning upon the first dawning of every attempt to alien any portion of our country from the rest, or to enfeeble the sacred ties which now link together the various parts.

"For this you have every inducement of sympathy and interest. Citizens by birth or choice, of a common country, that country has a right to concentrate your affections. The name of AMERICAN, which belongs to you in your national capacity, must always exalt the just pride of patriotism, more than any appellation derived from local discriminations. With slight shades of difference, you have the same religion, manners, habits, and political principles. You have, in a common cause, fought and triumphed together. The independence and liberty you possess are the work of joint councils, and joint efforts, of common dangers, sufferings, and successes.

"But these considerations, however powerfully they address themselves to your sensibility, are greatly outweighed by those which apply more immediately to your interest. Here every portion of our country finds the most commanding motives for carefully guarding and preserving the union of the whole.

"The NORTH, in an unrestrained intercourse with the SOUTH, protected by the equal laws of a common government, finds in the productions of the latter, great additional resources of maritime and commercial enterprise, and precious materials of manufacturing industry. The SOUTH, in the same intercourse benefiting by the agency of the NORTH, sees its agriculture grow, and its commerce expand. Turning partly into its own channels the seamen of the NORTH, it finds its particular navigation invigorated: and while it contributes, in different ways, to nourish and increase the general mass of the national navigation, it looks forward to the protection of a maritime strength, to which itself is unequally adapted.—The EAST, in a like intercourse with the WEST, already finds, and in the progressive improvement of interior communications, by land and water, will more and more find a valuable vent for the commodities which it brings from abroad, or manufactures at home.—The WEST derives from the EAST supplies requisite to its growth and comfort—and what is, perhaps, of still greater consequence, it must of necessity owe the SECURE enjoyment of indispensable OUTLETS for its own productions, to the weight, influence, and the future maritime strength of the Atlantic side of the union, directed by an indissoluble community of interest, as ONE NATION. Any other tenure by which the WEST can hold this essential advantage, whether derived from its own separate strength, or from an *apostate* and *unnatural* connexion with any foreign power, must be intrinsically precarious.

"While then every part of our country thus feels an immediate and particular interest in union, all the parties combined cannot fail to find, in the united mass of means and efforts, greater strength, greater resource, proportionably greater security from external danger, a less frequent interruption of their peace by foreign nations; and, what is of inestimable value, they must derive from union an exemption from those broils and wars between themselves, which so frequently afflict neighbouring countries, not tied together by the same government; which their own rivalships alone would be sufficient to produce, but which opposite foreign alliances, attachments, and intrigues, would stimulate and embitter. Hence, likewise, they will avoid the necessity of those overgrown military establishments, which, under any form of government, are inauspicious to liberty, and which are to be regarded as particularly hostile to republican liberty. In this sense it is, that your union ought to be considered as a main prop of your liberty, and that the love of the one ought to endear to you the preservation of the other.

"These considerations speak a persuasive language to every reflecting and virtuous mind, and exhibit the continuance of the UNION as a primary object of patriotic desire. Is there a doubt, whether a common government can embrace so large a sphere? Let experience solve it. To listen to mere speculation in such a case were criminal. We are authorized to hope, that a proper organization of the whole, with the auxiliary agency of governments for the respective subdivisions, will afford a happy issue to the experiment. 'Tis well worth a fair and full experiment. With such powerful and obvious motives to union, affecting all parts of our country, while experience shall not have demonstrated its impracticability, there will always be reason to distrust the patriotism of those, who in any quarter may endeavour to weaken its bands.

"In contemplating the causes which may disturb our union, it occurs as a matter of serious concern, that any ground should have been furnished for characterizing parties by GEOGRAPHICAL discriminations—NORTHERN and SOUTHERN—ATLANTIC and WESTERN; whence designing men may endeavour to excite a belief that there is a real difference of local interests and views. One of the expedients of party to acquire influence, within particular districts, is to misrepresent the opinions and aims of other districts. You cannot shield yourselves too much against the jealousies and heart-burnings which spring from these misrepresentations. They tend to render alien to each other those who ought to be bound together by fraternal affection. The inhabitants of our western country have lately had a useful lesson on this head. They have seen, in the negotiation by the executive, and in the unanimous ratification by the senate, of the treaty with Spain, and in the universal satisfaction at that event throughout the United States, a decisive proof how unfounded were the suspicions propagated among them, of a policy in the general government, and in the Atlantic states, unfriendly to their interest in regard to the MISSISSIPPI. They have been witnesses to the formation of two treaties, that with Great Britain, and that with Spain, which secure to them every thing they could desire, in respect to our foreign relations, towards confirming their prosperity. Will it not be their wisdom to rely for the preservation of these advantages on the union by which they were procured? Will they not henceforth be deaf to those advisers, if such there are, who would sever them from their brethren, and connect them with aliens?

"To the efficacy and permanency of your union, a government for the whole is indispensable. No alliances, however strict, between the parts, can be an adequate substitute. They must inevitably experience the infractions and interruptions which all alliances in all times have experienced. Sensible of the momentous truth, you have improved upon your first essay, by the adoption of a constitution of government better calculated than your former for an intimate union, and for the efficacious management of your common concerns. This government, the off-spring of your own choice, uninfluenced and unawed, adopted upon full investigation and mature deliberation, completely free in its principles, in the distribution of its powers, uniting security with energy, and containing within itself a provision for its own amendment, has a just claim to your confidence and your support. Respect for its authority, compliance with its laws, acquiescence in its measures, are duties enjoined by the fundamental maxims of true liberty. The basis of our political systems is the right of the people to make and alter their constitutions of government. But the constitution which at any time exists, till changed by an explicit and authentic act of the whole people, is sacredly obligatory upon all. The very idea of the power and the right of the people to establish government, pre-supposes the duty of every individual to obey the established government.

"All obstructions to the execution of the laws, all combinations and associations, under whatever plausible character, with a real design to direct, controul, counteract, or awe the regular deliberation and action of the constituted authorities, are destructive of this fundamental principle, and of fatal tendency. They serve to organize faction, to give it an artificial and extraordinary force—to put in the place of the delegated will of the nation the will of a party, often a small, but artful and enterprising minority of the community; and, according to the alternate triumphs of different parties, to make the public administration the mirror of the ill-concerted and incongruous project of faction, rather than the organ of consistent and wholesome plans, digested by common counsels, and modified by mutual interests.

"However combinations or associations of the above description may now and then answer popular ends, they are likely in the course of time and things to become potent engines, by which cunning, ambitious, and unprincipled men will be enabled to subvert the *power of the people;* and to usurp *to themselves* the reins of government; destroying afterwards the *very engines* which have lifted them to unjust dominion.

"Towards the preservation of your government, and the permanency of your present happy state, it is requisite, not only that you speedily discountenance irregular oppositions to its acknowledged authority, but also that you resist with care the spirit of innovation upon its principles, however specious the pretexts. One method of assault may be to effect, in the forms of the constitution, alterations which will impair the energy of the system, and thus to undermine what cannot be directly overthrown. In all the changes to which you may be invited, remember that time and habit are at least as necessary to fix the true character of government, as of other human institutions; that experience is the surest standard, by which to test the real tendency of the existing constitution of a country; that facility in changes, upon the credit of mere hypothesis and opinion, exposes to perpetual change, from the endless variety of hypothesis and opinion; and remember, especially, that for the efficient management of your common interests, in a country so extensive as ours, a government of as much vigour as is consistent with the perfect security of liberty is indispensable. Liberty itself will find in such a government, with powers properly distributed and adjusted, its surest guardian. It is, indeed, little else than a name, where the government is too feeble to withstand the enterprises of faction, to confine each member of the society within the limits prescribed by the laws, and to maintain all in the secure and tranquil enjoyment of the rights of person and property.

"I have already intimated to you the danger of the parties in the state, with particular reference to the founding of them on geographical discriminations. Let me now take a more comprehensive view, and warn you in the most solemn manner against the baneful effects of the spirit of party, generally.

"This spirit, unfortunately, is inseparable from our nature, having its root in the strongest passion of the human mind. It exists under different shapes in all governments, more or less stifled, controuled, or repressed; but in those of the popular form, it is seen in its greatest rankness, and is truly their worst enemy.

"The alternate domination of one faction over another, sharpened by the spirit of revenge natural to party dissention, which, in different ages and countries, has perpetrated the most horrid enormities, is itself frightful despotism. But this leads at length to a formal and permanent despotism. The disorders and miseries which result, gradually incline the minds of men to seek security and repose in the absolute power of an individual; and, sooner or later, the chief of some prevailing faction, more able or more fortunate than his competitors, turns this disposition to the purposes of his own elevation, on the ruins of public liberty.

"Without looking forward to an extremity of this kind (which nevertheless ought not to be entirely out of sight,) the common and continual mischiefs of the spirit of party are sufficient to make it the interest and duty of a wise people to discourage and restrain it.

"It serves always to distract the public councils, and enfeeble the public administration. It agitates the community with ill-founded jealousies and false alarms; kindles the animosity of one part against another; foments occasionally riot and insurrection; and opens the door to foreign influence and corruption, which find a facilitated access to the government itself through the channels of party passions. Thus the policy and will of one country are subjected to the policy and will of another.

"There is an opinion that parties in free countries are useful checks upon the administration of the government, and serve to keep alive the spirit of liberty. This, within certain limits, is probably true; and, in governments of a monarchical cast, patriotism may look with indulgence, if not with favour, upon the spirit of party. But in those of the popular character, in governments purely elective, it is a spirit not to be encouraged. From their natural tendency, it is certain there will always be enough of the spirit for every salutary purpose. And there being constant danger of excess, the effort ought to be, by force of public opinion, to mitigate and assuage it. A fire not to be quenched, it demands a uniform vigilance to prevent its bursting into a flame, lest, instead of warming, it should consume.

"It is important, likewise, that the habits of thinking in a free country should inspire caution, in those entrusted with its administration, to confine themselves within their respective constitutional spheres, avoiding in the exercise of the powers of one department to encroach upon another. The spirit of encroachment tends to consolidate the powers of all the departments in one, and thus to create, whatever the form of government, a real despotism. A just estimate of that love of power, and proneness to abuse it, which predominates in the human heart, is sufficient to satisfy us of the truth of this position. The necessity of reciprocal checks in the exercise of political power, by dividing and distributing it into different depositories, and constituting each the guardian of public weal against invasions by the others, has been evinced by experiments ancient and modern: some of them in our country, and under our own eyes. To preserve them must be as necessary as to institute them. If, in the opinion of the people, the distribution or modification of the constitutional powers be in any particular wrong, let it be corrected by an amendment in the way which the constitution designates.—But let there be no change by usurpation; for though this, in one instance, may be the instrument of good, it is the customary weapon by which free governments are destroyed.—The precedent must always greatly overbalance in permanent evil any partial or transient benefit which the use can at any time yield.

"Of all the dispositions and habits which lead to political prosperity, religion and morality are indispensable supports.—In vain would that man claim the tribute of patriotism, who should labour to subvert these great pillars of human happiness, these firmest props of the duties of men and citizens.—The mere politician, equally with the pious man, ought to respect and to cherish them.—A volume could not trace all their connexions with private and public felicity. Let it be simply asked, where is the security for property, for reputation, for life, if the sense of religious obligations DESERT the oaths, which are the instruments of investigation in courts of justice? And let us with caution indulge the supposition, that morality can be maintained without religion. Whatever may be conceded to the influence of refined education on minds of peculiar structure, reason and experience both forbid us to expect that national morality can prevail in exclusion of religious principle.

" 'Tis substantially true, that virtue or morality is a necessary spring of popular government. The rule indeed extends with more or less force to every species of free government. Who that is a sincere friend to it can look with indifference upon attempts to shake the foundation of the fabric?

"Promote then, as an object of primary importance, institutions for the general diffusion of knowledge.—In proportion as the structure of a government gives force to public opinion, it is essential that public opinion should be enlightened.

"As a very important source of strength and security, cherish public credit. One method of preserving it, is to use it as sparingly as possible; avoiding occasions of expense by cultivating peace; but remembering also that timely disbursements to *prepare* for danger frequently prevent much greater disbursements to *repel* it; avoiding likewise the accumulations of debt, not only by shunning occasions of expense, but by vigorous exertions in time of peace to discharge the debts which unavoidable wars may have occasioned, not ungenerously throwing upon posterity the burthen which we ourselves ought to bear.—The execution of these maxims belongs to your representatives; but it is necessary that public opinion should co-operate. To facilitate to them the performance of their duty, it is essential that you should practically bear in mind, that towards the payment of debts there must be revenue: that to have revenue there must be taxes; that no taxes can be devised which are not more or less inconvenient and unpleasant, that the intrinsic embarrassment inseparable from the selection of the proper object (which is always a choice of difficulties) ought to be a decisive motive for a candid construction of the conduct of the government in making it, and for a spirit of acquiescence in the measures for obtaining revenue, which the public exigencies may at any time dictate.

"Observe good faith and justice towards all nations: cultivate peace and harmony with all. Religion and morality enjoin this conduct: and can it be that good policy does not equally enjoin it? It will be worthy of a free, enlightened, and at no distant period a great nation, to give to mankind the magnanimous and too novel example of a people always guided by an exalted justice and benevolence. Who can doubt that, in the course of time and things, the fruits of such a plan would richly repay any temporary advantages which might be lost by a steady adherence to it? Can it be, that Providence has not connected the permanent felicity of a nation with its virtue? The experiment, at least, is recommended by every sentiment which ennobles human nature. Alas! is it rendered impossible by its vices?

"In the execution of such a plan, nothing is more essential than that permanent, inveterate antipathies against particular nations, and passionate attachments for others, should be excluded; and that in place of them just and amicable feelings towards all should be cultivated. The nation which indulges towards another a habitual hatred, or a habitual fondness, is in some degree a slave. It is a slave to its animosity or to its affection, either of which is sufficient to lead it astray from its duty and its interest. Antipathy in one nation against another disposes each more readily to offer insult and injury, to lay hold of slight causes of umbrage, and to be haughty and intractable, when accidental or trifling occasions of dispute occur. Hence frequent collisions, obstinate, envenomed, and bloody contests. The nation, prompted by ill-will and resentment, sometimes impels to war the government, contrary to the best calculations of policy. The government sometimes participates in the national propensity, and adopts, through passion, what reason would reject. At other times, it makes the animosity of the nation subservient to projects of hostility, instigated by pride, ambition, and other sinister and pernicious motives. The peace often, sometimes perhaps the liberty, of nations has been the victim.

"So, likewise, a passionate attachment of one nation for another produces a variety of evils. Sympathy for the favourite nation, facilitating the illusion of an imaginary common interest, in cases where no real common interest exists, and infusing into one the enmities of the other, betrays the former into a participation in the quarrels and wars of the latter, without adequate inducement or justification. It leads also to concessions to the favourite nation, of privileges denied to others, which is apt doubly to injure the nation, making the concessions: by unnecessarily parting with what ought to have been retained; and by exciting jealousy, ill-will, and a disposition to retaliate, in the parties from whom equal privileges are withheld. And it gives to ambitious, corrupted, or deluded citizens (who devote themselves to the favourite nation) facility to betray or sacrifice the interests of their own country, without odium, sometimes even with popularity; gilding, with the appearances of a virtuous sense of obligation, a commendable deference for public opinion, or a laudable zeal for public good, the base or foolish compliances of ambition, corruption, or infatuation.

"As avenues to foreign influence in innumerable ways, such attachments are particularly alarming to the truly enlightened and independent patriot. How many opportunities do they afford to tamper with domestic factions, to practise the arts of seduction, to mislead public opinion, to influence or awe the public councils! Such an attachment of a small or weak, towards a great and powerful nation, dooms the former to be the satellite of the latter.

"Against the insidious wiles of foreign influence (I conjure you to believe me, fellow citizens) the jealousy of a free people ought to be CONSTANTLY awake: since history and experience prove that foreign influence is one of the most baneful foes of republican government. But that jealousy, to be useful, must be impartial; else it becomes the instrument of the very influence to be avoided, instead of a defence against it.—Excessive partiality for one foreign nation, and excessive dislike of another, cause those whom they actuate to see danger only on one side, and serve to veil and even second the arts of influence on the other. Real patriots, who may resist the intrigues of the favourite, are liable to become *suspected and odious;* while its tools and dupes usurp the applause and confidence of the people, to surrender their interests.

"The great rule of conduct for us in regard to foreign nations, is, in extending our commercial relations, to have with them as little POLITICAL connexion as possible. So far as we have already formed engagements, let them be fulfilled with perfect good faith. Here let us stop.

"Europe has a set of primary interests, which to us have none, or a very remote relation. Hence she must be engaged in frequent controversies the causes of which are essentially foreign to our concerns. Hence, therefore, it must be unwise in us to implicate ourselves, by artificial ties, in the ordinary vicissitudes of her politics, or the ordinary combinations and collisions of her friendships or enmities.

"Our detached and distant situation invites and enables us to pursue a different course. If we remain one people, under an efficient government, the period is not far off, when we may defy material injury from external annoyance; when we may take such an attitude as will cause the neutrality , we may at any time resolve upon, to be scrupulously respected; when belligerent nations, under the impossibility of making acquisitions upon us, will not lightly hazard the giving us provocation; when we may choose peace or war, as our interest, guided by *justice,* shall counsel.

"Why forego the advantages of so peculiar a situation? Why quit our own, to stand upon foreign ground? Why, by interweaving our destiny with that of any part of Europe, entangle our peace and prosperity in the toils of European ambition, rivalship, interest, humour, or caprice?

" 'Tis our true policy to steer clear of permanent alliances with any portion of the foreign world; so far, I mean, as we are now at liberty to do it; for let me not be understood as capable of patronising infidelity to existing engagements. I hold the maxim no less applicable to public than to private affairs, that honesty is always the best policy. I repeat it, therefore, let those engagements be observed in their genuine sense. But, in my opinion, it is unnecessary and would be unwise to extend them.

"Taking care always to keep ourselves, by suitable establishments, in a respectable defensive posture, we may safely trust to temporary alliances for extraordinary emergencies.

"Harmony, liberal intercourse with all nations, are recommended by policy, humanity, and interest. But even our commercial policy should hold an equal and impartial hand; neither seeking nor granting exclusive favours or preferences; consulting the natural course of things; diffusing and diversifying by gentle means the streams of commerce, but forcing nothing; establishing, with powers so disposed, in order to give trade a stable course, to define the rights of our merchants, and to enable the government to support them, conventional rules of intercourse, the best that present circumstances and mutual opinion will permit, but temporary, and liable to be from time to time abandoned or varied, as experience and circumstances shall dictate; constantly keeping in view, that 'tis folly in one nation to look for disinterested favours from another; that it must pay with a portion of its independence for whatever it may accept under that character; that, by such acceptance, it may place itself in the condition of having given equivalents for nominal favours, and yet of being reproached with ingratitude for not giving more. There can be no greater error than to expect or calculate upon real favours from nation to nation. 'Tis an illusion which experience must cure, which a just pride ought to discard.

"In offering to you, my countrymen, these counsels of an old and affectionate friend, I dare not hope they will make the strong and lasting impression I could wish; that they will control the usual current of the passions, or prevent our nation from running the course which has hitherto marked the destiny of nations: but, if I may even flatter myself, that they may be productive of some partial benefit, some occasional good; that they may now and then recur to moderate the fury of party spirit; to warn against the mischiefs of foreign intrigues; to guard against the impostures of pretended patriotism; this hope will be a full recompense for the solicitude for your welfare, by which they have been dictated.

"How far, in the discharge of my official duties, I have been guided by the principles which have been delineated, the public records and other evidences of my conduct must witness to you and to the world. To myself, the assurance of my own conscience is, that I have, at least, believed myself to be guided by them.

"In relation to the still subsisting war in Europe, my proclamation of the 22d of April, 1793, is the index to my plan. Sanctioned by your approving voice, and by that of your representatives in both houses of congress, the spirit of that measure has continually governed me, uninfluenced by any attempts to deter or divert me from it.

"After deliberate examination, with the aid of the best lights I could obtain, I was well satisfied that our country, under all the circumstances of the case, had a right to take, and was bound in duty and interest to take, a neutral position. Having taken it, I determined, as far as should depend upon me, to maintain it with moderation, perseverance, and firmness.

"The considerations which respect the right to hold this conduct, it is not necessary on this occasion to detail. I will only observe, that, according to my understanding of the matter, that right, so far from being denied by any of the belligerent powers, has been virtually admitted by all.

"The duty of holding a neutral conduct may be inferred, without any thing more, from the obligation which justice and humanity impose on every nation, in cases in which it is free to act, to maintain inviolate the relations of peace and amity towards other nations.

"The inducements of interest for observing that conduct will best be referred to your own reflections and experience. With me, a predominate motive has been to endeavour to gain time to our country to settle and mature its yet recent institutions, and to progress without interruption to that degree of strength and consistency, which is necessary to give it, humanly speaking, the command of its own fortunes.

"Though, in reviewing the incidents of my administration, I am unconscious of intentional error, I am nevertheless too sensible of my defects, not to think it probable that I may have committed many errors. Whatever they may be, I fervently beseech the Almighty to avert or mitigate the evils to which they may tend. I shall also carry with me the hope that my country will never cease to view them with indulgence; and that, after forty-five years of my life dedicated to its service, with an upright zeal, the faults of incompetent abilities will be consigned to oblivion, as myself must soon be to the mansions of rest.

"Relying on its kindness in this as in other things, and actuated by that fervent love towards it, which is so natural to a man, who views in it the native soil of himself and his progenitors for several generations, I anticipate with pleasing expectation that retreat, in which I promise myself to realize, without alloy, the sweet enjoyment of partaking, in the midst of my fellow-citizens, the benign influence of good laws under a free government—the ever favourite object of my heart, and the happy reward, as I trust, of our mutual cares, labours, and dangers.

"G. WASHINGTON."

United States,
17th Sept. 1796."

The appearance of this piece in the gazettes of the U. States, struck every where a damp on the spirits of the people. To be thus bidden farewell by one to whom in every time of danger they had so long and so fondly looked up as under God their surest and safest friend, could not but prove to them a grievous shock. Indeed many could not refrain from tears, especially when they came to that part where he talked of being soon to be "consigned to the mansions of rest."

During the next and last session that he ever met congress, which was on the 7th of December, 1796, he laboured hard to induce that honorable body instantly to set about the following public works, which, to him, appeared all important to the nation.

1st. Societies and institutions for the improvement of agriculture.

2d. A navy.

3d. A military academy.

4th. A manufactory of arms.

5th. A national university.

On the 4th of March, 1797, he took his last leave of Philadelphia. Having ever been that enlightened and virtuous republican, who deems it the *first* of duties to honour the man whom the majority of his countrymen had chosen to honour, Washington could not think of going away, until he had first paid his respects to the man of their choice. It was this that retarded his journey—it was this that brought him to the senate chamber.

About eleven o'clock, while the members of congress with numbers of the first characters were assembled in the senate hall, anxiously awaiting the arrival of Mr. Adams, a modest rap was heard at the door. Supposing it to be the *president elect,* the attention of all was turned to the entry, when, lo! instead of Mr. Adams and his suite, who should appear but the honoured and beloved form of Washington, without attendants, and in his plain travelling dress! Instantly, the joy of filial love sprung up in all hearts, glowed in each face, and bursted forth in plaudits *involuntary* from every tongue. Presently Mr. Adams entered with his attendants, but passed on in great measure unnoticed. The father of his country was in the presence of his children, and perhaps for the last time; who then could divide their attentions? Rivetted on his face was every glistening eye, while busy memory, flying, over the many toils and dangers of his patriot life, gave them up to those delicious thoughts from which no obtruder could break them without a sigh.

Having just waited to congratulate Mr. Adams on his inauguration, and very heartily to pray that "his government might prove a great joy to himself, and a blessing to his country," he hastened to Mount Vernon, to close in peace the short evening of this laborious life, and to wait for a better, even for that *"rest which remaineth for the people of God."*

He carried with him the most fervent prayers of congress that *"Heaven would pour its happiest sunshine on the decline of his days."* But this their prayer was not fully answered. On the contrary, with respect to his *country,* at least, his evening sun went down under a cloud.

The French directory, engaged in a furious war with England, turned to America for aid. But Washington, wisely dreading the effects of war on his young republic, and believing that she had an unquestioned right to neutrality, most strictly enjoined it on his people by proclamation. This so enraged the directory, that they presently gave orders to their cruizers, to seize American ships on the *high seas*—that equal path which God had spread for the nations to trade on! Washington had sent out general Charles C. Pinckney, to remonstrate against such iniquitous proceedings. The directory would not receive him! but still continued their spoliations on our wide-spread and defenceless commerce, ruining numbers of innocent families. Still determined, according to Washington's advice, *"so to act as to make our enemy in the wrong,"* the American government, dispatched two other envoys, Marshall and Gerry, to aid Pinckney. But they fared no better. Though they only supplicated for *peace!* though they only prayed to be *permitted to make explanations,* they were still kept by the directors at a most mortifying distance, and, after all, were told, that America was not to look for a single smile of reconciliation, nor even a word on that subject, until her envoys should bring large tribute in their hands!! This, as Washington had predicted, instantly evaporated the last drop of American patience. He had always said, that "though some very *interested* or *deluded* persons were much too fond of *England* and *France* to value *America* as they ought, yet he was firmly persuaded that the great mass of the people were hearty lovers of their country, and, soon as their eyes were open to the grievous injuries done her, would assuredly resent them, like men, to whom God had given strong feelings, on purpose to guard their rights."

His prediction was gloriously verified. For, on hearing the word tribute, the American envoys instantly took fire!! while the brave Gen. Pinckney, (a revolutionary soldier, and neither *Englishman* nor *Frenchman,* but a true *American,*) indignantly exclaimed to the secretary of the directory—"*Tribute sir! no, sir! the Americans pay no tribute! tell the directory that we will give millions for defence, but not one cent for tribute.*"

Soon as this demand of the directory was told in America, the glorious spirit of '76 was kindled like a flash of lightning, from St. Mary's to Maine. "*What!*" said the people every where, "*shall we! shall Americans! who, rather than pay an unconstitutional three-penny tax on tea, bravely encountered a bloody war with Britain, now tamely yield to France to beggar us at pleasure!* No! *Millions for defence, but not a cent for tribute,*" was nobly reverberated throughout the continent.

War being now fully expected, the eyes of the nation were instantly turned towards Washington, to head her armies against the powers of France. He readily consented; but, at the same time, observed that there would be no war. "*The directory,"* said he, *"though mad enough to do almost any thing, are yet not quite so mad as to venture an attack when they shall find that the spirit of the nation is up."* The event showed the usual correctness of his judgment; for, on discovering that America, though very willing to be the *sister,* had no notion of being the *slave* of France—on learning that Washington was roused, and the strength of the nation rallying around him—and also that the American tars, led on by the gallant Truxtun, had spread the fiery stars of LIBERTY, blasting on every sea their sickly *fleurs-de-luce* of gallic piracy, the directory very sagaciously signified a disposition to accommodate. Mr. Adams immediately pushed off three new envoys to the French republic. By the time they got there the French republic was no more!! Bonaparte, believing that volatile people incapable of governing for themselves, had kindly undertaken to govern for them; and having, *en passant,* kicked the directory from their seats, he seized their ill-managed power, and very leisurely mounted, the throne of the Louis. Dazzled with the splendor of his talents and victories, the great nation quietly yielded to his reign, and, with a happy versatility peculiar to themselves, exchanged the tumultuous and bloody *"Ca ira,"* for the milder notes of *"vive l'empereur."* With this wonderful man, the American envoys found no difficulty to negotiate; for, having no wish to reunite America to his hated enemy, Britain, he received them very graciously, and presently settled all their claims in a satisfactory manner. Thus lovingly did the breath of God blow away once more the black cloud of war, and restore the bright day of peace to our favoured land! But Washington never lived to rejoice with his countrymen in the sunshine of that peace; for before it reached our shores, he had closed his eyes for ever on all mortal things.

CHAPTER XII

THE DEATH OF WASHINGTON

And when disease obstructs the labouring breath,
When the heart sickens and each pulse is death,
Even then religion shall sustain the just,
Grace their last moments, nor desert their dust.

If the prayers of millions could have prevailed, Washington would have been immortal on earth. And if fulness of peace, riches, and honours could have rendered that immortality happy, Washington had been blessed indeed. But this world is not the place of true happiness. Though numberless are the satisfactions, which a prudence and virtue like Washington's may enjoy in this world, yet they fall short, infinite degrees, of that pure, unembittered felicity, which the Almighty parent has prepared in heaven for the spirits of the just.

To prepare for this immensity of bliss, is the real errand on which God sent us into the world. Our preparation consists in acquiring those great virtues, purity and love, which alone can make us *worthy* companions of angels, and fit partakers of their exalted delights. Washington had wisely spent life in acquiring the IMMORTAL VIRTUES. *"He had fought the good fight"* against his own unreasonable affections; *he had glorified God,* by exemplifying the charms of virtue to men; *he had borne the heat and burden of the day*—his *great* day of duty; and the evening (of old age) being come, the servant of God must now go to receive his wages. Happy Washington! If crowns and kingdoms could have purchased such peace as thine, such hopes big with immortality, with what begging earnestness would crowns and kingdoms have been offered by the mighty conquerors of the earth, in their dying moments of *terror* and *despair!*

Engraving after Gilbert Stuart

Washington at Valley Forge

[illegible] ready for the press [illegible] piece
christen'd or to be christen'd "The Beauties of Washington" [illegible] artfully drawn up, enlivened with
anecdotes, and in my humble opinion, marvellously fitted "ad captandum — gustum populi
Americani"!!! What say you to printing it
for me and ordering a copper plate frontispiece
of that HERO, something in this way

George Washington Esqr.

"The Guardian Angel of his Country
"Go thy way [illegible] Die when thou wilt
we shall never look upon thy like again"

M Carey [illegible]

NB The whole will make but four sheets and will [illegible]
[illegible] at quarter of a dollar. I could make you [illegible]

Page of a Letter from Weems to Mathew Carey

The Frank Confession

On the 14th of December, 1799 (when he wanted but 9 weeks and 2 days of being 68 years old), he rode out to his mill, 3 miles distant. The day was raw and rainy. The following night he was attacked with a violent pain and inflammation of the throat. The lancet of one of his domestics was employed, but with no advantage. Early in the morning, Dr. Craik, the friend and physician of his youth and age, was sent for. Alarmed at the least appearance of danger threatening a life so dear to him, Dr. Craik advised to call in, immediately, the consulting assistance of his friends, the ingenious and learned Drs. Dick, of Alexandria, and Brown, of Port Tobacco. They came on the wings of speed. They felt the awfulness of their situation. The greatest of human beings was lying low: a life, of all others the most *revered,* the most *beloved,* was at stake. And if human skill could have saved—if the sword of genius, and the buckler of experience could have turned the stroke of death, Washington had still lived. But his *hour was come.*

It appears, that, from the commencement of the attack, he was favoured with a presentiment, that he was now laid down to rise no more. He took, however, the medicines that were offered him, but it was principally from a sense of *duty.*

It has been said that a man's death, is generally a copy of his life. It was Washington's case exactly. In his last illness he behaved with the firmness of a soldier, and the resignation of a christian.

The inflammation in his throat was attended with great pain, which he bore with the fortitude that became him. He was, once or twice, heard to say that, *had it pleased God, he should have been glad to die a little easier; but that he doubted not that it was for his good.*

Every hour now spread a sadder gloom over the scene. Despair sat on the faces of the physicians; for they saw that their art had failed! The strength of the mighty was departing from him; and death, with his sad harbingers, chills and paleness, was coming on apace.

Mount Vernon, which had long shone the queen of elegant joys, was now about to suffer a sad eclipse! an eclipse, which would soon be mournfully visible, not only through the United States, but throughout the whole world.

Sons and daughters of Columbia, gather yourselves together around the bed of your expiring father—around the last bed of him to whom under God you and your children owe many of the best blessings of this life. When Joseph the prime minister of Egypt heard his *shepherd father* was sick, he hastened up, to see him; and fell on his face and kissed him, and wept a long while. But Joseph had never received such services from Jacob as you have received from Washington. But we call you not to weep for Washington. We ask you not to view those eyes, now sunk and hollow, which fomerly darted their lightning flashes against your enemies—nor to feel that heart, now faintly labouring, which so often throbbed with more than mortal joys when he saw his young countrymen charging like lions, upon the foes of liberty. No! we call you not to weep, but to rejoice. Washington, who so often conquered himself, is now about to conquer the last enemy.

Silent and sad, his physicians sat by his bedside, looking on him as he lay panting for breath. They thought on the past, and the tear swelled in their eyes. He marked it, and, stretching out his hand to them, and shaking his head, said, *"O no! —don't! don't!"* then with a delightful smile added, *"I am dying, gentlemen: but, thank God, I am not afraid to die."*

Feeling that the hour of his departure out of this world was at hand, he desired that every body would quit the room. They all went out, and according to his wish, left him—with his God.

There, by himself, like Moses alone on the top of Pisgah, he seeks the face of God. There, *by himself,* standing as on the awful boundary that divides time from eternity, that separates this world from the next, he cannot quit the long-frequented haunts of the one, nor launch away into the untried regions of the other, until (in humble imitation of the world's great Redeemer) he has poured forth into the bosom of his God those strong sensations which the solemnity of his situation naturally suggested.

With what angel fervour did he adore that *Almighty Love,* which, though inhabiting the heaven of heavens, deigned to wake his sleeping dust—framed him so fearfully in the womb—nursed him on a tender mother's *breast*—watched his helpless infancy—guarded his heedless youth—preserved him from the dominion of his passions—inspired him with the love of virtue—led him safely up to man—and, from such low beginnings, advanced him to such unparalleled usefulness and glory among men! These, and ten thousand other precious gifts heaped on him, unasked, many of them long before he had the knowledge to ask, overwhelmed his soul with gratitude unutterable, exalted to infinite heights his ideas of eternal love, and bade him without fear resign his departing spirit into the arms of his Redeemer God, whose mercies are over all his works.

He is now about to leave the great family of man, in which he has so long sojourned! The yearnings of his soul are over his brethren! How fervently does he adore that *goodness,* which enabled him to be so serviceable to them! That *grace,* which preserved him from injuring them by violence or fraud! How fervently does he pray that the *unsuffering kingdom of God may come,* and that the earth may be filled with the richest fruits of righteousness and peace!

He is now about to leave his *country!* that dear spot which gave him birth!—that dear spot for which he has so long watched and prayed, so long toiled and fought; and whose beloved children he has so often sought to gather, even as a hen gathereth her chickens under her wings. He sees them now spread abroad like flocks in goodly pastures; like favoured Israel in the land of promise. He remembers how

God, by a mighty hand, and by an out-stretched arm, brought their fathers into this good land, a land flowing with milk and honey: and blessed them with the blessings of heaven above, and the earth beneath; with the blessings of LIBERTY and of PEACE, of RELIGION and of LAWS, above all other people. He sees that, through the rich mercies of God, they have now the precious opportunity to continue their country the GLORY of the earth, and a refuge for the poor and for the persecuted of all lands! The transporting sight of such a cloud of blessings, trembling close over the heads of his countrymen, together with the distressing uncertainty whether they will put forth their hands and enjoy them, shakes the *parent soul* of Washington with feelings *too strong* for his *dying frame!* The last tear that he is ever to shed now steals into his eye—the last groan that he is ever to heave is about to issue from his faintly labouring heart.

Feeling that the silver chord of life is loosing, and that his spirit is ready to quit her old companion the body, he extends himself on his bed—closes his eyes for the *last* time, with his own hands—folds his arms decently on his breast, then breathing out *"Father of mercies! take me to thyself,"*—he fell asleep.

Swift on angels' wings the brightening saint ascended; while voices more than human were heard (*in Fancy's ear*) warbling through the happy regions, and hymning the great procession towards the gates of heaven. His glorious coming was seen far off, and myriads of mighty angels hastened forth, with golden harps, to welcome the honoured stranger. High in front of the shouting hosts, were seen the beauteous forms of FRANKLIN, WARREN, MERCER, SCAMMEL, and of him who fell at Quebec, with all the virtuous patriots, who, on the side of Columbia, toiled or bled for *liberty* and *truth*. But oh! how changed from what they were, when, in their days of flesh, bathed in sweat and blood, they fell at the parent feet of their weeping country! Not the homeliest infant suddenly springing into a soul-enchanting Hebe—not dreary winter, suddenly brightening into spring, with all her bloom and fragrance, ravishing the senses, could equal such glorious change. Oh! where are now their wrinkles and grey hairs? Where their ghastly wounds and clotted blood? Their forms are of the stature of angels—their robes like morning clouds streaked with gold—the stars of heaven, like crowns glitter on their heads—immortal youth, *celestial rosy red,* sits blooming on their cheeks; while infinite benignity and love beam from their eyes. Such were the forms of thy sons, O Columbia! such the brother band of thy martyred saints, that now poured forth from heaven's wide-opening gates, to meet thy Washington; to meet their beloved chief, who in the days of his mortality, had led their embattled squadrons to the war. At sight of him, even these *blessed spirits* seem to feel new raptures, and to look more dazzling bright. In joyous throngs they pour around him—they devour him with their eyes of love—they embrace him in transports of tenderness unutterable; while from their roseate cheeks, tears of joy, such as angels weep, roll down.

All that followed was too much for the over-dazzled eye of *Imagination.* She was seen to return, with the quick panting bosom and looks entranced of a fond mother, near swooning at sudden sight of a dear loved son, deemed *lost,* but now *found,* and raised to *kingly honours!* She was heard passionately to exclaim, with palms and eyes lifted to heaven, *"O, who can count the stars of Jacob, or number the fourth part of the blessings of Israel!—Let me die the death of Washington, and may my latter end be like his!"*

Let us now return to all that remained of Washington on the earth. He had expressly ordered in his will that he should be buried in a private *manner, and without any parade.* But this was impossible; for who could stay at home when it was said, *"to-day general Washington is to be buried!"* On the morning of the 18th, which was fixed on for his funeral, the people poured in by thousands to pay him the *last respect, and,* as they said, *to take their last look.* And, while they looked on him, nature stirred that at their hearts, which quickly brought the best blood into their cheeks, and rolled down the tears from their eyes. About two o'clock, they bore him to his long home, and buried him in his own family vault, near the banks of the great Potomac. And to this day, often as the ships of war pass that way, they waken up the thunder of their loudest guns, pointed to the spot, as if to tell the sleeping hero that he is not forgotten in his narrow dwelling.

The news of his death soon reached Philadelphia, where congress was then in session. A question of importance being on the carpet that day, the house, as usual, was much interested. But, soon as it was announced—"GENERAL WASHINGTON IS DEAD"—an instant stop was put to all business—the tongue of the orator was struck dumb—and a midnight silence ensued, save when it was interrupted by deepest sighs of the members, as, with drooping foreheads rested on their palms, they sat, each absorbed in mournful cogitation. Presently, as utterly unfit for business, both houses adjourned; and the members retired slow and sad to their lodgings, like men who had suddenly heard of the death of a father.

For several days hardly any thing was done in congress; hardly any thing thought of but to talk of and to praise the departed Washington. In this patriotic work all parties joined with equal alacrity and earnestness. In this all were *federalists,* all were *republicans.* Elegant addresses were exchanged between the two houses of congress and the president, and all of them replete with genius and gratitude.

Then, by unanimous consent, congress came to the following resolutions:

1st. That a grand marble monument should be erected at the city of Washington, under which, with permission of his lady, the body of the general should be deposited.

2d. That there should be a funeral procession from congress hall to the German Lutheran church to hear an oration delivered by one of the members of congress.

3d. That the members of congress should wear full mourning during the session.

4th. That it should be recommended to the people of the United States, to wear crape on the left arm, as mourning, for 30 days.

But, thank God, the people of the United States needed not the hint contained in the last resolution. Though they could not all very elegantly speak, yet their actions showed that they all very deeply *felt* what they owed to Washington. For in every city, village, and hamlet, the people were so struck on hearing of his death, that long before they heard of the resolution of congress, they ran together to ease their troubled minds in talking and hearing talk of Washington, and to devise some public mode of testifying their sorrow for his death. Every where throughout the continent, churches and court houses were hung in black, mourning was put on, processions were made, and sermons preached, while the crowded houses listened with pleasure to the praises of Washington, or sighed and wept when they heard of his toils and battles for his country.

CHAPTER XIII

CHARACTER OF WASHINGTON

LET the poor witling argue all he can,
It is Religion still that makes the man.

WHEN the children of the years to come, hearing his great name re-echoed from every lip, shall say to their fathers, *"what was it that raised Washington to such height of glory?"* let them be told that it was HIS GREAT TALENTS, CONSTANTLY GUIDED AND GUARDED BY RELIGION. For how shall man, *frail man,* prone to inglorious ease and pleasure, ever ascend the arduous steps of virtue, unless animated by the *mighty hopes* of religion? Or what shall stop him in his swift descent to infamy and vice, if unawed by that dread power which proclaims to the guilty that their secret crimes are seen, and shall not go unpunished? Hence the wise, in all ages, have pronounced, that *"there never was a truly great man without religion."*

There have, indeed, been *courageous generals,* and *cunning statesmen,* without religion, but mere courage or cunning, however paramount, never yet made a man great.

ADMIT that this can conquer, that can cheat!
'Tis phrase absurd to call a villain *great!*
Who wickedly is wise, or madly brave,
Is but the more a fool, the more a knave.

No! to be truly great, a man must have not only great talents, but those talents must be constantly exerted on great, i. e. good actions—*and perseveringly* too—for if he should turn aside to vice—farewel to his heroism. Hence, when Epaminondas was asked which was the greatest man, himself or Pelopidas? he replied, *"wait till we are dead:*["] meaning that the all of heroism depends on *perseverance* in great good actions. But, sensual and grovelling as man is, what can incline and elevate him to those things like religion, that divine power, to whom alone it belongs to present those vast and eternal *goods* and *ills* which best alarm our fears, enrapture our hopes, inflame the worthiest loves, rouse the truest avarice, and in short touch every spring and passion of our souls in favour of virtue and noble actions.

Did SHAME restrain Alcibiades from a base action in the presence of Socrates? *"Behold,"* says religion, *"a greater than Socrates is here!"*

Did LOVE embolden Jacob to brave fourteen years of slavery for an earthly beauty? Religion springs that eternal love, for whose sake good men can even glory in laborious duties.

Did the ambition of a civic crown animate Scipio to heroic deeds? Religion holds a crown, at the sight of which the laurels of a Cæsar droop to weeds.

Did avarice urge Cortez through a thousand toils and dangers for wealth? Religion points to those treasures in heaven, compared to which all diamond beds and mines of massy gold are but trash.

Did good Aurelius study the happiness of his subjects for this world's glory? Religion displays that world of glory, where those who have laboured to make others happy, shall *"shine like stars for ever and ever."*

Does the FEAR of death deter man from horrid crimes? Religion adds infinite horrors to that fear—it warns them of a death both of soul and body in hell.

In short, what motives under heaven can restrain men from vices and crimes, and urge them on, full stretch, after individual and national happiness, like those of religion? For lack of these motives, alas! how many who once dazzled the world with the glare of their exploits, are now eclipsed and set to rise no more!

There was Arnold, who, in courage and military talents,

glittered in the same firmament with Washington, and, for a while, his face shone like the star of the morning; but alas! for lack of Washington's religion, he soon fell, like Lucifer, from a heaven of glory, into an abyss of never-ending infamy.

And there was general Charles Lee, too, confessedly a great wit, a great scholar, a great soldier, but, after all, not a great man. For, through lack of that magnanimous benevolence which religion inspires, he fell into the vile state of *envy,* and, on the plains of Monmouth, rather than fight to immortalize Washington, he chose to retreat and disgrace himself.

There was the gallant general Hamilton also—a gigantic genius—*a statesman* fit to rule the mightiest monarchy—a *soldier "fit to stand by Washington, and give command."* But alas! for lack of religion, see how all was lost! preferring the praise of man to that praise *"which cometh from God,"* and pursuing the phantom honour up to the pistol's mouth, he is cut off at once from life and greatness, and leaves his family and country to mourn his hapless fate.

And there was the fascinating colonel Burr. A man born to be *great*—brave as Cæsar, polished as Chesterfield, eloquent as Cicero, and, lifted by the strong arm of his country, he rose fast, and bade fair soon to fill the place where Washington had sat. But, alas! lacking religion, he could not wait the spontaneous fall of the rich honours ripening over his head, but in evil hour stretched forth his hand to the forbidden fruit, and by that fatal act was cast out from the Eden of our republic, and amerced of greatness for ever.

But why should I summon the Arnolds and Lees, the Hamiltons and Burrs of the earth to give sad evidence, that no valour, no genius alone can make men great? do we not daily meet with instances, of youth amiable and promising as their fond parents' wishes, who yet, merely for lack of religion, soon make shipwreck of every precious hope, sacrificing their gold to gamblers, their health to harlots, and their glory to grog—making conscience their curse, this life a purgatory, and the next a hell!! In fact, a young man, though of the finest talents and education, without religion, is but like a gorgeous ship without ballast. Highly painted and with flowing canvas, she launches out on the deep; and, during a smooth sea and gentle breeze, she moves along stately as the pride of ocean; but, as soon as the stormy winds descend, and the blackening billows begin to roll, suddenly she is overset, and disappears for ever. But who is this coming, thus gloriously along, with masts towering to heaven, and his sails white, looming like the mountain of snows? Who is it but *"Columbia's first and greatest son!"* whose talents, like the sails of a mighty ship spread far and wide, catching the gales of heaven, while his capacious soul, stored with the rich ballast of religion, remains firm and unshaken as the ponderous rock. The warm zephyrs of prosperity breathe meltingly upon him—the rough storms of adversity descend—the big billows of affliction dash, but nothing can move him; his eye is fixed on God! the *present joys* of an approving conscience, and the hope of that glory which fadeth not away; these comfort and support him.

"There exists," says Washington, *"in the economy of nature, an inseparable connexion between duty and advantage."* —The whole life of this great man bears glorious witness to the truth of this his favourite aphorism. At the giddy age of fourteen, when the spirits of youth are all on tiptoe for freedom and adventures, he felt a strong desire to go to sea; but, very opposite to his wishes, his mother declared that she could not bear to part with him. His trial must have been very severe; for I have been told that a midshipman's commission was actually in his pocket—his trunk of clothes on board the ship—his honour in some sort pledged—his young companions importunate with him to go—and his whole soul panting for the promised pleasures of the voyage; but religion whispered *"honour thy mother, and grieve not the spirit of her who bore thee."*

Instantly the glorious boy sacrificed inclination to duty—dropt all thoughts of the voyage, and gave tears of joy to his widowed mother, in clasping to her bosom a dear child who could deny himself to make her happy.

'Tis said, that, when he saw the last boat going on board, with several of his youthful friends in it—when he saw the flash and heard the report of the signal gun for sailing, and the ship in all her pride of canvas rounding off for sea, he could not bear it, but turned away, and, half choaked with grief, went into the room where his mother sat. *"George, my dear!"* said she, *"have you already repented that you made your mother so happy just now?"* Upon this, falling on her bosom, with his arms round her neck, and a gush of tears, he said, *"my dear mother, I must not deny that I am sorry; but, indeed, I feel that I should be much more sorry, were I on board the ship, and knew that you were unhappy."*

"Well," replied she embracing him tenderly, *"God, I hope, will reward my dear boy for this, some day or other."* Now see here, young reader, and learn that HE who prescribes our duty, is able to reward it. Had George left his fond mother to a broken heart, and gone off to sea, 'tis next to certain that he would never have taken that active part in the French and Indian war, which, by securing to him the hearts of his countrymen, paved the way for all his future greatness.

Now for another instance of the wonderful effect of religion on Washington's fortune. Shortly after returning from the war of Cuba, Lawrence (his *half* brother) was taken with the consumption, which made him so excessively fretful, that his *own* brother, Augustin, would seldom come near him. But George, whose heart was early under the softening and sweetening influences of religion, felt such a tenderness for his poor sick brother, that he not only put up with his peevishness, but seemed, from what I have been told, never so happy as when he was with him. He accompanied him to the island of Bermuda, in quest of health—and, after their return to

Mount Vernon, often as his duty to lord Fairfax permitted, he would come down from the back woods to see him. And while with him he was always contriving or doing something to cheer and comfort his brother. Sometimes with his gun he would go out in quest of partridges and snipes, and other fine flavoured game, to tempt his brother's sickly appetite, and gain him strength. At other times he would sit for hours and read to him some entertaining book—and, when his cough came on, he would support his drooping head, and wipe the cold dew from his forehead, or the phlegm from his lips, and give him his medicine, or smooth his pillow; and all with such alacrity and artless tenderness as proved the sweetest cordial to his brother's spirits. For he was often heard to say to the Fairfax family, into which he married, that *"he should think nothing of his sickness, if he could but always have his brother George with him."* Well, what was the consequence? Why, when Lawrence came to die, he left almost the whole of his large estate to George, which served as another noble step to his future greatness.

For further proof of *"the inseparable connexion between duty and advantage,"* let us look at Washington's conduct through the French and Indian war. To a man of his uncommon military mind, and skill in the arts of Indian warfare, the pride and precipitance of general Braddock must have been excessively disgusting and disheartening. But we hear nothing of his *threatening* either to leave or supplant Braddock. On the contrary, he nobly brooked his rude manners, gallantly obeyed his rash orders, and, as far as in him lay, endeavoured to correct their fatal tendencies.

And, after the death of Braddock, and the desertion of Dunbar, that weak old man, governor Dinwiddie, added infinitely to his hardships and hazards, by appointing him to the defence of the frontiers, and yet withholding the necessary forces and supplies. But though by that means, the western country was continually overrun by the enemy, and cruelly deluged in blood—though much wearied in body by marchings and watchings, and worse tortured in soul, by the murders and desolations of the inhabitants, he shrinks not from *duty*—still seeking the smiles of conscience as his greatest good; and as the sorest evil, dreading its frowns, he bravely maintained his ground, and, after three years of unequalled dangers and difficulties, succeeded.

Well, what was the consequence? why it drew upon him, from his admiring countrymen, such an unbounded confidence in his principles and patriotism, as secured to him the command of the *American armies,* in the revolutionary war!

And there again the connexion between *"duty and advantage"* was as gloriously displayed. For though congress was, in legal and political knowledge an enlightened body, and for patriotism equal to the senators of Republican Rome, yet certainly in military matters they were no more to be compared to him, than those others were to Hannibal. But still, though they were constantly thwarting his counsels, and in place of good soldiers sending him raw militia, thus compelling inactivity, or ensuring defeat—dragging out the war—dispiriting the nation—and disgracing him, yet we hear from him no gusts of passion; no dark intrigues to supplant congress, and, with the help of an idolizing nation and army, to snatch the power from their hands, and make himself king. On the contrary, he continues to treat congress as a virtuous son his respected parents. He points out wiser measures, but in defect of their adoption, makes the best use of those they give him, and at length, through the mighty blessing of God, established the independence of his country, and then went back to his plough.

Well, what was the consequence? why, these noble acts so completely filled up the measure of his country's love for him, as to give him that first of all felicities, the felicity to be the guardian angel of his country, and able by the magic of his name, to scatter every cloud of danger that gathered over her head.

For example, at the close of the war, when the army, about to be disbanded without their wages, was wrought up to such a pitch of discontent and rage, as seriously to threaten *civil war,* see the wonderful influence which their love for him gave him over themselves! In the height of their passion, and that a very natural passion too, he but makes a short speech to them, and the storm is laid! the tumult subsides! and the soldiers, after all their hardships, consent to ground their arms, and return home without a penny in their pockets!!!

Also, in that very alarming dispute between Vermont and Pennsylvania, where the furious parties, in spite of all the efforts of congress and their governors, had actually shouldered their guns, and were dragging on their cannon for a bloody fight—Washington only dropt them a few lines of his advice, and instantly they faced about for their homes, and laying by their weapons, seized their ploughs again, like dutiful children, on whose kindling passions a beloved father had shaken his hoary locks!!

And, in the western counties of Pennsylvania, where certain blind patriots, affecting to strain at the gnat of a small excise, but ready enough to swallow the hellish camel of rebellion, had kindled the flames of civil war, and thrown the whole nation into a tremor, Washington had just to send around a circular to the people of the union, stating the infinite importance of maintaining the SACRED REIGN OF THE LAWS, and instantly twenty thousand well-armed volunteers dashed out among the insurgents, and without shedding a drop of blood, extinguished the insurrection!

In short, it were endless to enumerate the many horrid insurrections and bloody wars which were saved to this country by Washington, and all through the divine force of *early religion!* for it was this that enabled him inflexibly to do his duty, by imitating God in his glorious works of wisdom and benevolence; and all the rest followed as naturally as light follows the sun.

We have seen at page 15 of this little work, with what pleasure the youthful Washington hung upon his father's lips, while descanting on the adorable wisdom and benevolent designs of God in all parts of this beautiful and harmonious creation. By such lessons in the book of nature, this virtuous youth was easily prepared for the far higher and surer lectures of revelation, I mean that blessed gospel which contains the MORAL philosophy of heaven. There he learnt, that *"God is love"*—and that all that he desires, with respect to men, is to glorify himself in their happiness—and since VIRTUE is indispensable to that happiness, the infinite and eternal weight of God's attributes must be for virtue, and against vice; and consequently that God will sooner or later gloriously reward the one and punish the other. This was the creed of Washington. And looking on it as the only basis of human virtue and happiness, he very cordially embraced it himself, and wished for nothing so much as to see all others embrace it.

I have often been told by colonel Ben Temple, (of King William county, Virginia), who was one of his aids in the French and Indian war, that he has frequently known Washington, on the sabbath, read the scriptures and pray with his regiment, in the absence of the chaplain; and also that, on sudden and unexpected visits into his marquee, he has, more than once, found him on his knees at his devotions.

The Reverend Mr. Lee Massey, long a rector of Washington's parish, and from early life his intimate, has assured me a thousand times, that "he never knew so constant a churchman as Washington. And his behaviour in the house of God," added my reverend friend, "was so deeply reverential, that it produced the happiest effects on my congregation, and greatly assisted me in my moralizing labours. No company ever kept him from church. I have been many a time at Mount Vernon on the sabbath morning, when his breakfast table was filled with guests. But to him they furnished no pretext for neglecting his God, and losing the satisfaction of setting a good example. For instead of staying at home out of a false complaisance to them, he used constantly to invite them to accompany him."

His secretary, judge Harrison, has frequently been heard to say, that, "whenever the general would be spared from camp on the sabbath, he never failed riding out to some neighbouring church, to join those who were publicly worshipping the Great Creator."

And while he resided at Philadelphia, as president of the United States, his constant and cheerful attendance on divine service was such as to convince every reflecting mind that he deemed no levee so honourable as that of his Almighty Maker; no pleasures equal to those of devotion; and no business a sufficient excuse for neglecting his supreme benefactor.

In the winter of '77, while Washington, with the American army lay encamped at Valley Forge, a certain good old FRIEND, of the respectable family and name of Potts, if I mistake not, had occasion to pass through the woods near head-quarters. Treading his way along the venerable grove, suddenly he heard the sound of a human voice, which as he advanced increased on his ear, and at length became like the voice of one speaking much in earnest. As he approached the spot with a cautious step, whom should he behold, in a dark natural bower of ancient oaks, but the commander in chief of the American armies on his knees at prayer! Motionless with surprise, friend Potts continued on the place till the general, having ended his devotions, arose, and, with a countenance of angel serenity, retired to headquarters: friend Potts then went home, and on entering his parlour called out to his wife, "Sarah, my dear! Sarah! All's well! all's well! George Washington will yet prevail!"

"What's the matter, Isaac?" replied she; "thee seems moved."

"Well, if I seem moved, 'tis no more than what I am. I have this day seen what I never expected. Thee knows that I always thought the sword and the gospel utterly inconsistent; and that no man could be a soldier and a christian at the same time. But George Washington has this day convinced me of my mistake."

He then related what he had seen, and concluded with this prophetical remark—"If George Washington be not a man of God, I am greatly deceived—and still more shall I be deceived if God do not, through him, work out a great salvation for America."

When he was told that the British troops at Lexington, on the memorable 19th of April, 1775, had fired on and killed several of the Americans, he replied, *"I grieve for the death of my countrymen, but rejoice that the British are still so determined to keep God on our side,"* alluding to that noble sentiment which he has since so happily expressed; viz. *"The smiles of Heaven can never be expected on a nation that disregards the eternal rules of order and right, which Heaven itself has ordained."*

When called by his country in 1775, to lead her free-born sons against the arms of Britain, what charming modesty, what noble self-distrust, what pious confidence in Heaven, appeared in all his answers. *"My diffidence in my own abilities,* says he, *was superseded by a confidence in the rectitude of our cause and the patronage of Heaven."*

And when called to the presidency by the unanimous voice of the nation, thanking him for his great services past, with anticipations of equally great to come, his answer deserves approbation.

"When I contemplate the interposition of Providence, as it was visibly manifested in guiding us through the revolution, in preparing us for the reception of a general government, and in conciliating the good will of the people of America towards one another after its adoption; I feel myself oppressed

and almost overwhelmed with a sense of the divine munificence. I feel that nothing is due to my personal agency in all those complicated and wonderful events, except what can simply be attributed to the exertions of an honest zeal for the good of my country."

And when he presented himself for the first time before that august body, the congress of the U. States, April 30th, 1789—when he saw before him the pride of Columbia in her chosen sons, assembled to consult how best to strengthen the chain of love between the states—to preserve friendship and harmony with foreign powers—to secure the blessings of civil and religious liberty—and to build up our young republic a great and happy people among the nations of the earth—never patriot entered on such important business with fairer hopes, whether we consider the unanimity and confidence of the citizens, or his own and the abilities and virtues of his fellow-counsellors.

But all this would not do; nothing short of the *divine friendship* could satisfy Washington. Feeling the magnitude, difficulty, and danger of managing such an assemblage of communities and interests; dreading the machinations of bad men, and well knowing the insufficiency of all second causes, even the *best;* he piously reminds congress of the wisdom of imploring the benediction of the *great first Cause,* without which he knew that his beloved country could never prosper.

"It would," says he, "be peculiarly improper to omit, in this first official act, my fervent supplications to that Almighty Being who rules over the universe; who presides in the councils of nations; and whose providential aids can supply every human defect, that his benediction may consecrate to the liberties and happiness of the people of the United States, a government instituted by themselves for these essential purposes, and may enable every instrument employed in its administration to execute with success the functions allotted to his charge. In tendering this homage to the great Author of every public and private good, I assure myself that it expresses your sentiments not less than my own; nor those of my fellow-citizens at large less than either. No people can be bound to acknowledge and adore the invisible hand which conducts the affairs of men, more than the people of the United States. Every step, by which they have advanced to the character of an independent nation, seems to have been distinguished by some token of providential agency. These reflections, arising out of the present crisis, have forced themselves too strongly on my mind to be suppressed. You will join with me, I trust, in thinking, that there are none, under the influence of which the proceedings of a new and free government can more auspiciously commence."

And after having come near to the close of this the most sensible and virtuous speech ever made to a sensible and virtuous representation of a free people, he adds—"I shall take my present leave: but not without resorting *once more* to the benign Parent of the human race in humble supplication, that, since he has been pleased to favour the American people with opportunities for deliberating with perfect tranquillity, and dispositions for deciding with unparalleled unanimity, on a form of government for the security of their union, and the advancement of their happiness; so his divine blessings may be equally conspicuous in the enlarged views, the temperate consultations, and the wise measures, on which the success of this government must depend."

In this constant disposition to look for national happiness only in national morals, flowing from the *sublime* affections and blessed hopes of religion, Washington agreed with those great legislators of nations, Moses, Lycurgus, and Numa. *"I ask not gold for Spartans,"* said Lycurgus: *"virtue is better than all gold."* The event showed his wisdom. The Spartans were invincible all the days of their own virtue, even 500 years.

"I ask not wealth for Israel," cried Moses.—"But O that they were wise!—that they did but fear God and keep his commandments! the Lord himself would be their sun and shield." The event proved Moses a true prophet. For while they were religious they were unconquerable. "United as brothers, swift as eagles, stronger than lions, one could chase a thousand, and two put ten thousand to flight."

"Of all the dispositions and habits which lead to the prosperity of a nation," says Washington, "religion is the indispensable support. Volumes could not trace all its connexions with private and public happiness. Let it simply be asked, where is the security for property, for reputation, for life itself, if there be no fear of God on the minds of those who give their oaths in courts of justice!"

But some will tell us, that *human laws* are sufficient for the purpose!

Human laws!—Human nonsense! For how often, even where the cries and screams of the wretched called aloud for lightning-speeded vengeance, have we not seen the sword of human law loiter in its coward scabbard, afraid of angry royalty? Did not that vile queen Jezebel, having a mind to compliment her husband with a vineyard belonging to poor Naboth, suborn a couple of villains to take a false oath against him, and then cause him to be dragged out with his little motherless, crying babes, and barbarously stoned to death?

Great God! what bloody tragedies have been acted on the poor ones of the earth, by kings and great men, who were *above* the laws, and had no sense of religion to keep them in awe!—And if men be not above the laws, yet what horrid crimes! what ruinous robberies! what wide-wasting flames! what cruel murders may they not commit in *secret,* if they be not withheld by the sacred arm of religion! "In vain, therefore," says WASHINGTON, "would that man claim the tribute of patriotism, who should do any thing to discountenance religion and morality, those great pillars of human happiness, those firmest props of the duties of men and citizens. The mere politician, equally with the pious man, ought to respect and cherish them."

But others have said, and with a serious face too, that a *sense of honour,* is sufficient to preserve men from base actions! O blasphemy to sense! Do we not daily hear of *men of honour,* by dice and cards, draining their fellow-citizens of the last cent, reducing them to a dung-hill, or driving them to a pistol? Do we not daily hear of *men of honour* corrupting their neighbours' wives and daughters, and then murdering their husbands and brothers in duels? Bind such selfish, such inhuman beings, by a sense of honour!! Why not bind roaring lions with cobwebs? "No," exclaims Washington, "whatever a sense of honour may do on men of refined education, and on minds of a peculiar structure, reason and experience both forbid us to expect that national morality can prevail, in exclusion of religious principles."

And truly Washington had abundant reason, from his own *happy experience,* to recommend religion so heartily to others.

For besides all those inestimable favours which he received from her at the hands of her celestial daughters, the *Virtues;* she threw over him her own magic mantle of *Character.* And it was this that immortalized Washington. By inspiring his countrymen with the profoundest veneration for him as the *best of men,* it naturally smoothed his way to supreme command; so that when War, that monster of hell, came on roaring against America, with all his death's heads and garments rolled in blood, the nation unanimously placed Washington at the head of their armies, from a natural persuasion that so good a man must be the peculiar favourite of Heaven, and the fastest friend of his country. How far this precious instinct in favour of goodness was corrected, or how far Washington's conduct was honourable to religion and glorious to himself and country, bright ages to come, and happy millions yet unborn, will, we hope, declare.

CHAPTER XIV

WASHINGTON'S CHARACTER CONTINUED

HIS BENEVOLENCE

This only can the bliss bestow
Immortal souls should prove;
From one short word all pleasures flow,
That blessed word is—LOVE.

IF ever man rejoiced in the divine administration, and cordially endeavoured to imitate it by doing good, George Washington was that man. Taught by religion that *"God is love,"* he wisely concluded those the most happy, who love the most; and, taught by *experience,* that it is love alone that gives a participation and interest in others, capacitating us to rejoice with those who rejoice, and to weep with those who weep, he early studied that BENEVOLENCE which rendered him so singularly the delight of all mankind.

The marquis De Chastellux, who visited him in camp, tells us that he was "astonished and delighted to see this great American living among his officers and men as a father among his children, who at once revered and loved him with a filial tenderness."

Brissot, another famous French traveller, assures us, that, "throughout the continent, every body spoke of Washington as of a father."

That dearest and best of all appellations, *"the father of his country,"* was the natural fruit of that *benevolence* which he so carefully cultivated through life. A singular instance of which we meet with in 1754, and the 22d year of his age.

He was stationed at Alexandria with his regiment, the only one in the colony, and of which he was colonel. There happened at this time to be an election in Alexandria for members of assembly, and the contest ran high between colonel

George Fairfax, and Mr. Elzey. Washington was the warm friend of Fairfax, and a Mr. Payne headed the friends of Elzey. A dispute happening to take place in the court-house-yard, Washington, a thing very uncommon with him, got warm, and, which was still more uncommon, said something that offended Payne; whereupon the little gentleman, who, though but a cub in *size,* was the old lion in heart, raised his sturdy hickory, and, at a single blow, brought our hero to the ground. Several of Washington's officers being present, whipped out their cold irons in an instant, and it was believed that there would have been murder off-hand. To make bad worse, his regiment, hearing how he had been treated, bolted out from their barracks, with every man his weapon in his hand, threatening dreadful vengeance on those who had dared to knock down their beloved colonel. Happily for Mr. Payne and his party, Washington recovered, time enough to go out and meet his enraged soldiers; and, after thanking them for this expression of their love, and assuring them that he was not hurt in the least, he begged them, as they loved him or their duty, to return peaceably to their barracks. As for himself, he went to his room, generously chastising his imprudence, which had thus struck up a spark, that had like to have thrown the whole town into a flame. Finding on mature reflection, that he had been the aggressor, he resolved to make Mr. Payne honourable reparation, by asking his *pardon* on the morrow! No sooner had he made this noble resolution, than recovering that delicious gaiety which accompanies good purposes in a virtuous mind, he went to a ball that night, and behaved as pleasantly as though nothing had happened! Glorious proof that great souls, like great ships, are not affected by those little puffs which would overset feeble minds with passion, or sink them with spleen!

The next day he went to a tavern, and wrote a polite note to Mr. Payne, whom he requested to meet him. Mr. Payne took it for a challenge, and repaired to the tavern, not without expecting to see a pair of pistols produced. But what was his surprise on entering the chamber, to see a decanter of wine and glasses on the table! Washington arose, and in a very friendly manner met him, and gave him his hand. "Mr. Payne," said he "to err is nature; to rectify error is glory; I find I was wrong yesterday, but I wish to be right to-day. You have had some satisfaction; and if you think that sufficient here's my hand, let us be friends."

Admirable youth! Noble speech! No wonder, since it charms us so, that it had such an effect on Mr. Payne, who from that moment became the most ardent admirer and friend of Washington, and ready at any time, for his sake, to charge up to a battery of two and forty pounders.

What a lesson for our young countrymen! Had Washington been one of the race of *little men,* how sadly different would have been his conduct on this occasion! Instead of going that night to the ball, and acting the lively agreeable friend, he would, like an angry viper that had been trod on, have retired to his chamber. There he would have found no such entertainments as Washington had at this ball; no sprightly music, no delicious wines, no sweetly smiling friends; on the contrary, all the tortures of a soul brooding over its indignities, until reflection had whipped it up into pangs of rage unutterable, while all the demons of hell, with blood-stained torches pointing at his bleeding honour, cried out revenge! revenge! revenge! There in his chamber, he would have passed the gloomy night in preparing his pistols, moulding his bullets, or with furious looks driving them through the body of his enemy chalked on the wall. The next morning would have seen him on the field, and, in language lately heard in this state, calling out to his hated antagonist, *You have injured me, sir, beyond reconciliation, and by G—d, I'll kill you if I can.* While his antagonist, in a style equally musical and christian, rejoins, *Kill and be damned!* Pop go the pistols—down tumbles one of the combatants; while the murderer with knocking knees and looks of Cain, flies from the avenger of blood! The murdered man is carried to his house, a ghastly, bloody corpse. Merciful God! what a scene ensues! some are stupified with horror, others sink lifeless to the floor. His tender sisters, wild-shrieking with despair, throw themselves on their dead brother, and kiss his ice-cold lips; while his aged parents, crushed under unutterable woe, go down in their snowy locks broken-hearted to the grave.

Thus bloody and miserable might have been the end of Washington or of Payne, had Washington been one of those poor deluded young men, who are determined to be *great,* and to be talked of in *newspapers,* in spite of God or devil. But Washington was not born to exemplify those horrid tragedies, which *cowards* create in society by *pusillanimously giving way to their bad passions.* No! he was born to teach his countrymen what sweet peace and harmony might for ever smile in the habitations of men, if all had the *courage,* like himself, to obey the sacred voice of JUSTICE and of HUMANITY. By firmly obeying these, he preserved his hands unstained by the blood of a fellow man; and his soul unharrowed by the cruel tooth of never-dying remorse. By firmly obeying these, he preserved a life, which, crowned with deeds of justice and benevolence, has brought more glory to God, more good to man, and more honour to himself, than any life ever lived since the race of man began.

Sons of Columbia! would you know what is true courage! see it defined, see it exemplified in this act of your great young countryman. Never man possessed a more undaunted courage, than Washington. But in him this noble quality was the life-guard of his reason, not the assassin; a ready servant to *obey* her commands, not a bully to *insult* them; a champion to defend his neighbour's rights, not a tyrant to invade them. Transported by a sudden passion, to which all are liable, he offended Mr. Payne, who resented it *rather too roughly,* by knocking him down on the spot. Washington had it in his power to have taken ample revenge; and *cowards,* who have *no command over their passions,* would have done it: but duty forbade him, and he had the *courage* to obey. Reason whispered the folly of harbouring black passions in his soul, poisoning his peace; he instantly banished them, and went to a ball, to drink sweet streams of friendship from the eyes of happy friends. Again reason whispered him, that having been the aggressor, he ought to ask Payne's pardon, and make friends with him. In this also he had the courage to obey her sacred voice.

In what history, ancient or modern, sacred or profane, can you find, in so young a man, only 22, such an instance of that TRUE HEROIC VALOUR which combats malignant passions—conquers unreasonable *self*—rejects the hell of *hatred,* and invites the heaven of *love* into our own bosoms, and into those of our brethren with whom we may have had a falling out? Joseph forgiving his brethren in the land of Egypt; David sparing that inveterate seeker of his life, Saul; sir Walter Raleigh pardoning the young man who spit in his face; afford, it is true, charming specimens of the *sublime* and *beautiful* in action, and, certainly, such men are the worthies of the world, and brightest ornaments of human nature. But yet, none of them have gone beyond Washington in the affair of Payne.

A few years after this, Payne had a cause tried in Fairfax court. Washington happened on that day to be in the house. The lawyer on the other side, finding he was going fast to leeward, thought he would luff up with a whole broadside at Payne's character; and, after raking him fore and aft with abuse, he artfully bore away under the lee of the jury's prejudices, which he endeavoured to inflame against him. "Yes, please your worships," continued he, "as a proof that this Payne is a most turbulent fellow, and capable of all I tell you, be pleased to remember, gentlemen of the jury, that this is the very man, who some time ago treated our beloved colonel Washington so barbarously. Yes, this is the wretch who dared, in this very court-house yard, to lift up his impious hand against that greatest and best of men, and knocked him down as though he had been a bullock of the stalls."

This, roared in a thundering tone, and with a tremendous stamp on the floor, made Payne look very wild, for he saw the countenance of the court beginning to blacken on him. But Washington rose immediately, and thus addressed the bench:

"As to Mr. Payne's character, may it please your worships," said he, "we have all the satisfaction to know that it is perfectly unexceptionable: and with respect to the little difference which formerly happened between that gentleman and myself, it was instantly made up, and we have lived on the best terms ever since: and besides, I could wish all my acquaintance to know, that I entirely acquit Mr. Payne of blame in that affair, and take it all on myself as the aggressor."

Payne used often to relate another anecdote of Washington, which reflects equal honour on the goodness of his heart.

"Immediately after the war," said he, "when the conquering hero was returned in peace to his home, with the laurels of victory green and flourishing on his head, I felt a great desire to see him, and so set out for Mount Vernon. As I drew near the house, I began to experience a rising fear, lest he should call to mind the blow I had given him in former days. However, animating myself, I pushed on. Washington met me at the door with a smiling welcome, and presently led me into an adjoining room, where Mrs. Washington sat. 'Here, my dear,' said he, presenting me to his lady, 'here is the little man you have so often heard me talk of, and who, on a difference between us one day, had the resolution to knock me down, big as I am. I know you will honour him as he deserves, for I assure you he has the heart of a true

Virginian.'—"He said this," continued Mr. Payne, "with an air which convinced me that his long familiarity with war had not robbed him of a single spark of the goodness and nobleness of his heart. And Mrs. Washington looked at him, I thought, with a something in her eyes which showed that he appeared to her greater and lovelier than ever."

A good tree, saith the divine teacher, *bringeth forth good fruit.* No wonder then that we meet with so many and such delicious fruits of CHARITY in Washington, whose soul was so rich in benevolence.

In consequence of his wealth and large landed possessions, he had visits innumerable from the poor. Knowing the great value of time and of good tempers to them, he could not bear that they should lose these by long waiting, and shuffling, and blowing their fingers at his door. He had a room set apart for the reception of such poor persons as had business with him, and the porter had orders to conduct them into it, and to let him know it immediately. And so affectionately attentive was he to them, that if he was in company with the greatest characters on the continent, when his servant informed him that a poor man wished to speak to him, he would instantly beg them to excuse him for a moment, and go and wait on him.

Washington's conduct showed that he disliked another practice, too common among some great men, who, not having the power to say yes, nor the heart to say no, to a poor man, are fain to put him off with a *"come again, come again,"* and thus trot him backwards and forwards, wasting his time, wearing out his patience and shoes, and, after all give him the mortification of a disappointment.

Washington could not away with such *cruel kindness.* If he could not oblige a poor applicant, he would candidly tell him so at once; but then the goodness of his heart painted his regret so sensibly on his countenance, that even his refusals made him friends.

A poor Irishman, wanting a little farm, and hearing that Washington had such a one to rent, waited on him. Washington told him that he was sincerely sorry that he could not assist him, for he had just disposed of it. The poor man took his leave, but not without returning him a thousand thanks! *Ah, do you thank me so heartily for a refusal?* "Yes, upon my shoul, now please your excellency's honour, and I do thank you a thousand times. For many a great man would have kept me waiting like a black negro; but your excellency's honour has told me strait off hand that you are sorry, and God bless you for it, that you can't help me, and so your honour has done my business for me in no time and less."

The Potomac abounds with the finest herrings in the world, which, when salted, furnish, not only to the wealthy a charming relish for their tea and coffee, but also to the poor a delicious substitute for bacon. But, fond as they are of this *small-boned bacon,* as they call it, many of them have not the means to procure it. Washington's heart felt for these poor people, and provided a remedy. He ordered a seine and a batteau to be kept on one of his best fishing shores on purpose for the poor. If the batteau was lost, or the seine spoilt, which was often the case, he would have them replaced with new ones immediately. And if the poor who came for fish were too weak handed to haul the seine themselves, they needed but to apply to the overseer, who had orders from Washington to send hands to help them. Thus all the poor had it in their power to come down in the season, and catch the finest fish for themselves and their families. In what silver floods were ever yet caught the herrings, which could have given to Washington what he tasted, on seeing the poor driving away from his shores, with carts laden with delicious fish, and carrying home, whooping and singing, to their smiling wives and children, the rich prize, a whole year's plenty.

In all his charities, he discovered great judgment and care in selecting proper objects. Character was the *main chance.*

Mount Vernon had no charms for lazy, drunken, worthless beggars. Such knew very well that they must make their application elsewhere. He never failed to remind them of the great crime of robbing the public of their services, and also the exceeding cruelty and injustice of snapping up from the really indigent, what little charity-bread was stirring. But if the character was good; if the poor petitioner was a sober, honest, and industrious person, whom Providence had by sickness or losses reduced to want, he found a brother in Washington. It is incredible what quantities of wool, corn, bacon, flour, clothes, &c. were annually distributed to the poor, from that almost exhaustless heap, which the blessings of Heaven bestowed on this, its *industrious* and *faithful* steward.

"I had orders," said Mr. Peake, a sensible, honest manager of one of Washington's plantations, "to fill a corn-house every year, for the sole use of the poor in my neighborhood! to whom it was a most seasonable and precious relief; saving numbers of poor women and children from miserable famine, and blessing them with a cheerful plenteousness of bread."

Mr. Lund Washington, long a manager of his Mount Vernon estate, had similar orders. One year when corn was so dear (a dollar per bushel), that numbers of the poor were on the point of starving, Mr. L. Washington, by order of the general, not only gave away all that could be spared from the granaries, but bought, at that dear rate, *several hundred bushels* for them!

Anecdote of Washington.—The town of Alexandria, which now flourishes like a green bay tree, on the waters of the Potomac, was, 50 years ago, but a small village. But though small, it was lovely. Situated on the fine plain which banks the western margin of the river, and with snow-white domes glistening through the trees that shook their green heads over the silver flood, it formed a view highly romantic and beautiful. Hence the name of the place at first was *Bellhaven.*

But, with all the beauties to the eye, Bellhaven had no charms for the palate. Not that the neighbourhood of Bellhaven was a *desert;* on the contrary, it was, in many places, a garden spot abounding with *luxuries.* But its inhabitants, though wealthy, were not wise. By the successful culture of tobacco they had made money. And having filled their coach-houses with gilt carriages, and their dining rooms with gilt glasses, they began to look down on the *poorer sort,* and to talk about *families.* Of course, it would never do for such great people to run *market carts!!* Hence the poor Bellhavenites, though embosomed in plenty, were often in danger of gnawing their nails; and, unless they could cater a lamb from some good-natured peasant or a leash of chickens from the Sunday negroes, were obliged to sit down with long faces to a *half-graced* dinner of salt meat and journey cake. This was the order of the day, A. D. '59, when Washington, just married to the wealthy young Mrs. Custis, had settled at Mount Vernon, nine miles below Bellhaven. The unpleasant situation of the families at that place soon reached his ear. To a man of his character, with *too much spirit* to follow a *bad* example, when he had the power to set a *good* one, and too much wit to look for happiness any where but in his own bosom, it could not long be questionable what part he had to act. A market cart was instantly constructed, and regularly, three times a week, sent off to Bellhaven, filled with nice roasters, kidney-covered lamb and veal, green geese, fat ducks, and goblers, chickens by the basket, fresh butter, new laid eggs, vegetables, and fruit of all sorts. Country gentlemen, dining with their friends in town, very soon marked the welcome change of diet. "*Bless us all!*" exclaimed they, "*what's the meaning of this? you invited us to family fare, and here you've given us a lord mayor's feast.*" "*Yes,*" replied the others, "*thank God for sending a Col. Washington into our neighbourhood.*" Thus it was discovered, to the extreme mortification of some of the *little great ones,* that

Col. Washington should *ever have run a market cart!!* But the better sort, who generally, thank God, have sense enough to be led right, provided they can get a leader, soon fell into the track—and market carts were soon seen travelling in abundance to town with every delicacy of the animal and vegetable republics.

Thus the hungry wall which pride had raised against Bellhaven was happily demolished; a flood-tide of blessings rolled in from the neighbouring country—the hearts of the merchants felt a fresh pulse of love for their brothers, the farmers; and even the little children, with cheeks red as the apples they seized, were taught to lisp the praises of God. And all this, reader, through the active benevolence of *one man.*

The following anecdote was related to me by his excellency, governor Johnson (Maryland), one of the few surviving heroes of '76.

"You seem, sir (said he, addressing himself to me), very fond of collecting anecdotes of Gen. Washington. Well, I'll tell you one, and one too, to which you may attach the most entire faith, for I have heard it a dozen times and oftener, from the lips of a very valuable man and magistrate, in Conostoga, a Mr. Conrad Hogmyer." "Just before the revolutionary war (said Mr. Hogmyer) I took a trip, for my *health's sake,* to the sweet springs of Virginia, where I found a world of people collected; some, like me, looking for health, others for pleasure. In consequence of the crowd, I was at first rather hard run for lodgings, but at length was lucky enough to get a mattress in the hut of a very honest baker of my acquaintance, who often visited those springs for the benefit of his oven. Being the only man of the trade on the turf, and well skilled in the science of dough, he met with no small encouragement; and it was really a matter of gratitude to see what heaps of English loaves, Indian pones, French bricks, cakes, and crackers, lay piled on his counter every morning. I often amused myself in marking the various airs and manners of the different waiters, who, in gay liveries and shining faces, came every morning, rattling down their silver, and tripping away with bread by the basket.—Among those gay-looking sons and daughters of Africa, I saw, every now and then, a poor Lazarite, with sallow cheek and hollow eye, slowly creeping to the door, and, at a nod from the baker, eagerly seize a fine loaf, and bear it off without depositing a cent. Surely, thought I to myself, this baker must be the best man, or the greatest fool in the world; but fearing that this *latter cap* best fitted his pericranium, I one morning could not hel[p] breaking my mind to him, for crediting his bread to such very unpromising dealers. 'Stophel,' for that was his name, 'you seem,' said I, 'to sell a world of bread here every day, but notwithstanding that, I fear you don't gain much by it.'

" 'No! 'squire: what makes you think so?'

" 'You credit too much, Stophel.'

" 'Not I indeed, sir not I; I don't credit a cent.'

" 'Ay! how do you make that out, Stophel; don't I see these poor people every day carrying away your bread, and yet paying you nothing?'

" 'Pshaw, no matter for that, 'squire, they'll pay me all in a lump at last.'

" '*At last! At last!!* Oh ho, at the *last day,* I suppose you mean, Stophel, when you have the conscience to expect that God Almighty will stand paymaster, and wipe off all your old scores for you, at a dash.'

" 'Oh no! 'squire we poor bakers can't give such long credit! but I'll tell you how we work the matter: the good man, colonel George Washington is here. Every season as soon as he comes, he calls and says to me "Stophel," says he, "you seem to have a great deal of company; and some, I fear, who don't come here for *pleasure,* and yet, you know, they can't do without *eating*. Though *pale* and *sickly,* they must have bread; but it will never do to make them *pay* for it.

Poor creatures! they seem already *low spirited* enough, through *sickness* and *poverty;* their spirits must not be sunk lower by taking from them every day what little money they have pinched from their poor families at home: I'll tell you what's to be done, Stophel; you must give each of them a good hot loaf every morning, and charge it to me; when I am going away, I'll pay you all." And believe me, 'squire, he has often, at the end of the season, paid me as much as 80 dollars, and that too for poor creatures who did not know the hand that fed them; for I had strict orders from him, not to mention a syllable of it to any body.' "

But though so kind to the *bodies,* Washington was still more kind and costly in his charities to the *minds* of the poor. Sensible that a republican government, that is, a government of the people, can never long subsist where the minds of the people are not enlightened, he earnestly recommended it to the citizens of the United States, to promote, as an object of *primary importance,* institutions for the general diffusion of knowledge. In this, as indeed in all other cases, where any thing great or good was to be done, Washington led the way.

He established a charity-school in Alexandria, and endowed it with a donation of *four thousand dollars!* The interest was regularly paid and expended on the education of fifteen boys. My young friend, the reverend Mr. Wiley, who, for talents, taste, and classical erudition, has few superiors in America, was educated by Washington.

In 1785, the assembly of his native state, Virginia, desirous "to embrace," as they said, "every suitable occasion of testifying their sense of the unexampled merits of George Washington, esq." presented him with fifty shares in the Potomac, and one hundred shares in the James River Navigation Company; making, in the whole, the enormous sum of ten thousand pounds sterling!

Of this public act, they requested the governor to transmit Washington a copy. In answer to which he addressed a letter to the governor, in which, "I take the liberty (says he) of returning to the general assembly, through your hands, the profound and grateful acknowledgments inspired by so signal a mark of their beneficent intentions towards me."

He goes on to beg that they would excuse his determined resolution not to accept a farthing of it for his *own use.*—"But (continued he) if it should please the general assembly to permit me to turn the destination of the fund vested in me, from my private emolument, to objects of a public nature, it shall be my study, in selecting, to prove the sincerity of my gratitude for the honour conferred on me, by preferring such as may appear most subservient to the enlightened and patriotic views of the legislature."

They were cheerfully submitted to his disposal; and, according to promise, he appropriated them to works of the greatest utility: viz. his shares in James River canal, to a college in Rockbridge county, near the waters of James River, and his Potomac shares to a national university, to be erected in the federal district, on the Great Potomac.

How immortal were his wishes for the good of his country! As if incapable of being satisfied with all that he had done for her while living, he endeavoured, by founding those noble institutions for the diffusion of knowledge and virtue, to make himself her benefactor when he could live no more.

Since the idea is perfectly correct, that the great Governor of the world must look with peculiar benignity on those of his children who have most nearly resembled him in benevolence, may we not indulge the pleasing hope, that these colleges, founded by *such a hand,* shall prove the nurseries of brightest genius and virtue, and that from their sacred halls will walk forth, in endless succession, the mighty *Washingtons* and *Jeffersons,* the *Franklins* and *Madisons* of future times! O that Columbia may live before God! and that the bright days of her prosperity may never have an end!

Washington's behaviour to the generous Fayette ought never to be forgotten.

When that glorious young nobleman heard that lord North had passed against America the decree of slavery; and that the American farmers, with their rusty firelocks and pitchforks, in front of their shrieking wives and children, were inch by inch disputing the soil against a hireling soldiery, the tears gushed from his eyes; he tore himself from the arms of the loveliest, fondest of wives—flew to his sovereign for leave to fight—turned into powder and arms every livre that he could raise, and, in a swift-sailing frigate rushing through the waves to America, presented himself before Washington. Washington received him as his son, and gave him command. Under the eye of that hero, he fought and conquered. Having aided to fix the independence of strangers, he hastened back to France, to liberate his own countrymen from the curses of monarchy, and to give them, like America, the blessings of a republic. A pupil of the temperate and virtuous Washington, he soon offended the hot-headed demogogues of France. Banished from his native country, he was presently thrown, by royal jealousy into a foreign prison. Most of us here in America, on hearing of his misfortunes, felt the kindly touch of sympathy; but alas! like those good people in the parable, we were so taken up with "buying land, proving oxen, or marrying wives," that we forgot our noble friend. But Washington did not forget him. His thoughts were often with him in his gloomy cell. He sent him a present of a thousand guineas—and, in a letter to the emperor of Germany, with equal delicacy and feeling solicited his discharge, and permission to come to America. The letter concluded with these remarkable words: —"As it is a maxim with me never to ask what, under similar circumstances, I would not grant, your majesty will do me the justice to believe, that this request appears to me to correspond with those great principles of magnanimity and wisdom which form the basis of sound policy and durable glory."

This letter produced, in part, the desired effect. For

immediately after the receipt of it the marquis experienced a great increase of attention; and in a short time was liberated. Such was the respect paid to our American farmer, by one of the greatest monarchs in Europe.

In 1795, the marquis's son made his escape from France, and arrived in Boston. Soon as Washington heard of it, he sent his parental respects to the youth and informed him, that, though, from motives of tenderness to his mother, who was in the power of the directory, he could not be seen publicly to notice him, yet begged to be considered by him as his father and protector—advised him to enter as a student in the university near Boston, and to draw on *him* for *whatever monies he should want.*

Congress, on hearing that a son of the noble marquis was in America, felt a deep interest in the youth, and ordered an immediate enquiry into his situation, intending generous things for him out of the national treasury. But, finding that on this, as on all other occasions, Washington had done honour to the American name, they rejoiced exceedingly, and let the matter drop.

CHAPTER XV

WASHINGTON'S CHARACTER CONTINUED

HIS INDUSTRY

Awake, my boy! and let the rising sun
Blush to see his vigilance still outdone;
In cheerful works consume the fleeting day,
Toil thy pleasure, and business all thy play.

But of all the virtues that adorned the life of this great man, there is none more worthy of our imitation than his admirable INDUSTRY. It is to this virtue in her Washington, that America stands indebted for services past calculation; and it is from this virtue, that Washington himself snatched a wreath of glory, that will never fade away. O that the good genius of America may prevail! that the example of this, her favourite son, may but be universally adopted! Soon shall our land be free from all those sloth-begotten demons which now haunt and torment us. For whence do all our miseries proceed, but from lack of industry? In a land like this, which heaven has blessed above all lands; a land abounding with the *fish* and *flesh pots* of Egypt, and flowing with the choicest *milk* and *honey* of Canaan; a land where the poorest Lazarus may get his *fifty cents* a day for the commonest labour; and buy the daintiest bread of corn flour for a *cent a pound!* why is any man hungry or thirsty, or naked, or in prison? Why but for his own unpardonable sloth?

But alas! what would it avail, though the blest shade of Washington were to descend from his native skies, and, with an angel's voice, recommend industry as the handmaid of *health, wealth, innocence,* and *happiness* to man. A notion, from the land of lies, has taken too deep root among some, that *"labour is a low-lived thing, fit for none but poor people and slaves! and that dress and pleasure are the only accomplishments for a gentleman!"* But does it become a *gentleman* to saunter about, living on the charity of his relations—to suffer himself to be dunned by creditors, and like a hunted wolf, to fly from the face of sheriffs and constables? Is it like a *gentleman* to take a generous woman from her parents, and reduce her to beggary—to see even her bed sold from under her, and herself and weeping infants turned out of doors. Is it like a *gentleman* to reduce one's children to rags, and to drive them, like birds of heaven, to hedges and highways, to pick berries, filling their pale bloated bodies with disease? Or is it like a *gentleman* to bring up one's sons in sloth, pleasure, and dress, as young noblemen, and then leave them without estates, profession, or trades, to turn gamblers, sharpers, or horse thieves? *"From such gentlemen, oh save my country, Heaven!"* was Washington's perpetual prayer, the emphatical prayer of his life and great example! In his ear, Wisdom was heard incessantly calling aloud, "He is the real gentleman, who cheerfully contributes his every exertion to accomplish heaven's favourite designs, the *beauty, order,* and *happiness of human life;* whose industry appears in a plentiful house and smiling wife; in the decent apparel of his children, and in their good education and virtuous manners; who is not afraid to see any man on earth, but meets his creditor with a smiling countenance, and with the welcome music of gold and silver in his hand; who exerts an honest industry for wealth, that he may become as a watercourse in a thirsty land, a source of refreshments to a thousand poor."

This was the life, this the example set by Washington. His whole inheritance was but a small tract of poor land in Stafford county, and a few negroes. This appearing utterly insufficient for those purposes of usefulness, with the charms of which his mind seems to have been early smitten, he resolved to make up the deficiency by dint of industry and economy. For these virtues, how excellent! how rare in youth! Washington was admirably distinguished when but a boy. At a time when many young men have no higher ambition than a fine coat and a frolic, *"often have I seen him* (says the reverend Mr. Lee Massey) *riding about the country with his surveying instruments at his saddle,"* enjoying the double satisfaction of obliging his fellow-citizens by surveying their lands and of making money, not meanly to hoard, but generously to lend to any *worthy* object that asked it. This early industry was one of the first steps to Washington's preferment. It attracted on him the notice and admiration of his numerous acquaintance, and, which was still more in his favour, it gave such uncommon strength to his constitution, such vigour to his mind, such a spirit for adventure, that he was ready for any glorious enterprise, no matter how difficult or dangerous. Witness the expedition from Williamsburgh, through the Indian country to the Ohio, which at the green age of twenty-one, he undertook for governor Dinwiddie. Indeed this uncommon attachment to industry and useful life, made such an impression on the public mind in his favour, that by the time he was *one and twenty* he was appointed major and adjutant general of the Virginia forces in the Northern Neck!

There was at this time a young fellow in *Williamsburgh* by the name of Jack B——, who possessed considerable vivacity, great good-nature, and several accomplishments of the *bon-companion* sort. He could tell a good story, sing agreeably, scrape a little on the fiddle, and cut as many capers to the tune of *old Roger* as any buck a-going: and being, besides, a young fellow of fortune, and son of an intimate acquaintance, Jack was a great favourite of the governor, and much at his house. But all this could not save poor Jack from the twinges of envy. For, on hearing every body talk in praise of major Washington, he could not help saying one day, at the governor's table, *"I wonder what makes the people so wrapped up in major Washington; I think, begging your excellency's pardon, I had as good a right to a major's commission." "Ah Jack," replied the governor, "when we want diversion, we send for you; but when we want a man of business, we send for major Washington."*

Never was the great Alfred more anxious to improve his time than our Washington; and it appears that, like Alfred, he divided his time into four grand departments, *sleep, devotion, recreation,* and *business.* On the hours of business, whether in his own or in his country's service, he would allow nothing to infringe. While in camp, no company, however illustrious; no pleasures, however elegant; no conversation, however agreeable, could prevail on him to neglect his business. The moment that his hour of duty was come, he would fill his glass, and with a smile call out to his friends around the social board, *"well, gentlemen, here is bon repos,"* and immediately withdraw to business. *Bon repos* is a French cant for good night. Washington drank it as a signal to break up; for the moment the company had swallowed the general's bon repos, it was *hats* and *off.* General Wayne, who, happily for America, understood fighting better than French, had some how or other taken up a notion, that this same bon repos, to whom Washington made such conscience of giving his last bumper, must have been some *great* warrior of the times of old. Having, by some extraordinary luck, gotten hold of two or three dozen of good old wine, he invited a parcel of hearty fellow-officers to dine with him, and help him to break them to the health of America. Soon as the cloth was removed and the bottles on the table, the hero of Stony Point cried out, *"come, my brave fellows, fill your glasses; here's old bon repos for ever."* The officers were thunderstruck; but, having turned off their wine, rose up, one and all to go. "Hey-day! what's all this, gentlemen, what's all this?" "Why, did not you drink *bon repos*—or *good night?"*

"What! is that the meaning of it?" "Yes," "Oh! then damn old bon repos, and take your seats again: for, by the life of

Washington, you shan't stir a peg till we have started every drop of our drink."[1]

While he was employed in choosing a place on the Potomac for the federal city, his industry was no less remarkable. Knowing how little is generally done before breakfast, he made it a rule to rise so early as to have breakfast over, and be on horseback by the time the sun was up. Let the rising generation remember that he then was sixty years of age!

On his farm, his husbandry of time was equally exemplary. He contemplated a great object; an object worthy of Washington. He aimed at teaching his countrymen the art of enriching their lands, and, consequently, of rendering the condition of man and beast more plentiful and happy. He had seen thousands of acres, which, by constant cultivation, had lost the power of covering their nakedness even with a suit of humble sedge; he had seen thousands of wretched cattle, which, driven out houseless and hayless into the cold wintry rains, presented such trembling spectacles of starvation and misery, as were enough to start the tear into Pity's eye. To remedy these *cruel evils* (which certainly they are, for He who lent us these animals never meant that we should make their lives a curse to them, much less to our children, hardened by such daily sights of misery), Washington generously set himself to make artificial meadows, to cultivate fields of clover, and to raise the most nutritious vegetables, such as *cabbage, turnips, scarcity,* and *potatoes;* of which last article he planted in one year 700 bushels! To render these vast supplies of food the more beneficial to his cattle, he built houses of shelter for them all. "He showed me a barn," says Brissot, "upwards of 100 feet square, and of brick, designed as a storehouse for his corn, potatoes, turnips, &c. around which he had constructed stables of an amazing length, for

[1] "Gen[l] Wayne says his father never committed that blunder about Old Bon Repos. He is displeas[d]—and I wish you w[d] put some other name. By the Bye he did commit it." (Weems to Carey, July 11, 1816; Skeel, I, 66.) Carey apparently ignored the suggestion.

his cattle." Every one of them had a stall well littered with leaves or straw; and a rack and manger well furnished with hay and provender.

The pleasure and profits arising from such an arrangement are incalculable. How delicious must it have been, to a man of Washington's feelings, to reflect that, even in the worst of weather, every creature, on his extensive farms, was warmly and comfortably provided; to have seen his numerous flocks and herds, gamboling around him through excess of joy, and fullness of fat; to have beheld his steps washed with butter, and his dairies floated with rivers of milk; to have seen his once naked fields and frog-croaking swamps, now, by clearance or manure, converted into meadows, standing thick with heavy crops of timothy and sweet-scented clover; while his farm-yards were piled with such quantities of litter and manure as afforded a constantly increasing fertility to his lands.

Here was an employment worthy of Washington; an employment, which we might indeed have expected from *him,* who, through life, had studied the best interests of his countrymen; who, first as a *soldier,* had defended them from slavery, and crowned them with liberty; then, as a statesman, had preserved them from war, and secured to them the blessings of peace; and now as the last, but not least service of his life, was teaching them the great arts of improving their farms, multiplying their cattle, enriching their lands, and thus pouring a flood of plenty and of comfort through the joyful habitations of man and beast.

Full of the greatly benevolent idea, no wonder that he was so frugal of his time. Though the most hospitable of all the hospitable Virginians, he would not suffer the society of his dearest friends to take him from his business. Long accustomed to find his happiness in doing his duty, he had attained to such a *royal arch degree* of virtue, as to be restless and uneasy while his duty was neglected. Hence, of all that ever lived, Washington was the most rigidly observant of those hours of business which were necessary to the successful management of his vast concerns. "*Gentlemen,* (he would often say to his friends who visited him) *I must beg leave of absence a few hours in the forenoon; here is plenty of amusements, books, music, &c. Consider yourselves at home, and be happy.*" He came in about twelve o'clock, and then, as if animated by the consciousness of having done his duty, and that all was going right, would give himself up to his friends and to decent mirth the rest of the evening.

But his mornings were always his own. Long before the sun peeped into the chambers of the sluggard, Washington was on horseback, and out among his overseers and servants, and neither himself nor any about him were allowed to eat the bread of idleness. The happy effects of such industry were obvious. Well manured and tilled, his lands yielded a grateful return, and it was at once pleasing and astonishing to behold the immense quantities of fine hay, of fat meats and choice grain that were raised on his farms; of wheat 7000 bushels in one year, and 5000 bushels of Indian corn! His servants fared plentifully; his cattle rarely had the *hollow horn;* and the surplus of his produce, sold to the merchants, furnished bread to the needy, and a revenue to himself more than sufficient to defray his vast expenditures, and to spread a table of true Virginian hospitality for those crowds of friends and foreigners whom affection or curiosity led to visit him.

Oh! divine Industry! queen mother of all our virtues and of all our blessings! what is there of GREAT or of GOOD in this wide world that springs not from thy royal bounty? And thou, O! infernal Sloth! fruitful fountain of all our crimes and curses! what is there of mean or of miserable in the lot of man that flows not from thy hellish malice?

What was it that betrayed David, otherwise the best of kings, into the worst of crimes? IDLENESS. Sauntering about *idly* on the terrace of his palace, he beheld the naked beauties of the distant bathing Bathsheba. Lust, adultery, and murder were the consequences.

What was it that brought on a ten years war between the Greeks and Trojans? IDLENESS. Young Paris, the coxcomb of Troy, having nothing to do, strolls over to the court of Menelaus (a Greek prince), whose beauteous wife Helen, the black-eyed queen of love, he corrupts and runs off with to Troy. A bloody war ensues; Paris is slain; his father, brothers, and myriads of wretched subjects are slaughtered; and Troy, the finest city of Asia, is reduced to ashes!

What was it that hurried poor Mr. A——d to that horrid act of suicide, which froze the blood of all who heard it? Idleness. His young wife, with all that we could conceive of sweetness, tenderness, and truth, in an angel's form; and his three beauteous babes were the three graces in smiling infancy. But oh, wretched man! having *nothing to do!* he strolled to a tavern, and to a card-table, where he lost his all! *five thousand pounds,* lately settled on him by a fond father! He awakes to horrors unutterable! What will become of his ruined wife! his beggared babes! Believing his torments little inferior to those of the damned, he seizes the fatal pistol; drives the scorching bullets through his brain; and flies a shrieking ghost to join the mournful throng!

O sad sight! See yon tall young man, in powder and ruffles, standing before his judges, trembling like an aspen, and pale and blank as the picture of guilt; while the crowded court-house, every countenance filled with pity or contempt, is fixed upon him. Alas! what could have brought him to this? Idleness. His father happening to possess 500 acres of poor land, and a few negroes, thought it would be an eternal disgrace to his family to bring up his son (though he had many) to be a *mechanic! No,* he must be a *gentleman!!* Grown to man's estate, and having no profession, trade, or habit of industry to support this pleasant life, he took to *horse-stealing!* If we had leisure to wait, we should presently see this unhappy youth, on receiving sentence of death bursting into sobs and cries sufficient to make us wish we had never been born. But let us leave these accursed scenes of *shame, misery,* and *death,* into which *idleness* never fails to bring poor deluded youth, and joyfully return to our beloved Washington, and to his health, wealth, and glory-giving goddess, *Industry.*

What is it that braces the nerves, purifies the blood, and hands down the flame of life, bright and sparkling, to old age? What, but *rosy-cheeked industry.* See Washington so invigorated by constant exercise, that, though hereditarily subject to the gout, of which all his family died, he entirely escaped it; and, even at the age of 66, continued straight and active as a young grenadier, and ready once more at his country's call, to lead her eager warriors to the field.

What is it that preserves the morals of young men unsoiled, and secures the blessings of unblemished character and unbroken health? What, but *snow-robed industry.* See Washington under the guardianship of industry, walking the slippery paths of youth, safe and uncorrupted, though born in a country whose fertility and climate furnished both the means and invitation to vice. Early smitten with the love of glory; early engaged in the noble pursuit of knowledge, of independence, and of usefulness, he had no eyes to see bad examples nor ensnaring objects, no ears to hear horrid oaths nor obscene language, no leisure for impure passions nor criminal amours; hence he enjoyed that purity of soul, which is rightly called its *sunshine;* and which impressed a dignity on his character, and gave him a beauty and loveliness in the eyes of men, that contributed more to his rise in the world, than young people are aware of.

And what is it that raises a young man from poverty to wealth, from obscurity to never-dying fame? What, but *industry?* See Washington, born of humble parents, and in humble circumstances—born in a narrow nook and obscure corner of the British plantations! yet lo! what great things wonder-working industry can bring out of this unpromising Nazareth. While but a youth, he manifested such a noble contempt of *sloth,* such a manly spirit to be always learning or doing something useful or clever, that he was the *praise* of all who knew him. And, though but 15, so high were the hopes entertained of him, he was appointed a surveyor! arduous task! But his industry was a full match for it. Such was the alertness with which he carried on his surveys; such the neatness and accuracy of his plats and drafts, that he met with universal applause. Full-fed and flushed with so much fare of *praise,* a fare of all others the most toothsome and wholesome to generous minds, our young eagle began to flap his wings of honest ambition, and to pant for nobler darings. A fair occasion was soon offered; a dangerous expedition through the Indian wilds, as before mentioned, to the French Mamelukes on the Ohio. Nobody else having ambition for such an adventure, Washington's offer was gladly accepted; and he executed that hazardous and important trust with such *diligence* and propriety, that he received the thanks of the governor and council. Honours came down on him now in showers: he was appointed major and adjutant-general of the Virginia forces; then a colonel; afterwards a member of the house of burgesses; next, generalissimo of the armies of the United States; and, finally, chief magistrate of the Union. All these floods of prosperity and honour, which in thousands would have but served to bloat with lust or pride, with him served but the more to rouse his industry, and to enlarge his usefulness; for such was his economy of time, and so admirable his method and regularity of business, that he always kept a head of it.* No letters of consequence

* He was taken ill on Friday. An intimate friend asked him if he wished to have any thing done on the arrangement of his *temporal affairs;* he shook his head and replied, "no, I thank you, for my books are all posted to Tuesday!" That industry and method must be truly astonishing, which in the management of possessions so vast and complicated as his, kept every thing so harmoniously adjusted as to be ready, at a moment's warning, to leave the world for ever without a wish to alter a tittle.

were unanswered; no reasonable expectations were disappointed; no necessary information was ever neglected; neither the congress, nor the governors of the several states, nor the officers of his army, nor the British generals, nor even the overseers and stewards on his farms, were uninformed what he expected from them; nobody concerned with him was *idle,* or *fretted* for want of knowing what to do.

Oh, admirable man! Oh, great preceptor to his country! no wonder every body honoured *him* who honoured every body; for the poorest beggar that wrote to him on business, was sure to receive a speedy and decisive answer. No wonder every body loved him, who, by his unwearied attention to the public good, manifested the tenderest love for every body. No wonder that his country delighted to honour *him,* who showed such a sense of her honours, that he would not allow even a leaf of them to wither; but so watered them all with the refreshing streams of his industry, that they continued to bloom with ever-increasing glory on his head.

Since the day that God created man on the earth, none ever displayed the power of industry more signally than did George Washington. Had he, as prince of Wales, or as dauphin of France rendered such great services, or attained such immortal honours, it would not have seemed so marvellous in our eyes. But that a poor young man with no king, lords, nor commons to back him—with no princes, nor strumpets of princes, to curry favour for him—with no gold but his virtue, no silver but his industry, should, with this old-fashioned coin, have stolen away the hearts of all the American Israel, and from a sheep-cot have ascended the throne of his country's affections, and gotten himself a name above the mighty ones of the earth! this is marvellous indeed! It is surely the noblest panegyric ever yet paid to that great virtue, industry, which has *"length of days in her right hand, and in her left hand riches and honours."*

Young Reader! go thy way, think of Washington, and

HOPE. Though humble thy birth, low thy fortune, and few thy friends, still think of Washington, and HOPE. Like him, honour thy God, and delight in glorious toil; then, like him, "thou shalt stand before kings; thou shalt not stand before common men."

CHAPTER XVI

WASHINGTON'S CHARACTER CONTINUED

HIS PATRIOTISM

"O eternal King of men and angels, elevate our minds! each low and partial passion thence dispel! till this great truth in every heart be known, that none but those who aid the public cause, can shield their country or themselves from chains."

LEONIDAS.

IN this grand republican virtue, with pleasure we can compare our Washington with the greatest worthies of ancient or modern times.

The patriotism of the Roman emperor, Alexander, has been celebrated through all ages, because he was never known to give any place through *favour* or *friendship,* but employed those only whom he believed to be best qualified to serve his country. In our Washington we meet this great and honest emperor over again. For, in choosing men to serve his country, Washington knew no recommendation but merit—had no *favourite* but worth. No relations, however near, no friends, however dear, stood any chance for places under him, provided he *knew* men *better qualified.* About *such* he never troubled himself to enquire, whether they were foreigners or natives, federalists or democrats. Some of the young officers of his native state, on hearing that colonel Washington was made COMMANDER IN CHIEF, were prodigiously pleased, counting to be made field officers in a hurry. But in this they were so utterly mistaken, that they used angrily to say, that *"it was a misfortune to be a Virginian."* Indeed, his great soul was so truly *republican,* that, during the whole of his administration, he was never known to advance an individual of his own name and family.

The British, with good reason, admire and extol admiral Blake as one of the bravest and best of patriots, because though he disliked Oliver Cromwell, yet he fought gallantly under him, and, with his dying breath, exhorted his men, *"to love their country as a common mother, and, no matter what hands the government might fall into, to fight for her like good children."*

Of the same noble spirit was Washington. Often was he called to obey men greatly his *inferiors,* and to execute orders which he entirely disapproved; but he was never known to faulter. Sensible of the infinite importance of union and order to the good of his country, he ever yielded a prompt obedience to her delegated will. And, not content with setting us, through life, so fair *an example,* he leaves us at death, this blessed advice: "Your government claims your utmost confidence and support. RESPECT for its AUTHORITY, *compliance* with its laws, *acquiescence* in its *measures,* are duties enjoined by the *fundamental maxims* of TRUE LIBERTY. The basis of our political system is the right of the people to make and alter their constitutions of government. But the constitution, which at any time exists, until changed by an explicit and authentic act of the whole people, is SACREDLY OBLIGATORY UPON ALL."

History has lavished its choicest praises on those magnanimous patriots, who, in their wars for liberty and their country, have cheerfully sacrificed their own wealth to defeat the common enemy.

Equal to this was the spirit of Washington. For, during the war, while he was with the army to the north, a British frigate came up the Potomac, to Mount Vernon, and threatened to lay the place in ashes, if provisions were not instantly sent on board. To save that venerable mansion, the manager sent aboard the requisite supplies. On hearing the matter, Washington wrote his manager the following letter:

"Sir—It gives me extreme concern to hear that you furnished the enemy with refreshments. It would have been a less painful circumstance to me to have heard, that, in consequence of your non-compliance with their request, they had laid my plantation in ruins. GEORGE WASHINGTON."

But, among all his splendid acts of patriotism, there is none that, with *so little noise,* may do us *more good* than his "Legacy, or Farewell to the People of the United States." In this admirable bequest, like a true teacher sent from God, he dwells chiefly on our union and brotherly love. That, the *first birth of true religion,* appears to him as the *one thing needful,* the spring of political life, and *bond* of perfection.

On this topic he employs all the energies of his mind, and, in words worthy to be written in gold, emphatically beseeches his countrymen to guard with holiest care *"the unity of the government,"* as the *"main pillar and palladium of their liberty, their independence, and every thing most dear to them on earth."*

Little did that illustrious patriot suspect, that, in so short a time after his death, the awful idea of DISUNION should have become familiar to the public eye!—so familiar as to have worn off half its horrors from the minds of many of our deluded citizens! *Disunion!* Merciful God! what good man can think of it but as of *treason,* and as a very Pandora's box, replete with every curse that can give up our dear country to desolation and havoc!

This disorganizing scheme has been three times brought forward, by what Washington terms *"cunning, ambitious, and unprincipled men,"* making use of a thousand arts to shut the eyes of the citizens on that yawning gulph to which they were so wickedly misleading them. And each time, Lucifer-like, these ministers of darkness have clothed themselves over as "angels *of light"* with the captivating plea of *public good.—"The disadvantages of the union! the disadvantages of the union!"* is their constant cry. Now admitting it to be true, that this so much *hated* union *has* its disadvantages, and where is there any human institution, even the noblest, that is free from them, yet is it not the parent of *blessings so many and great,* that no good man, as Washington says, "can *think of them without gratitude and rejoicing?*" and is it not equally true, that these disadvantages of the union would not, in fifty years, equal the ruinous consequences of a *disunion,* in probably, half a year.

At present, the plea for this most horrible measure,is, the mischievous effects of the *embargo.*—Well, grant that it is mischievous, highly mischievous and painful, for such we all feel it, yet how inexpressibly absurd it must be to put the loss of trade, for a year or two, in competition with the peace and happiness, the independence and sovereignty of our country? Would not this be an act a thousand times more mad and wicked than that of the accursed Esau, who, to remove the cravings of a momentary appetite, sold his BIRTH-RIGHT for a mess of pottage!

At this day, through the great mercies of God, we have cause to consider ourselves the happiest nation on earth.—List! oh list!

For many years past the greater part of christendom has been involved in all the horrors of the most bloody and destructive wars. Their kings and queens have been rudely hurled from their thrones; and the *"honourable men* and *the princes,"* verifying the mournful language of ancient prophecy, have been seen embracing the dunghill, or flying from their distracted countries; while the mass of the people, unable to fly, have been crushed to the earth with tythes and taxes—with impressments and conscriptions—with forced loans and arbitrary requisitions—with martial law, administered by military judges, with the bayonet at the breasts of the citizens! On the other hand, during all these horrid convulsions and miseries of other nations, WE, thoughtless, thankless WE, have enjoyed all the blessings of peace, plenty, and security. Our persons have been free from the violence of impressments and conscriptions; and our lives and property perfectly safe under the nightly staves of a few old watchmen! And while others have been over-run with devouring armies, and doomed to see their houses in flames, and the garments of their children rolled in blood, *we,* like favoured Israel, have been sitting under our vine and fig-tree, none daring to make us afraid: *we* have been advancing in riches and strength, with a rapidity unequalled in the history of man; we have been progressing in arts, manufactures, and commerce to an extent and success that has astonished the most enlightened Europeans; and, even at this moment, while suffering under the privations of the embargo, we are feasted with every necessary, and enjoying many of the elegancies of life.

And yet, with so many substantial blessings in our hands, with so much *heaven-sent manna in our mouths,* like *ungrateful Israel,* we are mourning for lack of European luxuries (as they did for the Egyptian flesh-pots), luxuries which we once enjoyed, but are now most unjustly deprived of, by our brethren, the nations of Europe, who are stronger than we. And as if that were not a sufficient *evil;* as if it were not grievous enough to suffer such a hindrance in trade, agriculture, and business of all kinds, we are now threatened with *one,* in comparison of which our present privations are but flea-bites; one that, of all others, Washington most dreaded, and was most startled at, I mean a SEPARATION OF THE STATES, and consequently, civil war.

This dreadful consequence is as obvious as it is dreadful. Yes, it is most obvious, that the separation of the states can never take place without civil war. For if the state, disposed to separate, were unanimous in the attempt, the general government could not look idly on their apostacy, but must resist it; and to that end must call out the force of the rest of the union to crush it. And here, merciful God! what scenes are rising before the eyes of horror-struck imagination? A whole nation suddenly filled with terror; "men's hearts failing them for fear, and for looking to those things that are coming on the land"—the drums and instruments of war beginning to sound—the warriors' guns and swords preparing; not for cheerful defence of liberty and country, which would make war glorious; but for the gloomy and worse than hellish work of civil discord. Sisters, mute with grief, and looking through swelling tears, on their brothers, as they gird on the hated swords; wives, shaking with strong fits, and, with their little children, filling their houses with lamentations for husbands and fathers tearing themselves away for the dismal war, whence they are to return no more! while aged parents, at parting with their sons, express the big grief only in groans; or, wringing their withered hands with tearful eyes to heaven, implore a speedy grave to put their griefs to rest.

But all this is but the beginning of sorrows. For who can paint the scenes which ensue when the two armies meet? when they meet, not in the liberal spirit of *stranger troops,* who, fighting merely for honour and pay, are ready in the first moment of victory to sheath their swords, and treat the vanquished with humanity and politeness; but in all the bitterness and exterminating spirit of a family quarrel, where men, after numberless acts of the blackest slander and of rancorous hate, have done every thing to destroy each other's souls, are now come together to destroy each other's bodies. Hence, the moment the ill fated parties meet, their fierce revengeful passions take fire: scarce can they wait the trumpet's dreadful signal. Then, rushing on each other, more like demons than men, they thrust and stab, and shout and yell, in the horrid work of mutual slaughter.

And when one of the wretched parties, nearly consumed by the sword, and unable to resist any longer, cry for quarters, they cry in vain.

The furious conquerors feel not the touch of pity, but regardless of uplifted hands and prayers, continue their cruel blows till all is hushed in death.

This is the horrid fate of all civil wars. The streets of ancient Rome; the fields of Culloden; the plains of modern

France; and even the piney woods of Georgia and South Carolina, strewed with mangled carcasses, all give awful proof, that when brethren turn their swords into each other's bowels, war degenerates into murder, and battles into butcheries.

Nor can even the grave set limits to their rage, but, like lions, turning from the mangled dead, they fly for new game to the living. All those, who by their wealth had most injured, or by their writings had most inflamed them, are sure to be the victims of their vengeance. Such persons, as was the case in the last war, between the whigs and tories in the southern states, have been dragged out of their houses, and, amidst the screams of their wives and children have been hung up to the trees, or cut to pieces with swords, with the most savage joy; while their furniture has been plundered, their houses burnt, their cattle and slaves carried off, and their widows and children driven out, crying, and without bread, into the barren woods.

Nor does this tragedy (of a free government madly divided and destroying itself) terminate here. Even this, as Solomon says, is but their *"way to hell and their going down by the chambers of death"* political (*slavery*). For when nations thus wickedly abuse their liberty, God will take it away. When they will not live in peace, out of *virtuous choice,* they shall be compelled by *brutal force.*

And, since they would not let God reign over them with a golden sceptre of reason and *equal laws,* he will set a master over them with a scourge of scorpions and an iron rod; some proud tyrant, who, looking on our country but as his estate, and ourselves as his cattle, shall waste our wealth on the pomps of his court, or the salaries of his officers; destroy our sons in his ambitious wars, and beggar us with exactions, as long as his ministers can invent, or we, by hard labour can raise money to pay them.

"Then," in the words of Washington, *"what a triumph for*

the advocates of despotism, to find that we are incapable of governing ourselves; and that systems founded on equal liberty are ideal and fallacious!" Then, how will the proud sons of despotism shake themselves with laughter on their thrones; and hell itself, responsive to their joy, clank her congratulating chains, that heaven is defeated, and the misery of man is sealed!

But, O ye favoured countrymen of Washington! your republic is not lost yet; yet there is hope. The arm that wrought your political salvation is still stretched out to save; then hear his voice and live! Hear the voice of the Divine Founder of your republic: "Little children love one another." Hear his voice from the lips of his servant Washington: "Above all things hold dear your NATIONAL UNION; accustom yourselves to estimate its immense, its infinite value to your individual and national happiness. Look on it as the palladium of your tranquillity at home; of your peace abroad; of your safety; of your prosperity; and even of that very liberty which you so highly prize! To this you are bound by every tie of gratitude and love to God or man. 1st. As to God, no people more than you can be bound to adore that invisible hand which rules the affairs of men. 'Twas he who fought your battles, and against such fearful odds established your independence; and afterwards disposed your hearts for the reception of a general and equal government. And for what did God perform all these miracles for you, but that he might glorify himself in your protection and happiness? And will you not now rise up with joy to co-operate with God in the glorious work of beautifying, with the fruits of righteousness, this goodly land, which he has so honoured, that he may place his own great name therein?"

"And remember, moreover, my countrymen, that you are now the favoured actors on a most conspicuous theatre: a theatre which seems peculiar[l]y, designated of Heaven for the display of human greatness and felicity. Far from the furious passions and politics of Europe, you are placed here by yourselves, the sole proprietors of a vast region, embracing all the soils and climates of the earth, and abounding with all the conveniences of life. And Heaven has crowned all its blessings by giving you a freer government and a fairer opportunity for political happiness than any other nation was ever favoured with. In this view, citizens of the United States, you are certainly responsible for the highest trust ever confided to any people. The eyes of long oppressed humanity are now looking up to you as to her last hope; the whole world are anxious spectators of your trial; and with your behaviour at this crisis, not only your own, but the destiny of unborn millions is involved. If, now, you make a wise use of the all-important opportunity; if your free constitution should be sacredly maintained; if honour, if patriotism, if union, and brotherly love should prevail, with all the good qualities which ennoble the character of nations, then the victory will be sure; your triumph will be complete; and the pressure of the present difficulties, instead of weakening, will give a firmer tone to the federal government, that shall probably immortalize the *blessings of* LIBERTY to our children and children's children."

"Then rouse! my generous countrymen, rouse! and, filled with the awfulness of our situation, with the glorious spirit of '76, rally around the sacred standard of your country. As good children give her all your support; *respect* her AUTHORITY!—comply with her laws! acquiesce in her *measures!*—Thus cemented by love, she shall become like the precious wedge of Ophir that defies the furnace; and coming forth from the fiery trial brighter than ever, she shall shed on the cause of freedom, a *dignity* and *lustre* which it never enjoyed before; a *lustre* which cannot fail to have a favourable influence on the rights of man. Other nations, finding from your example, that men are capable of governing themselves, will aspire to the same honour and felicity. Great and successful struggles will be made for liberty. Free governments (the pure mothers of nations) will at length be established; honouring all their virtuous children alike, jealousies and hatreds will cease, and cordial love prevail; inviting the industry of all, the blessing of plenty will be spread abroad, and shameless thefts be done away; and wisdom and worth (as in the choice of a free people) being called to *high places,* errors will be rare; vices, ashamed, shall hide their odious heads, cruelties seem abhorrent, and wars unknown. Thus, step by step progressing in virtue, the world will ripen for glory, till the great hour of her dissolution being come, the ready archangel shall lift his trumpet and sound her knell. The last refining flames shall then kindle on this *tear-bathed, blood-stained globe,* while from its ashes a new earth shall spring, far happier than the first. There, freed from all their imperfections, the spirits of *good* men (the *only* true *patriots*) shall dwell together and spend their ever brightening days in loves and joys eternal.

"May the Great Founder of your holy republic keep you all under his divine protection; incline your hearts to cultivate a spirit of cheerful subordination to government; to entertain a brotherly affection and love for one another; and finally dispose you all to do justice, to love mercy, and to demean yourselves with that charity, humility, and pacific temper of mind, which were the characteristics of the DIVINE AUTHOR of our blessed religion; without an humble imitation of whose example, in these things, we can never hope to be a GREAT AND HAPPY NATION."

CONCLUSION

WASHINGTON'S WILL

Few great men are great in every thing: but in the last testament of this extraordinary American, we see some things altogether characteristic.

When Benedict Arnold came to die, he said— *"I bequeath my soul to God."*

When Henry Laurens, president of the first congress, came to die, he said, *"My flesh is too good for worms: I give it to the flames,"* which was done.

But Washington makes no preamble about his soul or body. As to his soul, having made it his great business to reinstamp on it the image of God, he doubted not but it would be remembered when Christ should come *"to make up his jewels."*

And as to his body, that admirable piece of divine mechanism, so long the honoured servant of duty to his God and country, he trusted that, though *"sown in dishonour,* it would one day be *raised in glory;"* so leaving it to rest in hope, he proceeds to the following distribution of his worldly goods:

1st. Though an old husband of 68, yet, with the gallantry and warm affection of a young groom, he gives the whole of his estate (530,000 dollars) to his beloved wife Martha! during her life.

2d. Like a pure republican he orders all his slaves to be liberated, at certain ages, on his wife's death— lamenting, that from obstacles insurmountable, he could not do it earlier.

3d. He confirms his former donations, viz. 4000 dollars to a charity-school, in the town of Alexandria; 10,000 dollars to Liberty Hall academy, Rockbridge county, Virginia; and

20,000 dollars to a *national university,* to be founded in Washington, with this remark: "It has always been a source of serious regret with me, to see the youth of these United States sent to foreign countries for education, often before their minds were formed, or they had imbibed just ideas of the happiness of *their own;* contracting, too frequently, not only habits of dissipation and extravagance, but *principles unfriendly to republican government, and to the true and genuine liberties of mankind.*

"For these reasons, it has been my *ardent wish* to see a university in a central part of the *union,* to which the youths of fortune and talents, from all parts thereof, may be sent for the completion of their education in all the branches of polite and useful learning, and especially of POLITICS AND GOOD GOVERNMENT; and also that, by associating with each other, and forming friendships in early life, they may be enabled to free themselves from those *local prejudices* and *state jealousies,* which are never-failing sources of disquietude to the public mind, and pregnant of mischievous consequences to this country."

4th. Having no children, he bequeaths the whole of his estate, a few legacies excepted, to the children, 23 in number, of his *brothers* and *sister;* and, like a generous and affectionate relative, he gave to the children of his *half* brother, Augustin, as he did to those of his *own brothers.* And, 'tis a most pleasing fact, he gave to his wife's grand-children in like liberal measure with his own nieces and nephews! the part given to each has been computed at 20,000 dollars.

FINIS